# LAND NATIONALISATION

BY

ALFRED RUSSEL WALLACE

British Library Cataloguing-in-Publication Data
A catalogue record for this book is available from the
British Library

# Alfred Russel Wallace

Alfred Russel Wallace was born on 8th January 1823 in the village of Llanbadoc, in Monmouthshire, Wales.

At the age of five, Wallace's family moved to Hertford where he later enrolled at Hertford Grammar School. He was educated there until financial difficulties forced his family to withdraw him in 1836. He then boarded with his older brother John before becoming an apprentice to his eldest brother, William, a surveyor. He worked for William for six years until the business declined due to difficult economic conditions.

After a brief period of unemployment, he was hired as a master at the Collegiate School in Leicester to teach drawing, map-making, and surveying. During this time he met the entomologist Henry Bates who inspired Wallace to begin collecting insects. He and bates continued exchanging letters after Wallace left teaching to pursue his surveying career. They corresponded on prominent works of the time such as Charles Darwin's *The Voyage of the Beagle* (1839) and Robert Chamber's *Vestiges of the Natural History of Creation* (1844).

Wallace was inspired by the travelling naturalists of the day and decided to begin his exploration career collecting specimens in the Amazon rainforest. He explored the Rio Negra for four years, making notes on the peoples and languages he encountered as well as the geography, flora, and fauna. On his return voyage his ship, Helen, caught fire and he and the crew were stranded for ten days before being picked up by the Jordeson, a brig travelling from Cuba to London. All of his specimens aboard Helen had been lost.

After a brief stay in England he embarked on a journey to the Malay Archipelago (now Singapore, Malaysia, and Indonesia). During this eight year period he collected more than 126,000 specimens, several thousand of which represented new species to science. While travelling, Wallace refined his thoughts about evolution and in 1858 he outlined his theory of natural selection in an article he sent to Charles Darwin. This was published in the same year along with Darwin's own theory. Wallace eventually published an account of his travels *The Malay Archipelago* in 1869, and it became one of the most popular books of scientific exploration in the $19^{th}$ century.

Upon his return to England, in 1862, Wallace became a staunch defender of Darwin's landmark work *On the Origin of Species* (1859). He wrote responses to those critical of the theory of natural selection, including 'Remarks on the Rev. S. Haughton's Paper on the Bee's Cell, And on the Origin of Species' (1863) and 'Creation by Law' (1867). The former of these was particularly pleasing to Darwin. Wallace also published important papers such as 'The Origin of Human Races and the Antiquity of Man Deduced from the Theory of 'Natural Selection" (1864) and books, including the much cited *Darwinism* (1889).

Wallace made a huge contribution to the natural sciences and he will continue to be remembered as one of the key figures in the development of evolutionary theory.

Wallace died on 7th November 1913 at the age of 90. He is buried in a small cemetery at Broadstone, Dorset, England.

# LAND NATIONALISATION

## Its Necessity and Its Aims
## Being a Comparison of the System of Landlord and Tenant with That of Occupying Ownership in Their Influence on the Well-being of the People

**(1892 ed.)**

Ye friends to truth, ye statesmen who survey
The rich man's joys increase, the poor's decay--
'Tis yours to judge how wide the limits stand
Between a splendid and a happy land.
GOLDSMITH.

TO THE
WORKING MEN OF ENGLAND
THIS BOOK IS
*DEDICATED*,

IN THE HOPE THAT IT MAY REVEAL TO THEM THE CHIEF CAUSE OF SO MUCH POVERTY IN THE MIDST OF THE EVER-INCREASING WEALTH WHICH THEY CREATE, AND POINT OUT TO THEM THE GREAT REFORM WHICH WILL ENABLE LABOUR TO REAP ITS JUST REWARD, WHICH WILL SURELY TEND TO ABOLISH PAUPERISM, AND WHICH WILL GIVE TO ALL WHO INDUSTRIOUSLY SEEK IT A FAIR SHARE IN THE INCREASED PROSPERITY OF THEIR NATIVE LAND.

"Land is not, and cannot be property in the sense that moveable things are property. Every human being born into this planet must live upon the land if he lives at all. The land in any country is really the property of the nation which occupies it; and the tenure of it by individuals is ordered differently in different places, according to the habits of the people and the general convenience."--FROUDE.

"The land of Ireland, the land of every country, belongs to the people of that country."--JOHN STUART MILL.

"As land is necessary to the exertion of labour in the production of wealth, to command the land which is necessary to labour is to command all the fruits of labour save enough to enable the labourer to exist."--HENRY GEORGE.

"To make away into mercenary hands, as an article of trade, the whole solid area on which a nation lives, is astonishing as an idea of statesmanship."--PROF. F. W. NEWMAN.

"It may by-and-by be perceived that equity utters dictates to which we have not yet listened; and men may then learn that to deprive others of their rights to the use of the earth is to commit a crime inferior only in wickedness to the crime of taking away their lives or personal liberties."--HERBERT SPENCER.

"In my opinion, if it is known to be for the welfare of the community at large, the Legislature is perfectly entitled to buy out the landed proprietors. . . . Those persons who possess large portions of the earth's space are not altogether in the same position as the possessors of mere personalty. Personalty does not impose limitations on the action and the industry of man and the well-being of the community as possession of land does, and therefore, I freely own that compulsory expropriation is admissible, and even sound in principle."--W. E. GLADSTONE. (Speech at West Calder.)

# PREFACE.

The present work has been written with two main objects. In the first place, it is intended to demonstrate by a sufficient, though condensed, body of evidence, the widespread and crying evils--political and social, material and moral--which are not only the actual, but the necessary results of the system of Landlordism, while at the same time it shows, by a complementary series of facts, that a properly guarded system of Occupying Ownership under the State would afford a complete remedy for the evils thus caused. In the second place, it demonstrates that the proposed solution is a practicable one, by explaining in detail how the change may be effected with no real injury to existing landowners, and also how the scheme will actually work without producing any one of the evil results generally thought to be inseparable from a system of land-nationalisation.

It will be seen from this outline that the subjects here treated are of vast and momentous importance. So abundant are the available materials that it would have been easy to compile a work of several bulky volumes without exhausting the theme. To have done so might p. viii have added to the author's literary reputation, but would not have produced the effect which he desires to produce. It is the people at large--the middle and lower classes especially--who suffer by the present land-system, and it is by their mandate to their representatives in Parliament that the needed reform must be effected. Existing legislators can and will do nothing beyond removing the shackles which now prevent land from being freely bought and sold; but so limited a reform will only benefit landowners and capitalists, while the people will still suffer from all the evils which the monopoly of land by a class and the increase of land-speculation inevitably bring upon them. To reach the landless classes--to teach them what are their rights and how to gain these rights--is the object of this work; and it was therefore necessary that it should be at once clear and forcible, moderate in bulk, and issued at a low price. In effecting the required degree of condensation the historical part of the subject has been sketched in the briefest outline, because it appeared to the author much more important to demonstrate the evil results of our land-system than to prove that it had its origin in force or fraud in long-past ages. It also happens, that the history of the origin of landed property in general, as well as of our existing systems of land-tenure, are the portions of the subject which have been most fully treated, and which are best known to general readers.

p. ix Although so much has been written on the land-question, I am not aware of any single work which summarises the evidence and discusses the results of our system of land-tenure as compared with that of other civilised countries, in its bearing, not upon landlords and tenants alone but on all classes of the community; and I therefore venture to think that everyone who has at heart the advancement of the social condition of our people, and who feels the disgrace of our position as at once the wealthiest and the most pauperised country in the world, will find much to interest, and perhaps to instruct, in this small volume.

*Godalming, March, 1882.*

## TABLE OF CONTENTS.

shown to be comparatively Useless--Mr. Kay's Arguments in support of Free Trade in Land--Small Landed Estates are constantly absorbed by Great Ones--Free Trade in Land would not help either the Tenant or the Labourer--Nationalisation of the Land the only Effective Remedy--Occupancy and virtual Ownership must go together--To Secure this the State must be the real Owner or Ground-Landlord--The State must become Owner of the Land apart from the Improvements added to it--Mode of Determining the Value of the *Quit-rent* and of the *Tenant-Right*--How Existing Landowners may be compensated--Alleged unfairness of Compensation by means of Terminable Annuities--How Tenants may become Occupying Owners--Subletting must be absolutely prohibited--Evils of Subletting in Towns--Mortgaging should be strictly limited--Whether any Limits should be placed to the Quantity of Land personally occupied--Supposed Objections to Land Nationalisation--Mr. Fowler's Objections--Mr. Arthur Arnold's Objections--Mr. G. Shaw Lefevre's Objections--The Hon. George C. Brodrick's Objections--Mr. J. Boyd Kinnear's Objections--How Nationalisation will affect Towns--Free-Selection of Residential Plots by Labourers and Others--Objections to the Right of Free-Selection--Why Free-Selection should be restricted to Once in a Man's Life--Free-Selection would check the growth of Towns, and add to the Beauty and Enjoyability of Rural Districts--How Commons may be

# LAND NATIONALISATION.

## CHAPTER I.

## ON THE CAUSES OF POVERTY IN THE MIDST OF WEALTH.

INCREASE OF THE VALUE OF LAND DURING THE PRESENT CENTURY--GREAT INCREASE OF OUR TOTAL WEALTH--PAUPERISM DOES NOT DIMINISH IN PROPORTION TO OUR INCREASING WEALTH--FAILURE OF OUR SOCIAL ORGANISATION--INCREASE OF LABOUR-SAVING MACHINERY AND THE UTILISATION OF NATURAL FORCES--THE ANTICIPATED EFFECT OF MAN'S INCREASED POWER OVER NATURE--THE ACTUAL EFFECT--HOW TO DISCOVER THE CAUSE OF OUR SOCIAL FAILURE--WHY GREAT WEALTH IS OFTEN INJURIOUS--ACCUMULATED WEALTH MAY BE BENEFICIAL OR THE REVERSE--HOW GREAT ACCUMULATIONS OF CAPITAL AFFECT

THE LABOURER--THE NATURE OF THE REMEDY SUGGESTED--SCOPE OF THE PRESENT ENQUIRY.

Among the characteristics of the present century, none is, perhaps, more striking than the enormous increase of the national wealth, which, during the last fifty years especially, has progressed with a rapidity altogether unprecedented. During this period the land of Great Britain has more than doubled in value, while in the great centres of industry it has often increased a hundred or even a thousandfold, and this increase has been mainly due, not to any expenditure made by the owners or occupiers of the land, but almost wholly to the growth of population and of wealth, and to the great advance in all the arts and industries which minister to our modern civilisation. The total annual value of this landed property is enormous. The estates which exceed 3,000 acres in extent or £3,000 in annual value, amounting in all to twenty-one and a-half million acres, are valued at £35,000,000, while those of less area or less annual value amount to more than thirty-two million acres; and as these latter will consist to a great extent of highly-cultivated suburban lands, small residential estates, and building lots, while the former include all the poorest and least valuable mountain and moor-land of Scotland, Wales, and Ireland, their value can hardly be less than 65 millions, making a total of £100,000,000.[1] This large sum is, however, only an indication of the wealth of the country; for a considerable proportion of the 320,000 landowners who possess more than an acre derive large incomes from manufacturing industries and mercantile or financial pursuits, or have invested capital in the British or Foreign Funds, in railways, or in other securities, so that the amount of accumulated property and the number of persons who are supported on this property without personal exertion, are both probably larger in proportion to the whole population than at any other period of our history, or than in any other country in the world. The increase of our wealth, as well as its great amount, is sufficiently indicated by the fact, that the "Property and Profits" assessed to Income Tax have more than doubled in the 30 years from 1848 to 1878, being in the former year (for Great Britain) £256,413,354, and in the latter £542,411,545; and there can be no doubt that these amounts are, on the whole, greatly under-estimated.

*Pauperism does not Diminish with our Increasing Wealth.*--This enormous increase in the wealth of the country--and that far greater proportionate increase of its manufactures and commerce of which our legislators are so proud that rarely do they speak in public without calling attention to it--have not, however, been attended by any proportionate increase in the general well-being of the people. Nothing tests this well-being so surely as the number of paupers, since, if the condition of the people were generally raised to any considerable extent, this number must largely diminish. We find, however, that though the number fluctuates much from year to year, and figures can be picked to show a decrease, yet, taking a large early and late average, there is no decrease, the numbers of paupers in England and Wales fluctuating around an average of about six-sevenths of a million. This, however, is only the number in receipt of relief on the first day of each year. The total number relieved during the year is, according to Mr. Dudley Baxter, three and a-half times as much, or an average of upwards of three millions. Allowing for the same individuals being relieved more than once, we shall be quite within the mark if we take the mean of the two numbers, or a little less than two millions, as the actual average number of paupers; but it must be remembered that this does not include either the vagrants, or the casual poor, or the criminals in our jails, or that large body who are permanently dependent on private charity, which altogether must bring up the number to at least three millions. Let us consider for a moment what this implies. The three million paupers in any year are all persons who are actually unable to obtain a sufficiency of the coarsest food and clothing to support life; and they form, as it were, the failures from among a much larger body, who constantly live from hand to mouth on the scanty wages of their daily labour. If we take this class of the population who are ever trembling on the verge of pauperism at only half the number of the actual paupers, we arrive at a total of 4,500,000--more than one-sixth of the whole population--who live constantly in a state of squalid penury, unable to obtain many of the necessaries of a healthy existence, and one-half of them continually falling into absolute destitution, and becoming dependent on public or private charity.[2]

*Failure of our Social Organisation.*--This is, surely, a most anomalous and altogether deplorable state of things. On the one side, wealth and luxury and all the refinements of life to an unprecedented extent--on the other, a vast, seething mass of poverty and crime, millions living with their barest physical wants unsatisfied, in dwellings where common decency is impossible, and, so far as any development of the higher faculties is concerned, in a condition actually inferior to that of many savages. And these poverty-stricken millions consist largely of the tillers of that very soil which has of late years so vastly increased in value, and thus added so much to the wealth and luxury of its possessors. The political economist points with pride to the vast increase of our wealth; but he ignores the fact that the *distribution* of that wealth is more unequal than ever, and that for every single addition to the exceptionally rich there are scores or hundreds added to the exceptionally poor. But the legislator should look at the question from a different point of view. Every government which is not a despotism is bound to make the well-being of the whole community its object; and mere wealth is no indication whatever of this general well-being. So long as poverty and degradation are the characteristics of large classes of the community, society and government are alike proved to be failures; and the rapid increase of wealth, with the great advances of science, art, and literature, only render this failure the more glaring, and prove more clearly that there is something radically wrong in the social organisation that is incompetent to remedy such gross and crying evils.

For some generations, at all events, there has been no lack of will on the part of our legislators and philanthropists. Many serious evils have been remedied; much cruelty and injustice have been abolished; and, as we have seen, vast wealth has been created; but no one who knows the condition and mode of life of the large class of agricultural labourers, and the horrible degradation of great masses of the inhabitants of all our chief cities, with the periodical distress, and even famine, in the manufacturing districts and in Ireland, can doubt the utter failure of all their attempts.

*Increase of Labour-saving Machinery and Utilisation of Natural Forces.*--But there is another circumstance which adds immensely to our conception of the vastness and horror of this failure. During the present century there has been a continual and ever-increasing growth in the use of steam-power and labour-saving machinery, which has been equivalent to the possession by us of a body of industrious slaves, ever labouring, patiently and without complaint, and exceeding in effective power probably ten-fold that of our whole working population. In addition to each actual workman there are, therefore, ten of these willing slaves constantly labouring for us, and every day of our lives we derive the benefit of their labour.[3] Yet all this has only made the rich richer, the poor remaining as numerous, and, in many respects, even worse off than before we acquired this vast addition to our productive power.

Other sources of wealth have also been afforded us during the lives of the present generation altogether unique in the history of the world. In two hemispheres gold has been discovered in such quantities as to lead to a wonderful development of our commerce, while at the same time it has drawn off large numbers of our surplus population. Almost coincident with these great discoveries was the rise and rapid development of the railway systems of the world; and it was we English who, for a long time, had almost a monopoly of the construction of these railways. The demand for iron and coal for this purpose was enormous, and of this, too, we had the largest immediately available supply; and so eagerly did we make use of our opportunities that in one generation we have exhausted these stored-up treasures of our soil to an extent which would have supplied our home wants for centuries, and have thereby actually deteriorated our land for our descendants in order greedily to enrich ourselves.

The increase of the mere steam *power* employed does not, however, at all adequately represent the advantage we have over our immediate predecessors, for along with this increase of power has gone on an increased efficiency in our mode of applying that power to human uses, so that it is not improbable that each horse or man-power now employed in the production of all the countless forms of wealth which we enjoy, is five or ten times as efficient as it was a century ago. This will be clear if we think of the economy of the railway train as compared with the coach and waggon, and of the amount of clothing produced in a modern cotton-mill as compared with what was produced by the same actual *power* employed on the clumsy old machines of the hand-spinner and hand-weaver. Steam and electricity, and the thousand applications of modern science to the arts and industries, have economised *time* quite as much as they have economised mere *labour*. These various economies give us such an advantage over our ancestors that, although the average duration of life has been but little increased, yet, such is the intensity of modern existence that we may be said to live twice or thrice as long as they did.

*What might have been Anticipated as the Result of Man's Increasing Power over Nature.*--Let anyone ask himself what ought to have been the consequence of such a vast increase of man's power over nature? To quote the words of an eloquent and thoughtful modern writer:--"Could a man of the last century--a Franklin or a Priestly--have seen, in a vision of the future, the steamship taking the place of the sailing-vessel, the railroad-train of the waggon, the reaping-machine of the scythe, the thrashing-machine of the flail; could he have heard the throb of the engines that, in obedience to human will, and for the satisfaction of human desire, exert a power greater than that of all the men and all the beasts of burden of the earth combined; could he have seen the forest tree transformed into finished timber--into doors, sashes, blinds, boxes, or barrels, with hardly the touch of a human hand; the great workshops where boots and shoes are turned out by the case with less labour than the old-fashioned cobbler could have put on a sole; the factories where, under the eye of a girl, cotton becomes cloth faster than hundreds of stalwart weavers could have turned it out with their hand-looms; could he have seen steam-hammers shaping mammoth shafts, and delicate machinery making tiny watches; the diamond-drill cutting through the heart of the rocks, and coal-oil sparing the whale; could he have realised the enormous saving of labour resulting from improved facilities of exchange and communication--sheep killed in Australia eaten fresh in England, and the order given by the London banker in the afternoon executed in St. Francisco in the morning of the same day; could he have conceived of the hundred thousand improvements which these only suggest, what would he have inferred as to the social condition of mankind?

"It would not have seemed like an inference. Further than the vision went, it would have seemed as though he saw; and his heart would have leaped and his nerves would have thrilled, as one who from a height beholds just ahead of the thirst- stricken caravan the living gleam of rustling woods and the glint of laughing waters. Plainly in the sight of the imagination he would have beheld these new forces elevating society from its very foundations, lifting the very poorest above the possibility of want, exempting the very lowest from anxiety for the material needs of life; he would have seen these slaves of the lamp of knowledge taking on themselves the traditional curse, these muscles of iron and sinews of steel making the poorest labourer's life a holiday, in which every high quality and noble impulse could have scope to grow."[4]

*The Actual Effect.*--This the anticipation, but what the reality? The great cities have all become greater, and all contain within their bounds dense masses of people living in cellars and hovels and airless, filthy courts, again and again condemned as unfit for human habitation. Many fair valleys and once fertile plains have become blasted by the smoke of our engine fires and the noxious gases from our furnaces, while almost all our once bright and limpid streams have become fetid sewers. Everywhere the workers work harder than before; they live in unsightly and unwholesome houses, packed together in rows like pens for cattle; they have no field or garden ground for profitable occupation or healthy enjoyment; their young children can get no wholesome milk, and often no playground but the alley and the kennel.

Paupers and tramps abound everywhere. Men and women beg for work in all our streets, and many, failing to get it, die of want. Famine even attacks us as of old; and in the very same districts from which food or clothing is largely exported, the producers have now and again to be saved from starvation by public charity.

This is the outcome of our boasted civilisation. This is the final result of our unexampled increase in national wealth, of our improved laws, of our increased knowledge, of our vast strides in science. Our labourers not only do not participate in the comfort, refinement and relaxation which a fair share in our increased wealth would give them, but, so wretched is their condition that a great traveller in many barbarous lands solemnly declares that never among any savage tribe had he seen such utter wretchedness and degrading poverty as was to be found in Ireland at the present day. Nor is evidence wanting that the condition of some parts of England is hardly better. Professor Fawcett, in his work on "The British Labourer," asserts that "A large proportion of our working population are in a state of miserable poverty. Many of them live in dwellings that do not deserve the name of human habitations." In the same work he thus strongly supports the main allegations we have made in the present chapter:--

"The advance in the material prosperity of Liverpool, of Glasgow, and other centres of commerce is unprecedented, yet in close contiguity to this growing wealth there are still the same miserable homes of the poor, the same pestilential alleys, where fevers and other diseases decimate the infantile population with unerring certainty. . . . How is it that this vast production of wealth does not lead to a happier distribution? How is it that the rich seem to be constantly growing richer, while the poverty of the poor is not perceptibly diminished?"[5]

Neither in the work here quoted nor elsewhere can I find that Professor Fawcett has given, or even attempted to give, a complete answer to this momentous question--What is the cause, or what are the causes, of this complete, this utter, this awful failure? A failure under circumstances so extremely favourable that, to anyone having these circumstances set forth beforehand, failure of this kind would have seemed impossible. A failure, be it remembered, not confined to our country alone, but one which is also manifested, though usually with less intensity, in *every* civilised community. The cause must be a fundamental one. It cannot depend on anything in which one civilised community differs from another civilised community--on race or on religion, on government or on climate--for all suffer, though in very different degrees, and these differences of degree will perhaps afford an important clue to the true cause as well as to the true remedy.

*How to Discover the Cause of our Social Failure.*--The fundamental error shown to exist in our Social System may perhaps be detected by noting the leading idea which has governed all social and industrial legislation for the last fifty years, a period on the whole of enlightened and progressive government. That ruling idea seems to have been that whatever favours and assists the production of *wealth*, of whatever kind, and the accumulation of *capital* by individuals, necessarily advances the well-being of the whole community. This idea is seen in the constant references by public writers and public speakers to our increased trade and manufactures, to our enormous exports and imports, to the high price of our public funds, to the vast extent of our shipping, to the increased amount of Income Tax, and such like indications of growing wealth and accumulated capital. And it has found expression in most of the reforms in our fiscal and industrial legislation during the last half century--reforms which have been advocated on these grounds, and have been adopted by the Legislature with this avowed object. Of such a character are--the repeal of the coal duties, leading to the use of coal as ballast and an enormously increased export; the extensive enclosures of commons, and their division among the surrounding great landowners; the encouragement of railways, even when quite unprofitable; the opening of distant lands to our commerce, even at the expense of costly wars; the Limited Liability Act to favour the extension of Joint Stock Companies; the continued enlargement of our eastern possessions, and the acquisition of fresh additions to our already too extensive Colonial system. These, with many less important measures, all tending in the same direction and advocated for a similar purpose, have been successful even beyond expectation in adding to the total wealth of the country, and more especially to that of our hereditary landowners, great merchants, great capitalists, and astute speculators. The greatly increased wealth of these classes has added largely to the emoluments of the more successful professional men--lawyers and doctors--as well as to the profits of the more enterprising traders, and thus an upper middle class has arisen far exceeding in wealth and luxurious living anything before known in England or to be met with in any other European country. But none of these legislative acts, or the movements and tendencies of which they are the expression, have had any effect towards the diffusion or equalisation of wealth, or to the diminution of that large class ever hovering on the verge of pauperism; and (so far as I know) hardly any of our recognised teachers of political economy has pointed out that the increase in the number of very wealthy people or of great capitalists (which is what all our legislation favours), so far from being beneficial, is, in every respect, antagonistic to the well-being of the community at large.

*The Injurious Effects of Excessive Wealth-Accumulation.-* -This question is far too large to be adequately discussed here, but a few words of explanation will serve to indicate the idea sought to be conveyed, and may offer materials for deep consideration. The wealth of a country is produced solely by the working population of that country, including in that term all who produce anything that tends to human enjoyment or well-being. The laws of supply and demand, with freedom of exchange, will regulate the distribution of the products of labour, and, if all were producers and all had free access to those natural powers and agencies which furnish the raw material for human labour, the well-being of all would be ensured, since the exchangeable wealth each man could produce would far exceed what is necessary to supply the ordinary wants of existence. That this is so is proved by the fact that even the poorest countries--the poorest parts of Ireland, for example--always produce a large surplus over and above what is required for the subsistence of the inhabitants, the amount of this surplus being measured by the sum total of rent, taxes and savings. Accumulated wealth, however, introduces a disturbing agency. Just in proportion as it becomes great and can be made to produce a permanent income by investment in land or in the public funds, it leads to the existence of a large and ever-increasing class of non-producers, who necessarily live on the labour of the rest, since there is no other source from which they can live. This will be clear if we consider that the owners of the invested wealth purchase goods and pay for labour with money which the workers first supply them with in the shape of *rents* for the use of land, and *taxes* to pay the interest on the public funds. It is clear, therefore, that all the wealth represented by these two sources is not *real* wealth, but, however it originated, is *now* merely taxation for the purpose of supporting a portion of the community without work.

This, however, is not the worst feature of such nominal wealth, for it has a tendency and a power to divert labour from the production of articles of use and beauty--beneficial wealth--to the production of such as minister only to luxury and amusement, often of a more or less wasteful and even degrading nature--injurious wealth. If we could reckon up the amount of human labour, physical and mental, expended on jewellery and fancy goods, on costly toys or elaborate displays of clothing and equipages, on horse-racing and yachting, on luxurious dinners and fashionable entertainments, we should arrive at an enormous sum total of wasted labour, energy and talent, all of which is positively injurious to the productive workers, since it is they who really have to support, by their ill-paid labour, not only the rich individually, but also that vast array of servants, artisans, and labourers, who in so many varied ways minister to their luxuries, their pleasures, or their vices. This argument is not intended to show that all accumulation of wealth is bad, for it is only by the accumulation of wealth in the form of reproductive capital that civilisation progresses;

but merely that excessive wealth in the form of landed or funded property, which is perpetually transmitted from one generation to the next, is a perpetual and heavy tax on the producers of beneficial wealth.

*Accumulated Wealth may be Beneficial or the Reverse.*--Political economists, however, have glorified "capital" as the benefactor of mankind in general, and of the working-classes in particular; but they have not sufficiently distinguished between true productive capital--as expressed in roads and railways, mines, harbours, ships and buildings, machinery and tools, with a sufficient store of food, clothing and all other necessities of life--and the "capital" of the great fundholder or the great landholder, which, in both cases, is merely a power to appropriate the labour of others without any exertion on their part, a power not only to be supported themselves by the labour of the community, but to direct a large portion of that labour into wasteful, and even injurious, channels at their own will and pleasure. It is this latter form of capital that our recent increase in wealth has multiplied to a great and injurious extent--an extent to be measured by the immense number of persons of "independent means," the hosts who live in the "City" by the mere manipulation of money, and the general increase of luxury in dress and living among the wealthy classes.

We are here introduced to another great question, the justice or morality of permitting *permanent* burdens on the community to be created for *temporary* purposes. Such are the wars of one Government or generation, which remain as a burden on succeeding generations; but the principle is equally applicable to all expenditure which does not produce a *permanent* equivalent. Thus, in our railroads the only really permanent result of the capital expenditure is the earthwork; all the rest is temporary, requiring constant annual repairs and complete renewals at greater or less intervals. Yet the cost of a large proportion of these *temporary* works remains as a burden on the public long after they have been worn out, in the form of interest on capital and debenture stock, so that the present generation really pays twice over for much of what it enjoys. Honesty no less than sound policy would dictate that every expenditure not producing a permanent result should be repaid out of profits, by a sinking fund calculated at somewhat less than its probable duration. The result of not doing so is that the enormous capital of our railways and of many other great industrial enterprises to a considerable extent represents no actual existing wealth, and the interest paid on it is, therefore, a tax on the travelling community and on the shareholders, for which they receive no return whatever.

*How Great Accumulations of Capital Affect the Labourer.*--This, however, is a digression. Let us now come back to the primary question we were discussing, of the fundamental error of our legislators in favouring the *accumulation* of wealth rather than its wider *distribution*; and let us endeavour to see exactly how this affects the labourer, and how it leads to his poverty and pauperism amidst ever-increasing national wealth.

One of the most obvious causes which leads to this sad result is the almost complete dependence of the mass of labourers in this country (as in most civilised countries) on capitalists and landowners for the means of earning a livelihood. The absence of work for daily wages means for them starvation, since they have no other resource whatever. They are, therefore, not in a condition to refuse work, at whatever wages may be offered them, and the severe competition among capitalists and manufacturers for the means of employing their capital and adding to their wealth obliges them to force down the wages of unskilled labour to the lowest point at which the labourer can live. The labourers, as a class, are thus *absolutely* dependent on the comparatively few capitalists--dependent on *their* prudence, *their* capacity, *their* honesty, and *their* judgment--*wholly* dependent on the judicious application of capital, without having any voice or any direct or immediate interest in that application. They go blindly to any labour offered them; and when, owing to reckless competition, dishonest adulteration, foreign wars, and other causes, a time of depression arrives, they are helpless. They have no means of productive home industry, they have not even a home from which they cannot be ejected at any moment on failure to pay the weekly rent; they have no land, garden, or domestic animals, the produce of which might support them till fresh work could be obtained. If they have any savings these are soon spent, and they then inevitably fall into pauperism.

*The Nature of the Remedy Suggested.*--The remedy for these evils is sufficiently obvious, though how the remedy is to be generally applied is not so clear. The first great evil, of dependence on capitalists, would be remedied by small associated communities of workmen, by home manufactures, or co-operative workshops. The second evil, that the labourer has no independence, no fixed home, nothing to fall back on in time of depression, nothing on which to employ his spare time and that of his family, can only be cured by giving to every labourer freedom to enjoy and cultivate a portion of his native soil. It is by this latter reform alone that the first will be rendered possible. By it the great and important class of agricultural labourers may be at once raised from chronic pauperism to comparative affluence, comfort, and independence. By it the mechanic or artisan may find a refuge from distress when his industrial occupation temporarily fails him; while the enormously increased production of food, caused by every labourer and peasant possessing land, would at once renovate the home commerce and internal resources of the country so as to render prosperous many domestic industries now languishing. It will be shown in the present volume, by the unvarying experience of all civilised nations, that the *most* important of all classes of labourers for the permanent prosperity of a country are those who occupy and cultivate their own land. Just in proportion as this class is extensive and varied--comprising the wealthy farmer on the one hand and the agricultural labourer with an acre or two of ground on the other--so is the country free from poverty and the people prosperous and contented; and it is because this class is so rare with us, and especially because our labourers have for generations past been more and more divorced from the soil, that we are in the disgraceful position of being at once the wealthiest and most pauperised country in Europe--that, while boasting of our religion and our philanthropy, a large proportion of our labourers live in cottages and hovels that, by the most competent authorities, have been again and again declared unfit for human habitation, necessarily leading to disease and vice, and altogether unparalleled in the civilised world for every bad quality a dwelling can possess. The facts are so uniform in character and so clearly point to one conclusion, that nothing but the circumstance of our legislators having a vested interest in the existing state of things could have so long delayed the clear perception of the causes of the evil. For not only does the same system of land-tenure always coincide with the same social phenomena, but when the system has been changed the social condition has undergone a corresponding change. This has notably been the case with France before and since the Revolution--with Prussia before and since the reform effected by Stein and Hardenberg--and with Denmark before and since the somewhat similar change of land tenure which has been effected during the present century; though it must be noted that in none of these countries had the evils of landlordism ever attained the same proportions as with us. Neither our reform of Parliament, our Free Trade policy, our vast emigration, our enormous manufacturing system, our widespread colonial empire, our maritime supremacy, nor our unprecedented accumulations of capital, have had any apparent effect in elevating our labouring classes or securing them even that measure of well-being and contentment which they attain in every country where the land is widely held and cultivated by them. We are, therefore, warranted in concluding that, in order to effect a real and vital improvement in the condition of the great mass of the English nation, not only as regards physical well-being, but also socially, intellectually, and morally, we must radically change our system of land-tenure. It is when the cultivator of the soil is its virtual owner, and *all* the products of his labour as well as the increased value he can confer upon the land are his own, that the maximum of human food is produced by it, the maximum of human enjoyment is derived from its cultivation, while the cultivator is, as a rule, healthy, moral and contented. In order that the largest possible number of the people may be thus benefited, and that the evils necessarily resulting from the opposite system of landlordism may be totally abolished, it is essential that the ownership of land, merely as a source of income from its rent or for commercial speculation, shall cease, and a system be substituted for it which shall make every farmer and every occupier, large or small, the virtual (but for reasons to be afterwards explained, not the absolute or unrestricted) owner of the land he cultivates or dwells upon. If the facts which lead us to this conclusion are as above stated--and an overwhelming mass of evidence will be adduced that they are so--it follows that the present system of land-tenure in this country is incompatible with the national well-being, and that every enlightened legislator, every lover of truth and justice, and every true philanthropist is bound to seek the means of changing it.

*Scope of the Present Inquiry.*--In the present volume I propose, as briefly as is consistent with a clear presentation of the question, to lay before my readers a sketch of the condition of the different parts of our own country and of other civilised lands as regards land-tenure, and of the corresponding effects. I shall then point out the conclusions to which the facts invariably lead us, and shall show how the evils under which we suffer may be most effectually and justly remedied. My proposals will be founded entirely on the facts recorded by the best and most impartial authorities, and I claim for my work a purely inductive character. But there is another and a most important mode of discussing the same question as a strictly scientific problem, deducing results from the admitted principles and data of political economy. This has been done with great force of logic and wealth of illustration in Mr. George's work already alluded to. His conclusions support and his mode of argument supplements my own, and I shall, therefore, give a short summary of the essential part of his book before explaining in detail my practical scheme of Land Nationalisation.

*Notes, Chapter One*

1. The total annual value and rental of the landed property of the Kingdom given in the new Doomsday Book, is £131,470,360, but this appears to include the rental of all the buildings, factories, houses, &c. on the land, while it excludes the whole of London where land is of fabulous value. The above estimate, therefore, is probably below the mark as the rental value of the land itself of the United Kingdom. That the increase in the value of land during the present century is not overstated in the first paragraph, appears from a recent Return of the Board of Inland Revenue, which gives the gross value of Land, Tenements, and Tithes assessed to Income Tax in Great Britain, as £58,751,479 in 1814-15, and £172,136,183 in 1879-80, being an increase of almost threefold in sixty-five years. on

2. The average number of paupers in England and Wales on the 1st of January for the twelve years 1849-1860 was 863,338, and for the twelve years 1869-1880 it was 864,398. The numbers were lowest in 1876-78 and in 1853, while they continued at a maximum during the period from 1863 to 1873, when it averaged over a million; and it is very curious that this was the very period when our commerce was increasing so rapidly as to excite the admiration and pride of our legislators, reaching the highest point it has ever attained in the last-named year. Our population has of course been increasing all this time, and therefore the percentage of official pauperism has decreased, sometimes rapidly, sometimes very slowly. But it must be remembered that there are many causes which have been increasingly in operation during the period we are considering, all of which have a tendency to diminish the official number of paupers, even though the actual percentage of pauperism has increased. First, and perhaps most important, is the increasing perception among all poor-law officials of the evils of outdoor relief, which at once encourages improvidence and affords opportunities for deception. Year by year the poor-law has been worked with increased stringency in this respect, and this alone must have largely reduced the official record of paupers relieved. The establishment of casual wards for the relief of vagrants is another comparatively recent movement which has tended to diminish the list of official paupers. At the same time

there has been a continually increasing movement among philanthropists for the relief by private charity of true cases of distress. Such associations as the Charity Organisation Society, the Mendicity Society, the Metropolitan Visiting and Relief Association, and many others, indicate the amount of systematic efforts in relief of poverty and prevention of pauperism, while year by year we find new institutions formed to succour all those who fall into unmerited poverty. If the increasing effects of all these causes and agencies could be fully estimated, it would probably be found that they are more than sufficient to account for the nominal decrease in the percentage of pauperism, while their mere enumeration is sufficient to indicate that a reference to the official statistics of pauperism, however accurate these may be, does *not* prove that pauperism is diminishing, or even demonstrate that it is not actually increasing.

3. There seems to be no means of getting at the exact amount of the steam-power now employed in Great Britain. A writer in the *Radical* newspaper states it at two million horse power. Mr. Thomas Briggs in *The Peacemaker* states that "in 1851 we had steam machinery which represented 500 million pair of hands," but I am informed he means by this the number which would be required to do the same work by the old hand-power machines. In a periodical called *Design and Work* (Vol. X. 1881), it is stated that England now employs 9 million horse-power. Taking this last estimate

(which has been found for me by Mr. Anderson, one of the intelligent attendants in the British Museum Reading Room) as approximately correct, we have a power equal to 90 million men. One half our population (15 millions) consists of children and persons wholly dependent on the labours of others, and from the remainder we may deduct all the professional, literary, and independent classes, the army and navy, financiers and speculators, government officials, and most tradesmen and shopkeepers--none of whom are producers of wealth. Taking these, together with criminals, paupers, and tramps, at 6 millions, we have left 9 millions who do all the productive physical labour of the country, while the steam power at work for us is at least ten times as much.

4. "Progress and Poverty," by Henry George (, 2), a work which only became known to the present writer after the greater part of the MSS. of this volume was completed.

5. "The British Labourer," , 1865. In order to show that these statements of Professor Fawcett are as true now as when he wrote, I will quote a few passages from a speech of Mr. Jcssc Collings, M.P., at Ipswich, in October last year. He says:--"I have spent some time during the last two months in going down to the South of England to see what the increase of the labourers' wages has been. I visited districts in Worcestershire, in Hampshire, in Warwickshire, and in Wiltshire, and I found the labourer getting 10s. a week, and

in one large district the men are at this moment receiving 9s. a week, out of which they have to pay 1s. 6d. a week rent, and as I sat by the hedge-side with them they would make their dinner off bread and an onion. I felt serious then; and at night when I went into their cottages, as I have done scores of times, and found the everlasting bread again for their children and themselves, with no comfort in the present, no pleasant retrospect of the past, no apparent hope for the future--one might well be a serious politician. I went into one lovely village, for the villages are lovely in England, and one regrets to see men driven from them; and there again the mother was in mourning for her child who had died of disease. I came away and called it starvation." And when doubt was thrown on his statements Mr. Collings in reply said:--"I have spent considerable time to satisfy myself; my utterance has not been mere hearsay. Go through Wiltshire, Hampshire, Worcestershire, Devonshire, and Somersetshire. There, I say, outside the influence of the towns, there are at this moment men and women with families living on 10s. a week, with no art, no science, no literature, to enlighten their lives; nothing but the everlasting grind of human toil for them."

---

# CHAPTER II.

## THE ORIGIN AND PRESENT STATE OF BRITISH LAND-TENURE.

ANTIQUITY OF OUR PRESENT SYSTEM CAUSES IT TO APPEAR A NATURAL ONE--ANTIQUITY OF A SYSTEM NO PROOF OF ITS VALUE--ORIGIN OF BRITISH LAND TENURE--CHARACTERISTICS OF THE FEUDAL SYSTEM--GROWTH OF MODERN LANDLORDISM--THE LEGAL POWERS EXERCISED BY LANDLORDS--OUR LAND SYSTEM IS A MODIFIED FEUDALISM, IN WHICH THE LANDLORDS HAVE THROWN THEIR BURDENS ON THE PEOPLE, WHOSE RIGHTS IN THE LAND THEY HAVE ABSORBED.

The present tenure of land in this country is of such antiquity, it has so grown with the progress of society, and has become so interwoven with all the elements of rural, social, and political life, that to many persons the very conception of any other system is difficult, if not impossible. That land should be private property; that it should be bought and sold for pleasure or profit; that any man should be allowed to possess all that he inherits or is able to purchase; that it should be rented out to those who cultivate it; and that the owner should let it subject to whatever restrictions or stipulations he thinks proper--seem, to most people, not only natural but right; and even those who suffer by this state of things--the farmer who is injuriously restricted in his cultivation, or is turned out of his farm because he has voted against his landlord or otherwise offended him; and the labourer who sees the bit of green enclosed on which his father's donkey and geese used to run, who is liable to be turned out of his home at a week's notice, and who is obliged to walk three miles to his daily labour because there are no spare cottages in his employer's parish--rarely trace these evils to the general system of land-tenure, but rather to some deficiency in the character or conduct of their immediate landlords.

*Antiquity of a System no Proof of its Value.*--It is generally supposed that, when any system or institution has grown up with the growth of society, has persisted notwithstanding vast social and political changes, and has become interwoven with the very texture of a nation's life, it must necessarily be good in itself and adapted to the conditions under which it flourishes. But this is by no means universally, or even generally, the case; and it often happens that the worst evils inherent in a system may be so disguised by the good qualities of those who administer it that it is borne with long after its ill consequences are, in many cases, admitted. Sooner or later, however, the eyes of the people are opened to its faults; remedies of various kinds are proposed; and when all these remedies are resisted by those who benefit by the institution, a revolution sweeps away the whole, and a new system is introduced which is often far less beneficial or perfect than a carefully considered constitutional reform. Thus, despotic governments, notwithstanding their respectable antiquity, have in time to be modified by representative institutions, or are entirely destroyed in the throes of rebellion or revolution. Thus, too, slavery--the most ancient of all institutions, and one which has formed part of the essential character and social life of many communities--everywhere has to be abolished with advancing civilisation, if not voluntarily and peacefully, then by violence or civil war. So feudalism, with its accompanying remnant of serfdom, has been gradually modified in all civilised countries, while with us some of its essential features persist in the vast landed estates held by private individuals, and in the almost despotic power which the owners are able to exercise (and sometimes do actually exercise) over the population--a power so great that the supreme authority of the State is often unable to protect individuals in the occupation of their ancestral homes, in the right to live among the scenes of their childhood, or even in the possession of property created by their own industry.

Let us, then, see if there is anything in the history of modern landlordism which entitles it to continue to exist for ever, even though it may be shown to be incompatible with freedom, and adverse to the best interests of the people.

*Origin of British Land-Tenure.*--The actual system of land-tenure and all existing rights of property in land of this country may be said to have originated at the Norman Conquest, when the whole land of the kingdom became vested in the Crown. All the great landed estates were then granted as fiefs by the sovereign, and their holders were obliged to render military and other service proportionate to the extent and population of their lands. These estates were also subject to various fines, on marriage or on transmission to an heir; they were not allowed to be sold or alienated without the permission of the Sovereign; and on the death of the owner without heirs the whole reverted to the Crown. Any breach of fealty, or the commission of any act of felony, also entailed the loss of the estate. The great vassals were usually endowed with civil and criminal jurisdiction over the inhabitants of their estates, and were altogether more in the position of subordinate rulers than mere landlords in the modern sense of the term.

These immediate vassals of the Crown again granted lands in fief, on various payments or services, and in process of time these fiefs were allowed to be divided or sold, and the payment or service to be commuted for fixed sums of money. Military service, too, gradually ceased, and was changed into annual payments, which are now only represented by the small, fixed, land-tax; so that the greater part of the land of the kingdom became "freehold"--implying that it was "held" from the Crown "free" from all military service, dues and fines, and subject only to a fixed annual payment.

*Characteristics of the Feudal System.*--The system which was thus established was evidently very different from that of landlord and tenant at the present day. The great landlords were actual vassals of the Crown and subordinate rulers. They held their estates subject to military service; and this implied that the population on the land was the first essential, since this was the measure of its power in providing capable men-at-arms. Their tenants, the villeins or cultivators, held their farms subject to certain services, military or otherwise, and to the payment of certain dues; and these farms were held for life, and descended from father to son or other relation on payment of certain fines to the lord, whence, it is believed, arose the copyhold tenures by which so many small estates are held to this day. In those times the land was of less value than the men who lived on it, and the animal or vegetable produce of the land of less importance than the population of hardy villeins, who enhanced the lord's dignity, increased his revenues, and kept up the supply of his armed followers. The landowner then lived upon his estate, and his own power and influence in the country depended chiefly on the number and the well being of his tenants. Together they formed a little quasi-independent community, bound to each other by mutual interests and ancestral ties; and if the tenants were sometimes oppressed by their lords, they were as often guarded from robbery and plunder by wandering marauders, or saved from complete destruction during baronial feuds or civil wars.

*Growth of Modern Landlordism.*--During this rude period of our history, when the Central Government was lax and the means of communication imperfect, the feudal system possessed many advantages, and was, in some form or other, almost the only one possible. The "lords of the soil" were the chiefs and protectors of the community which lived on their estates, while every individual, down to the villein and serf, possessed definite rights and privileges in connection with the land, which, though they might be infringed by force or rapine, were fully recognised by custom and law.

But as time rolled on this system became modified in a variety of ways, though always for the benefit of the lord and to the injury of the inferior landholder. As the King obtained more power and the attractions of court life became greater, the nobles and great landowners came to look upon their estates chiefly as sources of revenue to be spent in the capital or in foreign lands. The employment of foreign mercenaries and the rise of standing armies enabled the King to dispense with the military service of his vassals, and by self-made laws this and other burdens on the land were gradually thrown off, and were replaced to a great extent by taxes on the mercantile and landless classes. The ingenuity of lawyers and direct landlord legislation steadily increased the powers of great landowners and encroached upon the rights of the people, till at length the monstrous doctrine arose that a landless Englishman has no right whatever to the enjoyment even of the unenclosed commons and heaths and the mountain and forest wastes of his native country, but is everywhere, in the eye of the law, a trespasser whenever he ventures off a public road or pathway. The Lord of the Manor is said to be the "owner of the soil," and the surrounding freeholders and copyholders have certain rights of pasture, fern or turf cutting; but the dwellers in the adjacent towns and villages, and all who are mere Englishmen, have no rights whatever, so that if the two former classes agree, the common can be (as hundreds of commons have been) enclosed, and divided among them. It has thus come to pass that at the present day the owners of land, whether acquired by inheritance or purchase, treat it solely as so much *property*, to be made the most of, quite irrespective of any rights in the *people* who live upon it. They now claim a power which no government, however despotic, has ever openly claimed--that of treating the land exclusively as a source of personal wealth, to which they have an indefeasible right, even at the sacrifice of all that the people who live upon the land hold most dear; and having rendered the exercise of this power legal by means of self-made laws and customs, they have at length come to look upon acts of oppression and cruelty of the most glaring kind as not only right, but such as are not incompatible with the condition and feelings of a people who pride themselves upon their freedom.

We find, then, neither in the origin of our land-system nor in the causes which have led to its present development, anything to render it sacred or immutable; but, on the contrary, very much to show that a radical change is needed to bring it into harmony with modern ideas, and to render possible the full use and enjoyment of the land of our country by the people who must necessarily inhabit it. Absolute private property in land logically carried out, denies the right of non-landholding Englishmen to live upon their native soil, except by sufferance and under conditions imposed by the will or caprice of the landlords. This power is, on the whole, moderately used, or the institution would have been long ago abolished in the throes of revolution. But it is not unfrequently exercised, and even abused, to the injury of individuals and of the community; and, as the sufferers have no legal redress, the institution itself stands thereby condemned.

*The Legal Powers Claimed and Exercised by Modern Landlords.*--Before proceeding (in the three following chapters) to exhibit in some detail the influence of landlordism on individuals and on the community at large, a few general observations and illustrative examples may here be given; but before doing so I wish to state, emphatically, that I have no desire to excite any ill-feeling against landowners as a body, or to make any accusation against them personally; still less is it my intention to propose any measure of confiscation as against existing landlords. The law places them in an anomalous position. It tells them that their rights over their land are absolute. They could, if it so pleased them, turn it into a waste given up wholly to wild animals, or might even destroy its surface-soil and convert it into a desert uninhabitable by man or beast. In doing this they might expatriate hundreds of families, and even cause many to die of exposure, want, or grief; and all this time the Government and the Law would stand by with no power to interfere. They would be acting within their legal rights. Public opinion would, no doubt, in such extreme cases condemn them, yet there are many who exercise similar rights to a partial extent; and so deadening is the influence of long custom and legal sanction that, whenever it can be shown that the result is profitable commercially, apologists are to be found who uphold the action as beneficial.

Mr. James Godkin well remarks: "According to this theory of proprietorship, the only one recognised by law, Lord Lansdowne may legally spread desolation over a large part of Kerry; Lord Fitzwilliam may send the ploughshare of ruin through the hearths of half the county Wicklow; Lord Digby, in the King's County, may restore to the bog of Allen vast tracts reclaimed during many generations by the labour of his tenants; and Lord Hertford may turn into a wilderness the district which the English settlers have converted into the garden of Ulster. If any or all of these noblemen took a fancy, like Colonel Bernard, of Kinnilty, and Mr. Allen, of Pollok, to become graziers and cattle-jobbers on a gigantic scale, the Government would be compelled to place the military power of the State at their disposal, to evict the whole population in the Queen's name, to drive all the families away from their homes, to demolish their dwellings, and turn them adrift on the highway, without one shilling compensation. Villages, schools, churches would all disappear from the landscape; and when the grouse season arrived, the noble owner might bring over a party of English friends to see his *improvements*! The right of conquest so cruelly exercised by the Cromwellians, is in this year of grace *a legal right*; and its exercise is a mere question of expediency and discretion. It is not law or justice, it is not British power that prevents the enactment of Cromwellian scenes of desolation in every county of that unfortunate island. It is self-interest, with humanity in the hearts of good men, and the dread of assassination in the hearts of bad men, that prevent at the present moment the immolation of the Irish people to the Moloch of territorial despotism. It is the effort to render impossible those human sacrifices, those holocausts of Christian households, that the priests of feudal landlordism denounce so frantically with loud cries of '*confiscation.*' " ("The Land War in Ireland," .)[1]

It may be thought that such cases as are here supposed are altogether imaginary, but it is not so. The *Daily News* special commissioner, a writer by no means unfavourable to the cause of the landlords, says, writing from Mayo (Oct. 30th, 1880):--"Tradesmen, farmers, and all the less wealthy part of the community still speak sorely of the evictions of thirty and forty years ago, *and point out the graveyards which alone mark the sites of thickly-populated hamlets abolished by the crowbar*. All over this part of the country people complain bitterly of the loneliness. According to their view, their friends have been swept away and the country reduced to a desert in order that it might be let in blocks of several square miles each to Englishmen and Scotchmen, who employ the land for grazing purposes only, and perhaps a score or two of people where once a thousand lived--after a fashion." The writer then goes on to explain that this was done in order that the landlords might get their rents more securely and more easily, even though the rents were somewhat less than those paid by the former occupants; and he seems to think that they acted very reasonably and that no one had any right to complain! Mr. Jonathan Pim, in his "Condition and Prospects of Ireland" (1848) says:--"Sometimes ejectments have been effected on a large scale. The inhabitants of whole villages have been turned adrift at once, without a home to go to, without the prospect of employment, or any certain means of subsistence." And one of the witnesses before the Devon Commission thus describes the condition of many of these poor people and the general results of that "consolidation of farms" which landlords and agents are said to approve so highly:--"It would be impossible for language to convey an idea of the state of distress to which the ejected tenantry have been reduced, or of the disease, misery, and even vice, which they have propagated in the towns wherein they have settled; so that not only they who have been ejected have been rendered miserable, but they have carried with them and propagated that misery. They have increased the stock of labour, they have rendered the habitations of those who received them more crowded, they have given occasion to the dissemination of disease, they have been obliged to resort to theft and all manner of vice and iniquity to procure subsistence; but, what is perhaps the most painful of all, a vast number of them have perished of want."[2]

Nor are these cruel evils confined to Ireland. A little more than half a century ago, the estate of the Marquis of Stafford in Sutherland, comprising 800,000 acres, or about two-thirds of the whole county, was forcibly cleared of a population of 15,000 herdsmen and farmers, in order to turn it into enormous sheep farms with a shepherd per square mile. Other landlords have since followed this example, till about 2,000,000 of acres, once crowded with farms and cottages in all the valleys, are now reduced to a vast desert wholly given up to sheep-runs and deer-forests. The amount of misery and destitution, and the various physical and social evils produced by this depopulation of the Highlands will be sketched in another chapter. We here adduce it only as an example of that terrible power over their fellow creatures which absolute property in land gives to individuals who possess large estates; and that this power is actually used with the most unsparing rigour, sometimes to obtain an increased or a more certain rental, sometimes in pursuance of views supposed to be in accordance with the teachings of political economy, sometimes merely to provide an extensive hunting-ground.

*Our Land System is a modified Feudalism, in which the Landlords have Thrown their Burdens on the People whose Rights in the Land they have Absorbed.*--I have now shown, by a few striking examples, that the land system under which we actually live is an abnormal development of feudalism, in which almost all the customary rights and privileges of the serfs, villeins, or tenants have been encroached upon and finally destroyed, while the great landowners under the Crown have, by means of self-made laws and customs, gradually absorbed the rights of the people, till they have become true *land-lords*, not only claiming, but actually exercising, such absolute rights of property in the soil that their fellow subjects can only live upon it at all by their gracious permission. And these terrible *rights* are not only theoretically permitted, but are actually enforced by all the executive power of the State whenever the landlord so wills! It only needs to state these facts to show, that the system which permits so vast and injurious a despotism in the midst of free institutions is radically wrong and cannot much longer be upheld; and if in exposing the evils of the *system* we are obliged to refer to the general or special results of landlordism, it is simply because the exposure can be made in no other way. The institution itself is necessarily evil--in the present state of society--just as slavery is necessarily evil; and this quite independently of the goodness or badness of individual landlords or slave-owners. But just as the evils of slavery would never have been generally acknowledged in our time if it had not been for the horrors resulting from the unrestrained passions of bad or careless or wealth-seeking slave-owners, so the evils of unrestricted private property in land can be best brought before the public by showing the effects it is calculated to produce, and does actually produce, in the hands of wealth-seeking capitalists and despotic landlords.

*Notes, Chapter Two*

1. This power still remains to the landlord in England and Scotland though the recent Land Act has abolished it in Ireland.

2. Parl. Re, vol. xix, page 19.

---

# CHAPTER III.

## A FEW ILLUSTRATIONS OF IRISH LANDLORDISM.

IRELAND AFFORDS EXAMPLES OF ALL THE EVILS THAT ARISE FROM PRIVATE PROPERTY IN LAND--ORIGIN OF IRISH LANDLORDISM--TENANT-RIGHT--CONFISCATION BY LANDLORDS--CONDITION OF THE IRISH COTTIER--FACTS IN POSSESSION OF THE LEGISLATURE FOR THIRTY YEARS; THE DEVON COMMISSION--GOVERNMENT NEGLECTS ITS FIRST DUTY--EVICTIONS AFTER THE FAMINE--SUGGESTED REMEDIES OF IRISH DISTRESS--CONTINUED BLINDNESS AND INCOMPETENCE OF THE LEGISLATURE--TREMENDOUS POWER OF AGENTS OVER THE TENANTS--THE CONDITION OF THE PEOPLE UNDER IRISH LANDLORDISM.

No part of the British Isles offers such striking examples of every kind of evil that results from unrestricted private property in land as Ireland. In that unfortunate country we find some of the largest estates; the greatest number of absentee landlords; the most complex settlements, perpetual leases, and other incumbrances; middlemen and sub-tenants in every variety; the greatest uncertainty of tenure; the most reckless competition for land; the most extravagant rack-rents; and the most merciless appropriation by the landlords of the improvements and actual property of the tenants. Nowhere else in our country do we find the land so generally treated as mere rent-producing property; nowhere else do a considerable proportion of the landowners exhibit an almost complete disregard for the welfare, or even the existence, of the native agricultural population.

*Origin of Irish Landlordism.*--The history of this island as regards the ownership of its land is a most distressing one, the greater portion of the country having been confiscated since the reign of Henry VIII. Extensive grants of land were made to court favourites or to successful soldiers, reign after reign; and every fresh rebellion of the oppressed people led to fresh confiscations and other transfers of land. Many of the new owners, not wishing to reside in the country, leased the land in perpetuity or for a very long term, at a low rent. The first leaseholder often again leased or subdivided the land, and this was sometimes repeated several times before coming to the actual cultivator. As an example, a townland in the county of Roscommon containing about 600 acres is owned by an English nobleman, but is leased in perpetuity for £30 rent. This first leaseholder has again leased it in perpetuity at £200 per annum. This third landlord has divided it, one man paying £150 a year rent for about one-third of the whole; and this fourth holder has divided a portion of his part among sixteen families, who are the actual cultivators of the soil. The superior landlords and leaseholders of course care nothing about the tenants, and have no interest in their welfare or in the condition of the estate, since their rents are amply secured and can never be increased; while the last middleman, who is landlord to the actual tenants, has a high rent to pay himself, and is obliged to let his land to the highest bidders in order to secure a profit. This is an actual case brought before the Relief Committee of the Society of Friends at the time of the great famine, and it is stated that the same condition of things, variously modified, is to be met with in all parts of the country.[1] Still more prejudicial is the fact that most of the large estates are under strict settlement, so that the actual owners have only a life interest in them; and as the estates are often laden with mortgages and family charges, it is impossible for the landlord, even if so disposed, to improve the land or to be lenient to his tenants. To add to the evil, most estates are managed by agents in the absence of the proprietors; and as their reputation and continued employment depends upon their success in collecting rents and punctuality in sending remittances, they are compelled to use all the powers the law gives them against defaulting tenants.

*Tenant-Right.*--The most fertile source of agrarian

disturbances in Ireland has been the general practice of leaving the occupier of the land to do everything that is done in the way of improvement--everything that is required to render the land capable of cultivation at all. The landlord usually does nothing but take rent. The whole process of changing the land from stony mountain slopes or boggy pastures into cultivated fields has been done by successive tenants. The tenants have made the fences, the roads, and the gates, they have dug the ditches and drains, and have even erected the farm houses and buildings. Of course they could not do this at all without some security or belief that they should enjoy it for a time, and thus arose a general custom, to consider the occupier as a co-partner with the landlord, who not only had a moral claim to the continued occupation of the land which he had reclaimed or improved, but who could also sell his share to a succeeding tenant or transmit it to his heirs. There have always, however, been some landowners who, either on account of their necessities or their greed, have refused to recognise this just claim, and have, at every opportunity, raised the rent to the full value of the tenants' improvements. Instances of this were common at the beginning of the century and appear to have increased rather than diminished to the present day; and they have naturally led to a feeling of utter insecurity in the smaller class of occupiers, who would rather remain idle than labour at any improvements which would only lead to an increase of their rent. Let us give a few examples of this legalised oppression and robbery from Mr. Tuke's moderate and trustworthy pamphlet, "Irish Distress and its Remedies" (1880).

*Confiscation by Landlords.*--At Glenties, in Donegal, a man took a piece of bog at a rent of £2 a year. This he fenced, drained, and cultivated, turning a wilderness into a tidy little farm, and was thereupon made to pay nearly four times the original rent for it. In another case, in Ulster, a man built a corn mill on land belonging to one of the London Companies. When the lease expired the rent was somewhat raised, but of this he did not complain, and again added to the value of the property by building a flax-mill. The rent was again raised and then the Company sold the land. The new purchaser still further raised the rent. This was too much to bear, so the occupier determined to sell his tenant-right; but the agent of the new owner declared at the sale that the rent would be still further raised to the purchaser, and this caused the tenant-right to bring far less than it would otherwise have done. This old man, thus robbed of what on every moral and equitable principle was his own property, then emigrated to America with his family, carrying with him the bitterest animosity against his oppressors and against the Government which allowed the oppression.

None cry out so loudly as landowners against any law which may possibly diminish the selling value of their property, however beneficial such law may be to the whole country. They exclaim against it as "confiscation." Yet they have allowed (as legislators) such cruel confiscation as this, which brings endless evils in its train. For these are not exceptional cases; indeed, a Member of Parliament recently stated with truth that there are "tens of thousands of instances where tenants paying five shillings an acre were evicted by their landlords that the landlords might let their occupations at a pound an acre, the increased value being entirely due to the labour expended upon the land by the evicted tenants." And then we wonder at the misery, and idleness, and deceit of the Irish peasantry! Why, it is forced upon them. They dare not become prosperous or look prosperous for fear of increased rent. Thus, they often live in filth. They come to the rent-audit in their worst clothes. They pay the rent in shillings and sixpences, to give the appearance of having collected it with the greatest difficulty. And they will be idle half the winter rather than improve their hovels, or mend their fences, or make any permanent improvement in their holdings. It is true that there are many good landlords who never commit such robbery; but good landlords do not live for ever, and are sometimes obliged to sell their property, and then the tenant's security is gone. It is just as it was in the days of American slavery. The good master did not voluntarily sell his slaves or part husband and wife, parent and child; but there was no security that at any moment they might not be transferred to a new owner who would do both.

*Condition of the Irish Cottier.*--The modern Irish cottier really lives in a state of hopeless and helpless degradation, comparable to that of the least fortunate serfs of the Middle Ages, who were not only subject to the payment of hard dues to their lord, but upon any appearance of wealth or even comfort were subject to extortion by the lord's followers or plunder by armed marauders. They were obliged to be poor and miserable to escape robbery. Ireland is a nation of small cultivators. There are 400,000 holdings under 30 acres, and 30,000 under 15 acres, while there are 156,000 mud cabins of only one room occupied by 228,000 families![2] Probably nowhere in the whole world is there a people living in such a state of degradation and barbarism under a civilised or even a semi-civilised government; and this is the direct result of pure landlordism, making its own laws, and carrying them out in its own way. It is a universal law that security to enjoy the produce of a man's labour is the only incentive to industry, and that incentive has been systematically denied to the Irish peasant. The injustice, the cruelty, the shortsightedness of this system had been urged again and again on our legislators, but wholly without effect, till the terrible calamity of the potato disease in 1846 and 1847, and the horrible events that ensued, forced them into action. But even then, so blind were they to the real cause of the evil, so convinced that landlordism was itself a perfect dispensation, that, instead of giving the occupier security for his labour, they established the Encumbered Estates Court as their great remedy, which, as is now universally admitted, only increased the evil, and gave the authority of an Act of Parliament to further confiscations of tenants' property. Mr. Tuke says: "It is notorious that the rights of the tenants were disregarded, and that this disregard was the occasion of grievous wrong in numerous instances, sometimes when the tenants were evicted without compensation to make room for new comers, and sometimes when the rents were raised by the new purchasers, with entire disregard to the peculiar position of the Irish tenant. It has often been noticed that the rack-rented estates are generally not the estates of the old Irish proprietors, in which the rents are for the most part moderate in amount, but estates purchased under the Act by speculators, who have resold them, after increasing the rental enormously." Can there be a more striking proof of the blindness and ignorance of those legislators who, against all evidence and repeated warnings, left the Irish peasantry to the tender mercies of new landlords armed with all the powers of the law, and were unable to see that the land of a country with the population dependent on it ought not to be subject to unrestricted sale and purchase, or to be allowed to minister to the reckless greed of capitalists and speculators.

*The Devon Commission*, 1847.--The Legislature which

passed the Encumbered Estates Act as a sufficient remedy for all the evils of the Irish land-system had before it the elaborate Report and Digest of Evidence of the Commission on the Occupation of Land in Ireland. This report, dated 1847, says: "It is admitted on all hands that, according to the general practice in Ireland, the landlord builds neither dwelling-house nor farm-offices, nor puts fences, gates, &c., into good order, before he lets the land to a tenant. The cases in which the landlord does any of these things are the exception." And with regard to the custom of tenant-right in Ulster, where the improvements made by the occupier are allowed to be sold by him to the incoming tenant, the same Report says: "Anomalous as this custom is, if considered with reference to all the ordinary notions of property, it must be admitted that the district in which it prevails has thriven and improved, in comparison with other parts of the country."

In the Digest of Evidence taken before the same Commission we find this weighty and important statement:--

"If a substantial security were offered to the occupying tenant for his judicious permanent improvements, a rapid change for the better would take place--a change calculated to increase the strength of the Empire and the tranquility of this country; to improve the food, raiment, and house-accommodation of the population; to remove that paralysis of industry which the sworn evidence of nearly every tenant, and of numerous landlords, examined on the subject, has proved to exist; to call into operation the active exertions of every occupier of land upon his farm; to add about five months in each year to the reproductive occupation of farmers and labourers, which are now passed in idly consuming produce, accumulating debts, or, for want of better employment, perhaps, in fomenting disturbance."

It is the want of this security that is the sole cause of those agrarian disturbances which for more than a century have been perennial in Ireland. This is authoritatively stated in the same Digest of Evidence, which tells us that "the great majority of outrages appear to have arisen from the endeavours of the peasantry to convert the possession of land into an indefeasible title," and that "in the northern counties, the general recognition of the tenant-right has prevented the frequent recurrence of these crimes." And again, the Report emphatically states: "The tenant's equitable right to a remuneration for his judiciously-invested labour and capital is not likely to be disputed in the abstract. This property is, undoubtedly, his own." And it adds:

"The importance and absolute necessity of *securing* to the occupying tenant in Ireland some distinct mode of remuneration for the judicious permanent improvements that he may effect upon his farm is sustained by a greater weight of concurrent evidence than any other subject which has been brought under the investigation of the Commissioners;" and

"The want of some measure of remuneration for tenants' improvements has been variously stated as productive, directly or indirectly, of most of the social evils of the country." And again we have this important statement: "It has been shown that the master evil--poverty--proceeds from the fact of occupiers of land withholding the investment of labour and capital from the ample and profitable field for it which lies within their reach on the farms they occupy; that this hesitation is attributable to the reasonable disinclination to invest labour or capital on the property of others without a security that adequate remuneration shall be derived from the investment."

The Report goes on to show that "the barbarous and unprofitable mode of tillage" is all due to this uncertainty that the tenants shall be allowed to reap the fruits of their labour; that many lucrative agricultural improvements may be made "without the investment of money capital, but merely by the judicious application of time and labour of his family, which are now wasted, whilst he is complaining that employment cannot be had;" that the larger farmers have the same ample opportunity of employing labourers on similar works, with a certainty of the most profitable results; but this is rarely done, "because they have no certainty of being permitted to reap the benefit of their expenditure," while, if tenants-at-will, "they may be immediately removed from the improved lands, after having invested their labour and capital, without receiving any compensation, or their rent may be raised to the full value of the improvements thus effected."

Yet with all these striking facts and authoritative statements before them--facts and statements, be it remembered, not of philanthropists or political economists, but of a Parliamentary Commission composed exclusively of landlords, who, with great labour, had collected this evidence for the express information of the Legislature--*no provision whatever was made to secure the tenant's right to the property created by himself*, but his position was in many cases rendered far worse than before by the sale of thousands of estates to the highest bidders, who *thereby obtained full legal power to seize and confiscate for their own use the wealth created by the life-long labours of Irish tenants!* Is it possible to imagine a more cruel mockery than this? Can there be a more complete condemnation of government by landlords, and, as this is almost a necessary result of their existence, of landlordism itself?

*Government Neglects its First Duty.*--We see, then, from the authoritative evidence of a Parliamentary Commission, that the chronic poverty of the Irish peasantry and farmers, their barbarous mode of tillage, their idleness for many months in the year, and their consequent inability to bear up against any distress caused by bad seasons or epidemic disease, were all clearly and directly traceable to the absence of any security for the improvements due to their labour on the land they occupied. The first duty of a civilised Government--the protection of property--was in their case systematically ignored, and the absence of protection for the fruits of human labour involved, in its results, the absence of protection to life, as surely as if bands of armed robbers and murderers had been allowed to range undisturbed over the country. Ignorance that such consequences might ensue could not be pleaded, since on many previous occasions famines of the most distressing kind, and due to the same causes, had occurred, notably in 1817 and 1822; yet still *nothing* was done to remove the causes of this perennial misery, which inevitably led to famine. When, therefore, in 1847 and 1848 the potato disease destroyed a large part of the food of the country, and--the extreme poverty of the people leaving them absolutely without resources--millions died of starvation, we cannot avoid seeing in this terrible calamity the direct results of ignorant and prejudiced government by a body of alien legislators.

*Evictions after the Famine*.--But what followed was still more dreadful, and, one would think, should have opened the eyes of the most bigoted to their fatal error. During the four years succeeding the famine, the miserable remnant of the agricultural population were in many districts subject to wholesale eviction from their homes, often resulting in loss of life. Mr. T. P. O'Connor tells us that in the four years

1849-1852 there were 221,845 evictions; whole townlands being depopulated, and their human inhabitants driven out to make room for cattle and sheep, as being more profitable to the landlords.[3] These poor people were often forced away from their homes, even though all rent due had been fully paid. The houses, which had been built by their own labour (or purchased from those who had built them), were pulled down; and when the houseless families, having nowhere to go, lighted fires in the ditches to cook some food, the fires were extinguished in order to drive them off the land. A Report to the Poor Law Commissioners states that many occupiers were forced out of their homes at night in winter, even sick women and children not being allowed to stay in the houses till morning!

And the power to do all this, be it remembered, is a necessary consequence of unrestricted private property in land. That such horrors do not occur more frequently is due to the good feeling and humanity of landlords, and to the absence of sufficient motive; but that they should have been ever possible, that they should have actually occurred in hundreds of cases, and that a Government which claims to rule over a free, prosperous, civilised, and Christian people was not only utterly powerless to prevent them, but was actually obliged to aid in carrying them into effect--for all was strictly legal, and the landlord was only enforcing his admitted rights--must, surely, make every one who is unfettered by prejudice see that the possession of land for any other purpose than *personal occupation* is incompatible with liberty, and therefore necessarily leads to evil results.

That fearful period of famine, and the emigration which succeeded it, reduced the population of Ireland from eight to five millions, and at the same time established in America a body of Irishmen imbued with the bitterest feelings of enmity against the British Government--an enmity whose natural fruit was that Fenian conspiracy which has been more really injurious to England than a great and unsuccessful war. For a time, however, all was thought to be going well. Many landlords had changed their once thickly-populated land into great grazing farms, supporting cattle and sheep instead of peasants, but returning a more secure if not a higher rent. The general prosperity caused by the gold discoveries and the great epoch of railway-making was felt by the diminished population of Ireland, and the landlords were for a time satisfied that their two great panaceas, emigration and large farms, would cure all the alleged evils. But the increased wealth of landowners in general, as well as of merchants and speculators, led to a more expensive style of living, and this could only be met by higher rents wherever they could be obtained. In Ireland, where to large numbers of the people a piece of land offers the sole means of subsistence, there is so much competition for land that rents may be raised to any amount the landlord or the agent chooses to demand; and, as a matter of fact, rents have been continually raised over a large part of the country so as to leave the tenants the barest possible subsistence.

*Suggested Remedies for Irish Distress.*--Before the great famine of 1847, European politicians and economists who visited Ireland were amazed at the spectacle of a country one-third of whose population lived perpetually on the very verge of starvation. The causes and the remedy for this disgraceful state of things were clear to them, and were pointed out in the plainest language by one of our greatest authorities on Political Economy--John Stuart Mill--in 1856. He demonstrated that a system of Cottier tenure such as prevailed in Ireland, in which a large agricultural population without capital, and with a low standard of living, have their rents determined by competition, must inevitably lead to all those social and physical evils which perennially exist there. He says:--"The rents which they promise they are almost invariably incapable of paying; and consequently they become indebted to those under whom they hold, almost as soon as they take possession. They give up in the shape of rent the whole produce of the land, with the exception of a sufficiency of potatoes for a subsistence; but as this is rarely equal to the promised rent, they constantly have against them an increasing balance. . . . Should the produce of the holding in any year be more than usually abundant, or should the peasant by any accident become possessed of any property, his comforts cannot be increased; he cannot indulge in better food nor in a greater quantity of it. His furniture cannot be increased, neither can his wife or children be better clothed. The acquisition must go to the person under whom he holds." And he goes on to show that such tenants have nothing to gain by industry and prudence, nothing to lose by any recklessness. If they doubled the produce of their farms by extra exertion, the only gainer would be their landlord. "Almost alone among mankind the Irish Cottier is in this condition, that he can scarcely be any better or worse off by any act of his own. If he were industrious or prudent, nobody but his landlord would gain; if he is lazy or intemperate, it is at his landlord's expense. A situation more devoid of motives to either labour or self-command imagination itself cannot conceive. The inducements of free human beings are taken away, and those of a slave not substituted. He has nothing to hope, and nothing to fear, except being dispossessed of his holding, and against this he protects himself by the *ultima ratio* of a defensive civil war."[4]

In the succeeding discussion on the "Means of Abolishing a Cottier Tenancy," Mill goes to the root of the question in the following passages:--"Rent paid by a capitalist, who farms for profit and not for bread, may safely be abandoned to competition; rent paid by labourers cannot, unless the labourers were in a state of civilisation and improvement which labourers have nowhere yet reached, and cannot easily reach, under such a tenure. Peasant rents ought never to be arbitrary--never at the discretion of the landlord; either by custom or law it is imperatively necessary that they should be fixed; and where no mutually advantageous custom has established itself, reason and experience recommend that they should be fixed by authority, thus changing the rent into a quit-rent, and the farmer into a peasant proprietor. For carrying this change into effect on a sufficiently large scale to accomplish the complete abolition of cottier tenancy, the mode which most obviously suggests itself is the direct one of doing the thing outright by Act of Parliament; making the whole land of Ireland the property of the tenants, subject to the rents now really paid (not the nominal rents) as a fixed rent-charge. This, under the name of 'fixity of tenure,' was one of the demands of the Repeal Association during the most successful period of their agitation, and was better expressed by Mr. Connor, its earliest, most enthusiastic, and most indefatigable apostle, by the words, 'A valuation and a perpetuity.' . . . To enlightened foreigners writing on Ireland, Von Raumer and Gustave de Beaumont, a remedy of this sort seemed so exactly and obviously what the disease required that they had some difficulty in comprehending how it was that the thing was not yet done."

As a milder and less radical, but still very efficacious, measure, if carried out to the fullest extent of which it is capable, Mill suggested an enactment "that whoever reclaims waste land becomes the owner of it, at a fixed quit-rent equal to a moderate interest on its mere value as waste;" and the proof that this measure would be successful is afforded by evidence given before Lord Devon's Commission, in 1847, by Colonel Robinson, the manager of the Waste Land Improvement Society. He states that "two hundred and forty-five tenants and their families have, by spade husbandry, reclaimed and brought under cultivation 1,032 plantation acres of land, previously unproductive mountain waste, upon which they grew last year crops valued at £3,896; and their live stock, consisting of cattle, horses, sheep, and pigs, now actually upon the estates, is valued at £4,162; and by the statistical tables and returns obtained annually by the Society, it is proved that the tenants, in general, improve their little farms, and increase their cultivation and crops, in nearly direct proportion to the number of available working persons of whom their family consist."

*Continued Blindness and Incompetence of the Legislature.*--Yet with all this mass of consentaneous evidence as to the law-made misery of the Irish people and its only effectual remedy, for another twenty-four long years the Legislature did nothing to give them that ownership of the soil which, wherever it exists, is the cause of untiring industry, thrift, peace, and contentment, till in the year 1880 famine again appeared, and again charity alone has saved thousands from death by starvation. To the landlord Government which has shut its ears to every word of truth and warning, even when coming from a Commission appointed by itself, the burning condemnation of Carlyle, written forty years ago, is surely applicable:--"Was change and reformation needed in Ireland? Has Ireland been governed in a wise and loving manner? A Government and guidance of white European men which has issued in perennial hunger of potatoes to the third man extant ought to drop a veil over its face, and walk out of Court under conduct of proper officers; saying no word; expecting now of a surety sentence either to change or die."[5]

In 1870, it is true, a Land Act was passed, which it was thought would settle the question; but it really settled nothing, because it did not go the root of the matter. As the late Mr. Charles Buxton, M.P., said in 1869: "It is security of tenure the Irish people want; and it is security of tenure the Irish people must and will have. It is no sort of good to put them off with talk about mere compensation for improvements, or other schemes for giving them what they do not ask for and do not want, instead of that which they do ask for, and do want." John Stuart Mill had said exactly the same thing a year before in his striking pamphlet, "England and Ireland," and all the evidence that had been collected for the previous twenty-five years demonstrated the same fact; yet our landlord Legislature, in its usual peddling and patchwork spirit, passed a most elaborate Act to secure compensation for a tenant's improvements in case he was ejected for any other cause than non-payment of rent, but guarded and modified by all kinds of stipulations and reservations, involving the employment of valuers and lawyers, and an indefinite amount of trouble and expense, but not securing the tenant either against arbitrary increase of rent or eviction at the will of his landlord, the two most important things the Irish tenants asked for, and without which the proposed compensation was a delusion and a snare. For, instead of evicting, the landlord simply raised the rent on a tenant who had made improvements, and thus confiscated these improvements in spite of the Act! And thus even the Ulster tenant-right has been made valueless by the very Act which was intended to extend some of its benefits over a wider area.[6]

*Tenant-Right Often Confiscated Even in Ulster.*--Even before this Act, however, tenant-right was only a *custom*, not a *law*, and was not unfrequently disregarded. Mr. Charles Wilson, writing in *The Statesman* (Feb., 1881), gives the following example:--"See the position of the tenants on a small estate in Ulster, which was bought some twenty years since, and the rents were doubled on the tenants. One had to pay £64 instead of £23, another £57 instead of £29; another lost his lease by accident, and though the landlord had the counterpart, instead of producing it, he raised the rent 50 per cent. Another, who holds in perpetuity, was charged £15 per annum for some years as a drainage rate; but, suspecting wrong, he applied to the Board of Works, and found that the landlord was paying only £5 19s., and pocketing the difference. The tenant got this put right and recovered the surcharge."

One of the tenants of Sir Richard Wallace stated at a recent meeting that the farm he now held at 25s. per acre was held by his grandfather at 2s. 6d. per acre, and that all the improvements which had so largely increased the rental value were made at the cost of the tenants. At another meeting of the tenants of the same estate resolutions were passed stating that, owing to the system which had been adopted by the late Marquis of Hertford, many reductions of rent had been purchased by the payment of a sum down, and that, owing to this system of "fining down leases," any reference to present rents as being low was fallacious; that tenants' improvements and agricultural property have been made a basis for continual rises of rent; that *tenants'* improvements are included in the Government valuation; and that, therefore, this forms no true basis for estimating the *landlord's* rent; that several vexatious "office rules," unknown formerly, have lately been instituted; that the tenants are charged five per cent. on the amount of the rent under the name of receiver's fees; that the ground rent of public roads and rivers is charged on the tenant; and many other complaints of a like nature.

*Tremendous Power of Agents over the Tenants.*--Against these and similar exactions of agents the tenants are powerless. As Mr. Godkin well puts it, "Armed with the 'rules of the estate,' and with a notice to quit, the agent may have almost anything he demands, short of possession of the farm and home of the tenant. The notice to quit is like a death warrant to the family. It makes every member of it tremble and agonise, from the grey-headed grandfather and grandmother to the bright little children, who read the advent of some impending calamity in the gloomy countenances and bitter words of their parents. The passion for the possession of land is the chord on which the agent plays, and at his touch it vibrates with the 'deepest notes of woe.'"[7]

Eviction is what the Irish peasant dreads as a sentence of misery or death, and it is well that my readers should realise what an Irish eviction really is. The following account of an eyewitness is taken from a published Pastoral Letter of the Roman Catholic Bishop of Meath:--

"It was a cruel, an inhuman eviction, which even still makes our hearts bleed as often as we allow ourselves to think of it. Seven hundred human beings were driven from their homes in one day, and sent adrift upon the world to gratify the caprice of one who, before God and man, probably deserved less consideration than the last and least of them. And we remember well that there was not a single shilling of rent due on the estate at the time except by one man; and the character and acts of that man made it perfectly clear that the agent and himself quite understood each other. The crowbar brigade, employed on the occasion to extinguish the hearths and demolish the homes of honest, industrious men, worked away with a will at their awful calling until evening. At length an incident occurred that varied the monotony of the grim, ghastly ruin which they were spreading all around. They stopped suddenly, and recoiled, panic-stricken with terror, from two dwellings which they were directed to destroy with the rest. They had just heard that a frightful typhus fever held those houses in its grasp, and had already brought pestilence and death to their inmates. They therefore supplicated the agent to spare these houses a little longer; but the agent was inexorable, and insisted that the houses should come down. He ordered a large winnowing sheet to be secured over the beds in which the fever victims lay--fortunately they happened to be perfectly delirious at the time--and then directed the houses to be uprooted cautiously and slowly, because, he said, 'He very much disliked the bother and discomfort of a coroner's inquest.' I administered the last sacrament of the Church to four of these fever victims next day; and, save the above-mentioned winnowing sheet, there was not then a roof nearer to me than the canopy of heaven.

"The horrid scenes that I then witnessed I must remember

all my life long. The wailing of women; the screams, the terror, the consternation of children; the speechless agony of honest, industrious men, wrung tears of grief from all who saw them. *I saw the officers and men of a large police force*, who were obliged to attend on the occasion, *cry like children* at beholding the cruel sufferings of the very people whom they would be obliged to butcher, had they offered the least resistance. The heavy rains that usually attend the autumnal equinoxes descended in cold, copious torrents throughout the night, and at once revealed to those houseless sufferers the awful realities of their condition. I visited them next morning, and rode from place to place administering to them all the comfort and consolation I could. The appearance of men, women and children, as they emerged from the ruins of their former homes--saturated with rain, blackened and besmeared with soot, shivering in every member from cold and misery--presented positively the most appalling spectacle I ever looked at. *The landed proprietors in a circle all round--and for many miles in every direction--warned their tenantry, with threats of direct vengeance, against the humanity of extending to any of them the hospitality of a single night's shelter*. Many of these poor people were unable to emigrate with their families; while at home the hand of every man was thus raised against them. They were driven from the land on which Providence had placed them; and, in the state of society surrounding them, every other walk of life was rigidly closed against them. What was the result? After battling in vain with privation and pestilence, they at last graduated from the workhouse to the tomb, *and in little more than three years nearly a fourth of them lay quietly in their graves.*"[8]

*The Condition of the People under Irish Landlordism.*--When we remember that a plot of land is the sole means of subsistence to the mass of the rural population of Ireland, that there are "at least 500,000 families, amounting to about 3,000,000 persons, competing for the land as the sole stay between themselves and starvation," how absurd is it to talk of "freedom of contract," or to wonder that the Irish peasants submit to any rent and any conditions that the landlords or their agents choose to impose, rather than suffer the barbarous punishment of eviction.

The natural, the inevitable result of such a state of things is thus described by recent observers. Mr. Charles Russell says:--"In a country whose fruitfulness would suffice to feed and maintain a greatly increased population in decent condition, there exists at this moment in a population which famine and emigration have reduced from eight millions to about five millions, a more intense degree of wretchedness and poverty, and that more general, than in any known country in the world." And Mr. De Courcy Atkins, in his "Case of Ireland Stated," after describing what he saw in Cork and Kerry, concludes thus:--"There have been many countries, both ancient and modern, in which slavery was part of the acknowledged law, but I submit to all men who have studied the question of slavery, whether in any such country the producing slave has been so limited in the enjoyment of the produce as the nominally free Irish labourer or cottier tenant is in Ireland."

It may perhaps be said, "All this is now at an end. The Government has done justice to Ireland by the new Land Act. Why tell old tales?" But no law, even if far more efficient and more beneficial than the recent Act, can recall the past, or undo the misery and degradation brought upon the bulk of the Irish people by the action of landlordism and landlord-made law, such as still exists in England and Scotland. Some of their worst effects have no doubt now been locally remedied, but the root of the evil still remains; and it is important to show the natural and inevitable results of a system which requires to be held in check by exceptional legislation in order to prevent horrors and catastrophes like those it has produced in Ireland.

*Notes, Chapter Three*

1. Pim's Condition and Prospects of Ireland, 1848, .

2. Speech of Mr. Cowen, M.P., at Newcastle.

3. These figures are approximate, but they are generally supported by those given in a Parliamentary Report issued in April 1881. This gives 35,061 families, consisting of 194,603 persons, evicted in two years (1849-50). And the

same Report shows that again in 1880, during the height of the last famine, there were 2,110 evictions of 10,457 persons. It is to be noted that these are only the evictions that have come to the knowledge of the constabulary, and are doubtless considerably below the actual number, since many are carried into effect by persons employed by the agent.

4. Political Economy, Book II, Chap. ix.

5. Mr. Tuke in his "Irish Distress and its Remedies," gives 72,864 as the number of persons who received relief in the County of Donegal, the whole population of which, in 1871, was 218,000. This was one of the ten distressed counties, and if taken as an average one, here, too, every third man had been living in "perennial hunger of potatoes."

6. See numerous examples of this in Mr. Charles Russell's "New Views of Ireland," as well as in the daily press.

7. It will hardly be credited what kind of "rules" prevail on some estates. Mr. Thomas Crosbie, of Cork, an agent himself, published in 1858 an account of "The Lansdowne Estates." He declares that the "rules of the estate," which were rigidly enforced, forbid tenants to build houses for their labourers; forbid marriage without the agent's permission, so that a young couple having transgressed the rule were chased away to America, and the two fathers-in-law were punished for harbouring their son and daughter by a fine of a gale of rent. Another rule was that no stranger be lodged or

harboured in any house on the estate, lest he should become sick or idle, or in some way chargeable on the poor-rates. A tenant, who sheltered his sister-in-law while her husband was seeking work, was so afraid of the agent that, at the woman's approaching confinement, he removed her to a shed on a relative's land, where her child was born. This man was fined a gale of rent, and was made to pull down the shed. Then the poor sick woman went to a cavern in the mountain, and for this two other fines were levied from the tenants who jointly grazed the land. A still worse case is given; but these are sufficient to show that Irish tenants live under a system of penal laws, unknown to the Legislature, and are punished by fines enforced by the dread of eviction. (Godkin's "Land War in Ireland," .)

8. Quoted from Mr. T. Walter's pamphlet--"Irish Wrongs and How to Mend Them--1881," .

# CHAPTER IV.

## LANDLORDISM AND ITS RESULTS IN SCOTLAND.

CHIEFS AND CLANSMEN IN THE HIGHLANDS--HIGHLAND CHIEFS CHANGED INTO LANDLORDS--CHARACTER OF THE HIGHLAND TENANTRY EIGHTY YEARS AGO--THE CHANGE EFFECTED BY LANDLORDS AND AGENTS--THE STORY OF THE SUTHERLAND EVICTIONS--OTHER EXAMPLES OF HIGHLAND CLEARANCES--WIDE EXTENT AND LONG CONTINUANCE OF THESE CLEARANCES--THEY WERE EXPOSED AND PROTESTED AGAINST IN VAIN--CONTINUANCE OF HIGHLAND CLEARANCES AND CONFISCATIONS DOWN TO THIS DAY--THESE EVILS INHERENT IN LANDLORDISM: AN ILLUSTRATIVE CASE--THE GENERAL RESULTS OF LANDLORDISM IN THE HIGHLANDS--FURTHER CLEARANCES AND DEVASTATION FOR THE SAKE OF SPORT--THE GROSS ABUSE OF POWER BY

HIGHLAND LANDLORDS REQUIRES A RADICAL AND IMMEDIATE REMEDY--LANDLORDISM IN THE LOWLANDS OF SCOTLAND: CONDITION OF THE LABOURERS--THE CAUSE OF THIS STATE OF THINGS IS THE LANDLORD SYSTEM--SOME RECENT IMPROVEMENTS IN THE CONDITION OF SCOTCH LABOURERS--GENERAL RESULTS OF SCOTCH LANDLORDISM.

In a large part of Scotland landlordism presents peculiar features, and has produced its normal evil results on a larger scale and in a more striking manner than in any other part of the kingdom. This has been mainly due to the continued existence of the old Celtic Clans, with their hereditary Chieftains possessing many of the powers and privileges of a barbarous age, down to so recent a period as the middle of the last century, and the comparatively sudden transformation of these chiefs into landlords, who soon claimed and exercised all those absolute and despotic powers which the law of England bestowed upon them.

*Chiefs and Clansmen in the Highlands.*--Under the old system the Highland Chief was a petty sovereign, who retained civil and criminal jurisdiction over his clansmen and the power of making war on other chiefs and clans. But these clansmen were never either serfs or vassals, but free men; and the clan was really a great family, all the members of which were supposed to be, and often actually were, of one blood. It was a true patriarchal system, totally distinct from the feudal system of Europe; and though every clansman owed fealty and military service, as well as certain dues or payments, to his chief, these were given through love and duty rather than through fear, and every petty clansman held his land and his rights to pasture and wood and turf, and to hunt and fish over the mountains and lakes, by the same title as the chieftain held his more extensive lands and privileges. As well expressed by an able writer in the *Westminster Review*--"No error could be grosser than that of viewing the chiefs as unlimited proprietors, not only of the arable land, but of the whole territory of the mountain, lake, river, and seashore, held and won during hundreds of years by the broadswords of the clansmen. Could any MacLean admit, even in a dream, that his chief could clear Mull of all the MacLeans and replace them with Campbells; or the MacIntosh people his lands with MacDonalds, and drive away his own race, any more than Louis Napoleon could evict all the population of France and supply their place with English and German colonists?" Yet this very power and right the English Government, in its aristocratic selfishness, bestowed upon the chiefs, when, after the great rebellion of 1745, it took away their privileges of war and criminal jurisdiction, and endeavoured to assimilate them to the nobles and great landowners of England. The rights of the clansmen were entirely left out of consideration.

*Highland Chiefs Changed into Landlords.*--For some time the change was not materially felt. Tracts of land were assigned to the more important members of the clan on payment of an annual rent, and these often sublet the land to the poorer Highlanders. The English system of entail soon became common in Scotland, and by marriage, inheritance, and purchase, the great estates became still greater and passed into fewer hands, while the feeling of clanship became weaker and the rights of the clansmen less clearly recognised. When, shortly afterwards, England became engaged in the great American and Continental wars, the Highland noblemen raised recruits from among their clansmen and formed the famous Highland regiments; and, as this added to their dignity and importance, they favoured the increase of small farmers whose hardy sons would swell the ranks of the army. The larger of these tenants were called "tacksmen," the smaller "crofters," and thus most of the Highland valleys were filled with a peaceful, hardy, industrious, and contented population.

*Character of Highland Tenantry Eighty Years Ago.*--The testimony on this subject is of a very uniform nature. The tacksmen, or small gentlemen farmers, lived in rude houses but with much comfort, and were almost always men of good education and refined manners; while their hospitality was unbounded, and they freely supported among them the poor of the district. Dr. Norman MacLeod tells us, as a proof of the sterling qualities and high character of this class of Highlanders, that, since the beginning of the last wars of the French Revolution, the island of Skye alone sent forth from her wild shores 21 lieutenant and major-generals, 48 lieutenant-colonels, 600 commissioned officers, 10,000 soldiers, 4 governors of colonies, 1 governor-general, 1 adjutant-general, 1 chief baron of England, and 1 judge of the Supreme Court of Scotland. Besides such men as these, the same class supplied the whole of the clergy, doctors and lawyers of the North of Scotland, as well as many to other parts of the empire. Now, through the changes brought about by the despotism of the landlords, this class of men has almost entirely ceased to exist, and few soldiers or officers are supplied by the Highlands.[1]

In Sir John McNeill's "Report on the Western Highlands and Islands," he describes the crofter as often a permanent or even hereditary tenant, at a rent fixed for long periods, occupying a few acres of arable land, with right of peat and pasture on the mountain, and of fishing, if near the sea or a loch. His rude house was often built by himself, the byre for the cows and the barn for his crop being under the same roof. He usually possessed some cattle, sheep, and a pony or two, a boat, nets, and fishing gear, and a good supply of needful implements and household furniture. His croft supplied him with food and a great part of his clothing, his annual sale of cattle paid his rent, he had abundance of dried fish or salt herrings for winter use, and he thus lived in a rude abundance, with little labour, and knew nothing of the unremitting daily toil by which labourers in other parts of the country gain their livelihood. And what was the character of these men? Dr. McLeod says: "The real Highland peasantry are, I hesitate not to affirm, by far the most intelligent in the world. I say this advisedly, after having compared them with those of many countries. Their good breeding must strike every one who is familiar with them." The Highlander is said to be lazy, but when removed to another clime he exhibits a perseverance and industry which makes him rise very rapidly. Hugh Miller says that, in the golden age of the Highlands, between the rebellion of 1745 and the commencement of the clearance system, the Highland peasantry were contented and comfortable, and continuously supplied those Highland regiments which were composed of at once the best men and the best soldiers in the service; and he declares that, when he has seen them labouring to extract a miserable crop from a barren soil of quartz rock and peat, his chief wonder has been at their great industry.

*The Change Effected by Landlords and Agents.*--The happy and contented lot of the Highlanders, both of the "tacksman" and the "crofter" class, might doubtless, under a wise and liberal system of permanent tenure and free use of the land of their native country, have been extended and perpetuated with the most beneficial results; but in the hands of landlords and agents this could hardly be expected. In order to obtain the highest rents the agents and some of the tacksmen favoured the subdivision of the crofts till they would hardly support a family, and the crofters were then forced to add to their means either by the wages of labour, by the manufacture of kelp, or other expedients. Poverty and distress increased; and the landlords, tempted by offers of large rents from Lowland sheep-farmers, began to seek means of getting rid of the burdensome population of small farmers--whose rents were difficult to collect and often in arrear--in order to let out their vast territories as sheep farms. The great landlords argued, and perhaps persuaded themselves, that the land could not support more small farmers, but might be more profitably employed in feeding sheep, thus producing wool and mutton for the whole community, and, therefore, that the proposed change was for the public benefit. Accordingly, the full rights of possession given by the English law were now insisted on. The pasture of the hill-tops, the game on the moors, the wood and the peat of the forests, the salmon in the rivers, and even the very shell-fish and sea-weed on the wild sea-shore were declared the sole and exclusive property of the landlords. Then began the clearances and evictions dignified by the name of "improvements." By hundreds and thousands at a time the occupiers of the soil were driven from their homes, and were many of them forced to leave the country which they had so bravely defended on many a hard-won battle-field.

One of the most celebrated of these wholesale clearances was made on the great estate of the lords of Sutherland, then in the possession of an English nobleman, the Marquis of Stafford, who had acquired it by marriage. This estate consisted of more than 700,000 acres, or the larger half of the entire county, and was inhabited by a population of 15,000 herdsmen or small farmers, occupying the numerous valleys and secluded glens which penetrate among its bleak and barren mountains. In the course of a few years these were almost all forcibly removed, some to the sea-coast, where small plots of land were allotted to them, others to Canada; and this large population was replaced by thirty-nine sheep farmers and their few shepherds. As there is a general belief among educated people (who alone have heard that any such events took place) that these clearances were conducted with gentleness and humanity, and that they were really beneficial to the inhabitants--as they were no doubt intended to be by the Marquis and Marchioness of Stafford--it becomes necessary to give a few authentic statements of what actually took place under their general orders. Our authority is a series of letters by Donald M'Leod, one of the tenants on the Sutherland Estate an eye-witness of much that he relates, and a personal sufferer. These letters first appeared in the *Edinburgh Weekly Chronicle*, and were republished at Greenock, in 1856, in a pamphlet form, by four gentlemen of that town, who append their names to an introductory address in which they state that "Deeds have been done of a character so base and heartless on these unoffending Highlanders that it almost exceeds belief," and that as a consequence of the clearances, the land under tillage in Scotland *decreased, between* 1831 *and* 1855, *by no less than one million five hundred and thirteen thousand three hundred and eighty-two acres.*

*The Story of the Sutherland Evictions.*--The Sutherland clearances commenced in 1807 by the ejection of 90 families, who were provided with smaller lots near the coast, and allowed to remove the timber of their houses, wherewith to build new ones. During the removal their crops suffered greatly; they and their families had to sleep out of doors; some died through fatigue and exposure, while others contracted diseases which shortened their lives. At a later period the evictions were carried out with much greater severity; the lots given to the people were often patches of moor and bog quite unfit for cultivation, the houses were often burned down, crops and furniture destroyed, and general misery spread among the people. The following is Donald M'Leod's account of some of these proceedings:--"In former removals the tenants had been allowed to carry away the timber of their old dwellings to erect houses on their new allotments, but now a more summary mode was adopted--by setting fire to them. The able-bodied men were by this time away after their cattle or otherwise engaged at a distance, so that the immediate sufferers by the general house-burning that now commenced were the aged and infirm, the women and children. . . . The devastators proceeded with the greatest celerity, demolishing all before them, and when they had overthrown all the houses in a large tract of country, they set fire to the wreck. Timber, furniture, and every other article that could not be instantly removed was consumed by fire or otherwise utterly destroyed. The proceedings were carried on with the greatest rapidity and the most reckless cruelty. The cries of the victims, the confusion, the despair and horror painted on the countenances of the one party, and the exulting ferocity of the other, beggar all description. . . . Many deaths ensued from alarm, from fatigue, and cold, the people having been instantly deprived of shelter, and left to the mercies of the elements. Some old men took to the woods and to the rocks, wandering about in a state approaching to, or of absolute insanity; and several of them in this situation lived only a few days. Pregnant women were taken in premature labour, and several children did not long survive their sufferings. To these scenes I was an eye-witness, and am ready to substantiate the truth of my statements, not only by my own testimony, but by that of many others who were present at the time. In such a scene of devastation it is almost useless to particularise the cases of individuals; the suffering was great and universal. I shall, however, notice a very few of the extreme cases of which I was myself an eye-witness. John Mackay's wife, Ravigill, in attempting to pull down her house, in the absence of her husband, to preserve the timber, fell through the roof. She was in consequence taken in premature labour, and in that state was exposed to the open air and to the view of all the bystanders. Donald Munro, Garvott, lying in a fever, was turned out of his house and exposed to the elements. Donald Macbeath, an infirm and bedridden old man, had the house unroofed over him, and was in that state exposed to the wind and rain until death put a period to his sufferings. I was present at the pulling down and burning of the house of William Chisholme, Badinloskin, in which was lying his wife's mother, an old bedridden woman of nearly 100 years of age none of the family being present. . . . Fire was set to the house, and the blankets in which she was carried out were in flames before she could be got out. She was placed in a little shed, and it was with great difficulty they were prevented from firing it also. Within five days she was a corpse."

In 1819 the parish of Kildonan, and parts of three others, were cleared by parties with faggots, who burnt down 300 houses. The following is M'Leod's account of what took place:--"The consternation and confusion were extreme; little or no time was given for the removal of persons or property; the people striving to remove the sick and the helpless before the fire should reach them, and struggling to save the most valuable of their effects. The cries of the women and children, the roaring of the affrighted cattle, hunted at the same time by the yelling dogs of the shepherds amid the smoke and fire, altogether presented a scene that completely baffles description--it required to be seen to be believed. A dense cloud of smoke enveloped the whole country by day, and even extended far out to sea; at night an awfully grand, but terrific, scene presented itself--all the houses in an extensive district in flames at once. I myself ascended a height about eleven o'clock in the evening, and counted 250 blazing houses, many of the owners of which were my relations, and all of whom I personally knew, but whose present condition--whether in or out of the flames--I could not tell. The conflagration lasted six days, till the whole of the dwellings were reduced to ashes or smoking ruins. During one of these days a boat actually lost her way in the dense smoke as she approached the shore, but at night was enabled to reach a landing-place by the lurid light of the flames."

The "allotments" to which the expelled and burnt-out inhabitants were removed are thus described by M'Leod:--

"These allotments were generally situated on the sea-coast, the intention being to force those who could not, or would not leave the country, to draw their subsistence from the sea by fishing; and in order to deprive them of any other means the lots were not only made small (varying from one to three acres), but their nature and situation rendered them unfit for any useful purpose . . . To the sea-coasts, then, which surround the greatest part of the county, where the whole mass of the inhabitants, to the amount of several thousand families, driven by their unrelenting tyrants in the manner I have described, to subsist as they could on the sea or the air; for the spots allowed them could not be called land, being composed of narrow strips, promontories, cliffs and precipices, rocks and deep crevices, interspersed with bogs and morasses. The whole quite useless to the superiors, and evidently never designed by nature for the habitation of man or beast. . . . The patches fit for cultivation were so small that few of them would afford room for more than a few handfuls of seed, and in harvest if there happened to be any crop, it was in continual danger of being blown into the sea, in that bleak, inclement region, where neither tree nor shrub could exist to arrest its progress."

No less disastrous were the immediate results of forcibly removing an inland agricultural population to one of the wildest and stormiest of the sea-coasts of our islands, and forcing them to attempt to eke out a scanty subsistence by fishing. Some in time, became expert fishermen, but many lost their lives in the attempt. The following are a few cases given by Donald M'Leod:--

"William M'Kay, a respectable man, shortly after settling on his allotment on the coast, went one day to explore his new possession, and in venturing to examine more nearly the ware growing within the flood-mark was suddenly swept away by a splash of the sea, and lost his life before the eyes of his miserable wife and three helpless children, who were left to deplore his fate. James Campbell, a man also with a family, on attempting to catch a peculiar kind of small fish among the rocks, was carried away by the sea and never seen afterwards. Bell M'Kay, a married woman, and mother of a family, while in the act of taking up salt water to make salt of was carried away in a similar manner, and nothing more seen of her. Robert M'Kay, who, with his family, were suffering extreme want, in endeavouring to procure some sea-fowls' eggs among the rocks, lost his hold, and, falling from a prodigious height, was dashed to pieces, leaving a wife and five destitute children behind him. John M'Donald, while fishing, was swept off the rocks, and never seen more."

Scenes like these went on for fourteen years, unknown to the English people, unnoticed by the English Government. Hugh Miller, speaking of them, says:--"The clearing of Sutherland was a process of ruin so thoroughly disastrous that it might be deemed scarcely possible to render it more complete. Between the years 1811 and 1820, 15,000 inhabitants of this northern district were ejected from their snug inland farms by means for which we would in vain seek a precedent, except, perhaps, in the history of the Irish massacre. A singularly well-conditioned and wholesome district of country has been converted into one wide ulcer of wretchedness and woe."

*Other Examples of Highland Clearances.*--Other great landlords soon followed the example thus set them, but in many cases with even more disastrous results, driving away their tenants without troubling themselves about their means of support or what became of them. An example of two of these later evictions must be quoted from a pamphlet recently published by Alex. Mackenzie, F.S.A., Scot., editor of the *Celtic Magazine*, and author of several works on the Highlands:--

"The Glengarry property at one time covered an area of nearly 200 square miles, and to-day, while many of their expatriated vassals are landed proprietors and in affluent circumstances in Canada, not an inch of the old possessions of the ancient and powerful family of Glengarry remains to the descendants of those who caused the banishment of a people who, on many a well-fought field, shed their blood for their chief and country. In 1853 every inch of the ancient heritage was possessed by the stranger except Knoydart, in the west, and this has long ago become the property of one of the Bairds. In the year named young Glengarry was a minor, his mother, the widow of the late chief, being one of his trustees. She does not appear to have learned any lesson of wisdom from the past misfortunes of her house. Indeed, considering her limited power and possessions, she was comparatively the worst of them all. The tenants of Knoydart, like all other Highlanders, had suffered severely during and after the potato famine in 1846 and 1847, and some of them got into arrear with a year's and some with two years' rent, but they were fast clearing it off. Mrs. Macdonell and her factor determined to evict every crofter on her property, to make room for sheep. In the spring of 1853 they were all served with summonses of removal, accompanied by a message that Sir John Macneil, Chairman of the Board of Supervision, had agreed to convey them to Australia. Their feelings were not considered worthy of the slightest consideration. They were not even asked whether they would prefer to follow their countrymen to America and Canada. They were to be treated as if they were nothing better than Africans, and the laws of their country on a level with those which regulated South American slavery. The people, however, had no alternative but to accept any offer made to them. They could not get an inch of land on any of the neighbouring estates, and any one who would give them a night's shelter was threatened with eviction themselves. It was afterwards found not convenient to transport them to Australia, and it was then intimated to the poor creatures, as if they were nothing but common slaves to be disposed of at will, that they would be taken to North America, and that a ship would be at Isle Ornsay, in the Island of Skye, in a few days to receive them, and that they *must* go on board.

The *Sillery* soon arrived, and Mrs. Macdonell and her factor came all the way from Edinburgh to see the people hounded across in boats, and put on board this ship, whether they would or not. An eye-witness who described the proceeding at the time, in a now rare pamphlet, and whom I met last year in Nova Scotia, characterises the scene as indescribable and heart-rending. 'The wail of the poor women and children as they were torn away from their homes would have melted a heart of stone.' Some few families, principally cottars, refused to go, in spite of every influence brought to bear upon them; and the treatment they afterwards received was cruel beyond belief. The houses, not only of those who went, but of those who remained, were burnt and levelled to the ground. The Strath was dotted all over with black spots, showing where yesterday stood the habitations of men. The scarred, half-burnt wood--couples, rafters, and bars--were strewn about in every direction. Stooks of corn and plots of unlifted potatoes could be seen on all sides, but man was gone. No voice could be heard. Those who refused to go aboard the *Sillery* were in hiding among the rocks and the caves, while their friends were packed off like so many African slaves to the Cuban market.

"No mercy was shown to those who refused to emigrate; their few articles of furniture were thrown out of their houses after them--beds, chairs, tables, pots, stoneware, clothing, in many cases rolling down the hill. What took years to erect and collect was destroyed and scattered in a few minutes. From house to house, from hut to hut, and from barn to barn, the factor and his menials proceeded carrying on the work of demolition, until there was scarcely a human habitation left standing in the district. Able-bodied men, who, if the matter should rest with a mere trial of physical force, would have bound the factor and his party hand and foot and sent them out of the district, stood aside as dumb spectators. Women wrung their hands and cried aloud, children ran to and fro dreadfully frightened; and while all this work of demolition and destruction was going on, no opposition was offered by the inhabitants, no hand was lifted, no stone cast, no angry word was spoken."

Mr. Mackenzie proceeds to give a large number of detailed cases of these evictions, of which the following two may be taken as average samples:--

"Archibald Macisaac, crofter, aged 66; wife 54, with a family of ten children. Archibald's house, byre, barn, and stable were levelled to the ground. The furniture of the house was thrown down the hill, and a general destruction then commenced. The roof, fixtures, and wood work were smashed to pieces, the walls razed to the very foundation, and all that was left for poor Archibald to look upon was a black, dismal wreck. Ten human beings were thus deprived of their homes in less than half an hour. It was grossly illegal to have destroyed the barn, for, according *even* to the law of

Scotland, the outgoing or removing tenant is entitled to the use of the barn until his crops are disposed of. But, of course, in a remote district, and among simple and primitive people like the inhabitants of Knoydart, the laws that concern them and define their rights are unknown to them."

"John Mackinnon, a cottar, aged 44, with a wife and six children, had his house pulled down, and had no place to put his head in, consequently he and his family, for the first night or two, had to burrow among the rocks near the shore! When he thought that the factor and his party had left the district, he emerged from the rocks, surveyed the ruins of his former dwelling, saw his furniture and other effects exposed to the elements, and now scarcely worth the lifting. The demolition was so complete that he considered it utterly impossible to make any use of the ruins of the old house. The ruins of an old chapel, however, were near at hand, and parts of the walls were still standing, and thither Mackinnon proceeded with his family, and having swept away some rubbish, and removed some grass and nettles, they placed some cabars up to one of the walls, spread some sails and blankets across, brought in some meadow hay, and laid it in a corner for a bed, stuck a piece of iron into the wall in another corner, on which they placed a crook, then kindled a fire, washed some potatoes, and put a pot on the fire and boiled them, and when these and a few fish roasted on the embers were ready, Mackinnon and his family had *one* good diet, being the first regular food they tasted since the destruction of their house!

"Mackinnon is a tall man, but poor and unhealthy-looking. His wife is a poor weak woman, evidently struggling with a diseased constitution and dreadful trials. The boys, Ronald and Archibald, were lying in 'bed'--(may I call a 'pickle' hay on the bare ground a bed?)--suffering from rheumatism and cholic. The other children are apparently healthy enough as yet, but very ragged. There is no door to their wretched abode, consequently every breeze and gust that blow have free ingress to the inmates. A savage from Terra-del-Fuego, or a Red Indian from beyond the Rocky Mountains, would not exchange huts with these victims, nor humanity with their persecutors. Mackinnon's wife was pregnant when she was turned out of her house among the rocks. In about four days thereafter she had a premature birth; and this and the exposure to the elements, and the want of proper shelter and a nutritious diet, has brought on consumption, from which there is no chance whatever of her recovery.

"There was something very solemn indeed in this scene. Here, amid the ruins of the old sanctuary, where the swallows fluttered, where the ivy tried to screen the grey moss-covered stones, where nettles and grass grew up luxuriantly, where the floor was damp, the walls sombre and uninviting, where there were no doors nor windows nor roof, and where the owl, the bat, and the fox used to take refuge, a Christian family was necessitated to take shelter! One would think that as Mackinnon took refuge amid the ruins of this most singular place he would be let alone, that he would not any longer be molested by *man*. But, alas! he was molested. The manager of Knoydart and his minions appeared, and invaded this helpless family, even within the walls of the sanctuary. They pulled down the sticks and sails he set up within its ruins--put his wife and children out on the cold shore--threw his tables, stools, chairs, &c., over the walls--burnt up the hay on which they slept--put out the fire--and then left the district. Four times have these officers broken in upon poor Mackinnon in this way, destroying his place of shelter, and sending him and his family adrift on the cold coast of Knoydart. Had Mackinnon been in arrears of rent, which he was not, even this would not justify the harsh, cruel, and inhuman conduct pursued towards himself and his family. No language of mine can describe the condition of this poor family, exaggeration is impossible. The ruins of an old chapel is the last place in the world to which a poor Highlander would resort with his wife and children unless he was driven to it by dire necessity."

Particulars are also given of similar clearances in Strathglass, Kintail, Glenelg, and several islands of the Hebrides. These people were generally shipped off to Canada without any provision whatever for them on their arrival there. We have only room here for the following statement, made by the passengers of one of the vessels which conveyed them there:--

"We, the undersigned passengers per *Admiral*, from Stornoway, in the Highlands of Scotland, do solemnly depose to the following facts:--That Colonel Gordon is proprietor of estates in South Uist and Barra; that among many hundred tenants and cottars whom he has sent this season from his estates to Canada, he gave directions to his factor, Mr. Fleming, of Cluny Castle, Aberdeenshire, to ship on board of the above-named vessel a number of nearly 450 of said tenants and cottars, from the estate in Barra; that accordingly, a great majority of these people, among whom were the undersigned, proceeded voluntarily to embark on board the *Admiral*, at Loch Boisdale, on or about 11th Aug., 1851; but that several of the people who were intended to be shipped for this port, Quebec, refused to proceed on board, and, in fact, absconded from their homes to avoid the embarkation. Whereupon Mr. Fleming gave orders to a policeman, who was accompanied by the ground officer of the estate in Barra, and some constables, to pursue the people who had run away among the mountains; which they did, and succeeded in capturing about twenty from the mountains and islands in the neighbourhood; but only came with the officers on an attempt being made to handcuff them; and that some who ran away were not brought back, in consequence of which four families at least have been divided, some having come in the ships to Quebec, while other members of the same families are left in the Highlands.

"The undersigned further declare that those voluntarily embarked did so under promises to the effect that Colonel Gordon would defray their passage to Quebec; that the Government Emigration Agent there would send the whole party free to upper Canada, where, on arrival, the Government agents would give them work, and furthermore, grant them land on certain conditions.

"The undersigned finally declare that they are now landed in Quebec so destitute that, if immediate relief be not afforded them, and continued until they are settled in employment, the whole will be liable to perish with want."

(Signed) HECTOR LAMONT, and 70 others.

The *Quebec Times*, which prints this statement, adds:--"This is a beautiful picture! Had the scene been laid in Russia or Turkey, the barbarity of the proceeding would have shocked the nerves of the reader; but when it happens in Britain, emphatically the land of liberty, where every man's house, even the hut of the poorest, is said to be his castle, the expulsion of these unfortunate creatures from their homes--the man-hunt with policemen and bailiffs--the violent separation of families--the parent torn from the child, the mother from her daughter--the infamous trickery practised on those who did embark--the abandonment of the aged, the infirm, women, and tender children, in a foreign land--forms a tableau which cannot be dwelt on for an instant without horror. Words cannot depict the atrocity of the deed. For cruelty less savage the dealers of the South have been held up to the execration of the world."

*Wide Extent and Long Continuance of these Clearances: They are Exposed and Protested against in Vain.*--The reader will perhaps exclaim "These accounts must be exaggerated, or they would have been protested against at the time, and Parliament would have interfered." Protests, however, were made. General Stewart of Garth protested immediately after the Sutherland clearances; while Hugh Miller's paper, *The Witness*, again and again called attention to them; but in vain. In a series of articles which appeared in 1849 the wide extent and cruel severity of these clearances were forcibly exhibited, as the following extracts will show:--

"Men talk of the Sutherland clearings as if they stood alone amidst the atrocities of the system; but those who know fully the facts of the case can speak with as much truth of the Ross-shire clearings, the Inverness-shire clearings, the Perthshire clearings, and, to some extent, the Argyleshire clearings. The earliest was the great clearing on the Glengarry estate about the end of the last century. . . . Crossing to the south of the great glen, we may begin with Glencoe. How much of its romantic interest does the glen owe to its desolation? Let us remember, however, that the desolation, in a large part of it, is the result of the extrusion of its inhabitants. Travel eastward, and the footprints of the destroyer cannot be lost sight of. Large tracts along the Spean and its tributaries are a wide waste. The southern bank of Loch Lochy is almost without inhabitants, though the symptoms of former occupancy are frequent. When we enter the country of the Frasers, the same spectacle presents itself--a desolate land. Across the hills in Stratherrick, the property of Lord Lovat, with the exception of a few large sheep farmers and a very few tenants, is one wide waste. To the north of Loch Ness, the territory of the Grants, both Glenmorison and the Earl of Seafield, presents a pleasing feature amidst the sea of desolation. But beyond this, again, let us trace the large rivers of the east coast to their sources. Trace the Beauly through all its upper reaches, and how many thousands upon thousands of acres, once peopled, are, as respects human beings, a wild wilderness! The lands of the Chisholm have been stripped of their population down to a mere fragment; the possessors of those of Lovat have not been behind with their share of the same sad doings. Let us cross to the Conon and its branches, and we will find that the chieftains of the Mackenzies have not been less active in extermination. Breadalbane and Rannoch, in Perthshire, have a similar tale to tell, vast masses of the population having been forcibly expelled. The upper portions of Athole have also suffered, while many of the valleys along the Spey and its tributaries are without an inhabitant, if we except a few shepherds. Sutherland, with all its atrocities, affords but a fraction of the atrocities that have been perpetrated in following out the ejectment system of the Highlands. In truth, of the habitable portion of the whole country, but a small part is now really inhabited. We are unwilling to weary our readers by carrying them along the west coast, from the Linnhe Loch northwards; but if they inquire, they will find that the same system has been, in the case of most of the estates, relentlessly pursued. These are facts of which, we believe, the British public know little, but they are facts on which the changes should be rung until they have listened to them and seriously considered them. May it not be that part of the guilt is theirs, who might, yet did not, step forward to stop such cruel and unwise proceedings?

"Let us leave the past, however (he continues), and considers the present. And it is a melancholy reflection that the year 1849 has added its long list to the roll of Highland ejectments. While the law is banishing its tens for terms of seven or fourteen years, as the penalty of deep-dyed crimes, irresponsible and infatuated power is banishing its thousands for life for no crime whatever. This year brings forward, as leader in the work of expatriation, the Duke of Argyll. Is it possible that his vast possessions are over-densely populated? And the Highland Destitution Committee co-operate. We had understood that the large sums of money at their disposal had been given them for the purpose of relieving, and not of banishing, the destitute. Next we have Mr. Bailie of Glenelg, professedly at their own request, sending five hundred souls off to America. Their native glen must have been made not a little uncomfortable for these poor people, ere they could have petitioned for so sore a favour. Then we have Colonel Gordon expelling upwards of eighteen hundred souls from South Uist; Lord Macdonald follows with a sentence of banishment against six or seven hundred of the people of North Uist, with a threat, as we learn, that three thousand are to be driven from Skye next season; and Mr. Lillingston of Lochalsh, Maclean of Ardgour, and Lochiel, bring up the rear of the black catalogue, a large body of people having left the estates of the two latter, who, after a heartrending scene of parting with their native land, are now on the wide sea on their way to Australia. Thus, within the last three or four months, considerably upwards of three thousand of the most moral and loyal of our people--people who, even in the most trying circumstances, never required a soldier, seldom a policeman, among them to maintain the peace--are driven forcibly away to seek subsistence on a foreign soil."

Professor Leoni Levi, who has made a special study of the condition of the Highlands, in an article in the Journal of the London Statistical Society, Vol. XXVIII, makes the following statement:--"Again and again these clearances have been continued, down even to the present time; and it is impossible to read the accounts of such transactions without feeling sympathy for those large bands of men, women, and children, who, with their scanty household furniture, and all their *lares* and *penates* with them, were driven out from their own soil to find shelter where best they could."

Later on, Mrs. Hugh Miller bears similar testimony:--"At this date, 1862, the depopulation of the Highlands is still rapidly going on. Not half a mile from the spot where we write, in the North-West Highlands, many families were ejected from their holdings but a few months ago. The factor--that dreaded middleman of the people--came with the underlings of the law, with spade and pickaxe, and left literally not one stone upon another of their poor cottages standing. I can see a miserable hovel into which several families have crowded who had before separate holdings of their own. Such scenes ought not to be allowed to disgrace a Christian country. But even where the inhabitants are allowed to remain in their miserable and insufficient crofts, the able-bodied--that is, the choicest of the population--are rapidly emigrating. 'There is not a lad worth anything,' said a person the other day who had just left a very large strath at some twenty miles distance--'there is not a lad worth anything who is not going away to New Zealand or some other place.' The people are indeed oppressed with a sense of utter poverty, and a total inability to rise above it. In many places their circumstances are made as wretched as possible on purpose to starve them out. There are a few proprietors--such as Sir Kenneth M'Kenzie, of Gairloch--who respect the feelings of those who have been for generations located on their properties; but these are *very* few. . . . Nothing can ever make the Highlander what he was but that interest in the soil which he has lost. Every Highlander formerly was possessed of all those feelings which constitute much that is valuable in the birthright of true gentlemen--a long-descended lineage, a sense of status and property, and an intense attachment to home and country."

Speaking of the general results of these clearings, a well-informed writer in the *Westminster Review* in 1868 says:--

"The Gaels, rooted from the dawn of history on the slopes of the northern mountains, have been thinned out and thrown away like young turnips too thickly planted. Noble gentlemen and noble ladies have shown a flintiness of heart and a meanness of detail in carrying out their clearings upon which it is revolting to dwell; and, after all, are the evils of over-population cured? Does not the disease still spring up under the very torture of the knife? Are not the crofts slowly and silently taken at every opportunity out of the hands of the peasantry? Where a Highlander has to leave his hut there is now no resting-place for him save the cellars or attics of the closes of Glasgow, or some other large centre of employment; and it has been noticed that the poor

Gael is even more liable than the Irishman to sink under the debasement in which he is then immersed."[2]

*Continuance of Highland Clearances and Confiscations Down to this Day.*--Lest our readers should think that these cruel wrongs are things of the past, and that the exposure of them by so many eminent writers has led the proprietors of Highland estates to adopt a different system of management, or has caused the Government to interfere, it is necessary to call attention to a remarkable pamphlet by Dr. D. G. F. Macdonald, consisting of letters published recently in the *Echo* newspaper and some correspondence arising out of them. These show us that almost all the evils so prevalent in Ireland exist as fully and to as disastrous an extent in Scotland at the present day. There, also, rents are systematically raised on the improvements made by the tenant--there, too, is found the same general absence of leases, and the same monstrous powers of oppression and eviction in the hands of factors and agents, owing to a prevalence of absenteeism--there, too, the holdings are insufficiently small, and the destitution caused by this very insufficiency is made the excuse for wholesale eviction and the creation of large grazing farms. The following extracts will indicate what Dr. Macdonald has to say on these matters, as to which--being an agriculturist and estate-manager by profession, having written many works of repute on these subjects, having been largely employed on Highland estates, and being himself a native of the Highlands--he must be considered one of the very highest authorities. As to insecurity of tenure, he says:--

"I know that many crofters are never safe in improving their land, for as soon as they begin to reap the benefit the landlord or factor steps in and raises their rents, or gives notice to quit, thus robbing the poor people of their just rights as much as if he dipped his hands into their pockets and walked away with their cash."

Again:--"Amongst the crying evils of the Highland crofters is the ball-room size of his holding, and the want of security of occupation. Crofters often complain--and complain very justly--of a want of sympathy on the part of the owners, and of being extruded from their holdings at the caprice of the landlord or factor, without a farthing of compensation for their improvements. . . . Such breaches of good faith are indeed atrocious, oppressive, and a violation of rights."

As to absenteeism and eviction he bears testimony as follows:--"The curse of Scotland is that so many of the proprietors are non-resident. . . . Because agents, forsooth! find that they can with less trouble collect rents from a few large tenants than from a number of small ones they recommend wholesale evictions. Neither understanding nor respecting the real manhood and sterling qualities of the Highland character, they heartlessly wage a war of extermination against the helpless crofters and small farmers; and this is in nine cases out of ten the result of absenteeism."

As to the nature and extent of this extermination Dr. Macdonald writes in the strongest manner. He says:--

"The extermination of the Highlanders has been carried on for many years as systematically and relentlessly as of the North American Indians. . . . Who can withhold sympathy as whole families have turned to take a last look at the heavens red with their burning houses? The poor people shed no tears, for there was in their hearts that which stifled such signs of emotion; they were absorbed in despair. They were forced away from that which was near and dear to their hearts, and their patriotism was treated with contemptuous mockery."

Again:--"I know a glen, now inhabited by two shepherds and two gamekeepers, which at one time sent out its thousand fighting men. And this is but one out of many that might be cited to show how the Highlands have been depopulated. Loyal, peaceable, and high-spirited peasantry have been driven from their native land--as the Jews were expelled from Spain, or the Huguenots from France--to make room for grouse, sheep, and deer. A portly volume would be needed to contain the records of oppression and cruelty perpetrated by many landlords, who are a scourge to their unfortunate tenants, blighting their lives, poisoning their happiness, and robbing them of their improvements, filling their wretched homes with sorrow, and breaking their hearts with the weight of despair."

These statements, strong though they are, are fully supported by the testimony of other witnesses. Mr. John Somerville, of Lochgilphead, writes:--"The watchword of all is exterminate, exterminate the native race. Through this monomania of landlords the cottier population is all but extinct; and the substantial yeoman is undergoing the same process of dissolution." The following examples are then given:--"About nine miles of country on the west side of Loch Awe, in Argyleshire, that formerly maintained 45 families, are now rented by one person as a sheep-farm; and in the island of Luing, same county, which formerly contained about 50 substantial farmers, beside cottiers, this number is now reduced to about six. The work of eviction commenced by giving, in many cases, to the ejected population, facilities and pecuniary aid for emigration; but now the people are turned adrift, penniless and shelterless, to seek a precarious subsistence on the seaboard, the nearest hamlet or village, and in the cities, many of whom sink down helpless paupers on our poor-roll, and others, festering in our villages, form a formidable Arab population, who drink our money contributed as parochial relief. This wholesale depopulation is perpetrated, too, in a spirit of invidiousness, harshness, cruelty, and injustice, and must eventuate in permanent injury to the moral, political, and social interests of the kingdom."

Again:--"The immediate effects of this new system are the dissociation of the people from the land, who are virtually denied the right to labour on God's creation. In L___, for instance, garden ground and small allotments of land are in great demand by families, and especially by the aged, whose labouring days are done, for the purpose of keeping cows, and by which they might be able to earn an honest independent maintenance for their families, and whereby their children might be brought up to labour, instead of growing up vagabonds and thieves. But such, even in our centres of population, cannot be got; the whole is let in large farms and turned into grazing. The few patches of bare pasture, formed by the delta of rivers, the detritus of rocks, and tidal deposits are let for grazing cows, at the exorbitant rent of £3 10s. each for a small Highland cow; and the small space to be had for garden ground is equally extravagant. The consequence of these exorbitant rents and the want of agricultural facilities is a depressed, degraded, and pauperised population."

Similar facts were proved before the last Game Law Committee. It was shown that in Ross-shire and Inverness about 200,000 acres had been laid waste in order to make room for the deer. On one estate in Ross-shire from sixty to eighty thousand acres had been cleared of inhabitants, and the arable land turned into waste in order to form deer forests, while the few crofters in that county were confined to a few patches by the loch sides, for which they paid exorbitant rents of from thirty to forty shillings an acre.

*These Evils Inherent in Landlordism--An Illustrative Case.*--The facts stated in this chapter will possess, I feel sure, for many Englishmen, an almost startling novelty; the tale of oppression and cruelty they reveal reads like one of those hideous stories of violence peculiar to the dark ages rather than a simple record of events happening upon our own land and within the memory of the present generation. For a parallel to this monstrous power of the landowner, under which life and property are entirely at his mercy, we must go back to mediæval times, or to the days when, serfdom not having been abolished, the Russian noble was armed with despotic authority; while the more pitiful results of this landlord tyranny, the wide devastation of cultivated lands, the heartless burning of houses, the reckless creation of pauperism and misery out of well-being and contentment, could only be expected under the rule of Turkish Sultans or greedy and cruel Pashas. Yet these cruel deeds have been perpetrated in one of the most beautiful portions of our native land. They are not the work of uncultured barbarians or of fanatic Moslems, but of so-called civilised and Christian men, and--worst feature of all--they are not due to any high-handed exercise of power beyond the law, but are all strictly legal, are in many cases the act of members of the Legislature itself, and, notwithstanding that they have been repeatedly made known for at least sixty years past, no steps have been taken, or are even proposed to be taken, by the Legislature to prevent them for the future! Surely it is time that the *people* of England should declare that such things shall no longer exist--that the rich shall no longer have such legal power to oppress the poor--that the land shall be *free* for all who are willing to pay a fair value for its use--and, as this is not possible under landlordism, that landlordism shall be abolished.

Dr. Macdonald, to whose writings we are so much indebted, like most other writers on the subject, does not seem to contemplate any such radical change, but thinks that protection to the tenants might be given by special legislation. But a little consideration will, I think, show that any such legislation, to be an adequate remedy for the various phases and evils of landlordism, must necessarily be complex and therefore difficult of application, must involve legal procedure of some sort, and must therefore be totally illusive--a mere mockery and delusion--when one party to every case brought before the courts would be the wealthy landlord, the other the poverty-stricken or ruined tenant. So long as the relation of landlord and tenant exists, the law can only, at the best, provide a legal--and therefore an uncertain and costly--remedy, for evils already caused and wrongs already committed. I maintain that it would be infinitely better to prevent the wrong and evil from ever coming into existence, which, as will be shown in succeeding chapters, can be done with ease and certainty when once we abolish landlordism and substitute for it occupying ownership.

To show how inherent are evil results in the very nature of landlordism (always supposing that no universal and miraculous change occurs in the nature of landlords) it will be instructive to give a sketch of the correspondence as to the island of Lewis, the property of Sir James Matheson, Bart. This gentleman is declared by Dr. Macdonald, who has long known him personally, to be "one of the most benevolent and popular men of the age," and one "who lives almost constantly among his people, dispensing bounty with a liberal hand, and diffusing much good by example." Yet, it is admitted that under so good a landlord as this, a body of tenants were subjected for years to such cruel injustice by the factor that they at last broke into a mild form of rebellion, *and then only did the landlord know anything about the matter*, and of course dismissed the offending factor. Estates in Scotland seem to be like some great empires, in this respect, that the subordinate rulers are able to oppress their dependents for years, only being found out when they goad their unhappy subjects into rebellion. Even Mr. Hugh Matheson, who styles himself "Commissioner for Sir J. Matheson," does not appear to know much of what really goes on. For, in a letter to the *Glasgow Weekly Mail*, of the

7th April, 1877, he states as follows:--"I can say, without fear of contradiction, that he (Sir James Matheson) has never in his life evicted a tenant in order to make room for deer, or to turn small farms into large ones." Yet the following week a correspondent signing himself "A Native" gives case after case in detail, in which these very things have been done by Sir James Matheson's factors, while another correspondent compares the excellent roads and the great skill and taste manifested in the Castle and its demesne with the hovels of the tenants, which he says "are simply a scandal and an outrage on the civilisation of this century;" and the reason for this is stated to be that "the people are refused a lease of their holdings, and in cases where improvements have been made, the treatment the holders have been subjected to is not encouraging to those whose means are limited." Yet another correspondent, Mr. D. Mackinlay, gives details of the case of the eviction of one of the Coll crofters by the factor, Mr. Mackay. It appears that this man had paid his rent punctually, had drained and trenched the land, and had built himself a house on it; yet he was evicted by the factor because (as it was alleged) he did not abide by the "rules of the estate" (which the crofter denied), his sick wife and himself were turned out by force on a bitterly cold day, he was sent to a hut unfit for human habitation, and given a piece of poor, neglected land on which hardly anything will grow. His former house is valued by the factor at £1 10s.

and by himself at £10; and he assured Mr. Mackinlay that he was "a bruised, down-trodden creature, now weary of this world."

Now, as Dr. Macdonald, who is a great admirer of Sir James Matheson, publishes these several statements in July, 1878 and gives no further explanation of them, we may probably assume that they are fairly accurate; and we must then ask--What are we to think of the system which renders such things possible on the estate of a resident landlord, who is "one of the most benevolent and popular men of the age?"[3] And further, What kind of treatment may the crofters expect when the landlord is *not* resident, and neither benevolent nor popular, but leaves all to his factor, and looks upon his estate as a rent-producing property and nothing more? It is clear that the system is one of almost unchecked despotism on one side and hardly mitigated serfdom on the other. The arguments for and against landlordism are very much the same as those for and against slavery. Both are essentially wrong, and must produce evil results, though the evil may be greatly mitigated in the case of wise and benevolent men. To allow the average citizen to possess and exercise such monstrous powers over fellow citizens, and still more, to allow these powers to be exercised by deputy with the one object of producing a revenue, is surely the greatest and most deplorable of political errors. The law which arms the landowner with this pernicious power is incompatible with every principle of equality of rights, protection of property, and liberty of enjoyment, and more than any other demands immediate and radical reform.

*The General Results of Landlordism in the Highlands.*--The general results of the system of modern landlordism in Scotland are not less painful than the hardship and misery brought upon individual sufferers. The earlier improvers, who drove the peasants from their sheltered valleys to the exposed sea-coast, in order to make room for sheep and sheep farmers, pleaded, however erroneously, the public benefit as the justification of their conduct. They maintained that more food and clothing would be produced by the new system, and that the people themselves would have the advantage of the produce of the sea as well as that of the land for their support. The result, however, proved them to be mistaken, for thenceforth the perennial cry of Highland destitution began to be heard, culminating at intervals into actual famines, like that of 1836-37 when £70,000 were distributed to keep the Highlanders from death by starvation. The evidence taken before the Select Committee on Emigration, Scotland, showed much the same state of chronic poverty as prevails in Ireland--and from the very same causes--great landlords, few of whom were resident, and a cottier population of tenants-at-will, with plots of land too small to occupy the labour of a family and to support them on its produce. And the only remedy our wise landlord Legislature could find for this state of things was emigration! Just as in Ireland, there was abundance of land capable of cultivation, but the people were driven to the coast and to the towns, to make way for sheep, and cattle, and lowland farmers; and when the barren and inhospitable tracts allotted to them became overcrowded, they were told to emigrate.[4] As the Rev. J. Macleod says:--"By the clearances one part is depopulated and the other overpopulated; the people are gathered into villages where there is no steady employment for them, where idleness has its baneful influence and lands them in penury and want."

The actual effect of this system of eviction and emigration--of banishing the native of the soil and giving it to the stranger--is shown in the steady increase of poverty indicated by the amount spent for the relief of the poor having increased from less than £300,000 in 1846 to more than £900,000 now; while in the same period the population has only increased from 2,770,000 to 3,627,000, so that pauperism has grown about nine times faster than population![5] This shows plainly that the system has failed, as every unjust system does fail in one way or another. But even had it succeeded in this respect--had more of the poor Highlanders been banished, and had the new comers succeeded in abolishing, or at least in not increasing, pauperism, and in producing general content, even then the system would be equally cruel and equally opposed to every principle of justice and good government. The fact that a whole population could be driven from their homes like cattle at the will of a landlord, and that the Government which taxed them, and for whom they freely shed their blood on the battle-field, neither would nor could protect them from this cruel interference with their personal liberty, is surely the most convincing and most absolute demonstration of the incompatibility of landlordism with the elementary rights of a free people.

*Further Clearances and Devastation for the Sake of Sport.*--As if, however, to prove this still more clearly, and to show how absolutely incompatible with the well-being of the community is modern landlordism, the great lords of the soil in Scotland have for the last twenty years or more been systematically laying waste enormous areas of land for purposes of sport, just as the Norman Conqueror laid waste the area of the New Forest for similar purposes. At the present time more than two millions of acres of Scottish soil are devoted to the preservation of deer alone--an area larger than the entire counties of Kent and Surrey combined. Glen Tilt Forest includes 100,000 acres; the Black Mount is sixty miles in circumference; and Ben Aulder Forest is fifteen miles long by seven broad. On many of these forests there is the finest pasture in Scotland, while the valleys would support a considerable population of small farmers. Yet all this land is devoted to the sport of the wealthy, farms being destroyed, houses pulled down, and men, sheep and cattle all banished to create a wilderness for the deer-stalkers! At the same time the whole people of England are shut out from many of the grandest and most interesting scenes of their native land, gamekeepers and watchers forbidding the tourist or naturalist to trespass on some of the wildest Scotch mountains.[6]

*The Gross Abuse of Power by Highland Landlords Requires an Immediate Remedy.*--Now, when we remember that the right to a property in these unenclosed mountain lands was most unjustly given to the representatives of the Highland chiefs little more than a century ago, and that they and their successors have grossly abused their power ever since, it is surely time to assert those fundamental maxims of jurisprudence which state that--"No man can have a vested right in the misfortunes and woes of his country," and that--"The sovereign ought not to allow either communities or private individuals to acquire large tracts of land in order to leave it uncultivated." If the oft-repeated maxim that "property has its duties as well as its rights" is not altogether a mockery, then we maintain that in this case the *total* neglect of all the duties devolving on the owners of these vast tracts of land affords ample reason why the State should take possession of them for the public benefit. A landlord Government will, of course, never do this till the people declare unmistakably that it must be done. To such a Government the rights of property are *sacred*, while those of their fellow citizens are of comparatively little moment; but we feel sure that when the people of England fully know and understand the doings of the landlords of Scotland, the reckless destruction of homesteads, and the silent sufferings of the brave Highlanders, they will make their will known, and, when they do so, that *will* must soon be embodied in law. We will conclude this brief sketch of what by Highland landlords is termed "improvement" with a quotation from the work of a respected Scotch pastor, the Rev. John Kennedy, a lifelong resident among the scenes which he describes. He tells us that it was at a time when the people of the Highlands became distinguished as the most peaceable and virtuous peasantry in Britain that they began to be driven off by their landlord oppressors, to clear their native soil for strangers, red-deer, and sheep. He then describes the action of the landlords in these forcible words:--"With few exceptions the owners of the soil began to act as if they were also the owners of the people, and, disposed to regard them as the vilest part of their estate, they treated them without respect to the requirements of righteousness or the dictates of mercy. Without the inducement of gain, in the very recklessness of cruelty, families by hundreds were driven across the sea, or were gathered as the sweepings of the hill-sides into wretched hamlets on the shore. By wholesale evictions wastes were formed for the red deer, that the gentry of the nineteenth century might indulge in the sports of the savages of three centuries before."[7]

*Landlordism in the Lowlands of Scotland: Condition of the Labourers.*--Now let us turn from this picture of what unrestricted landlordism has effected in the Highlands to that part of the country which is its pride and glory--the Lowlands. For here are the highest agricultural rents and the best farming in Great Britain. Here the landlords are wealthy and the farmers are thriving. Here everything is neat, thrifty, and elegant; the rude husbandry of the Highlands has been left more than a thousand years behind; the furrows are straight as an arrow, the fences closely dressed, the farm-houses commodious, and the gentlemen's seats bear all the evidences of taste, luxury, and refinement. Such being the case, we should naturally expect that some portion of this prosperity would have descended to the labourers, and we should look for neat and roomy cottages, with ample gardens, so essential to the well-being of the poor. Let us first see what was their condition thirty years ago, as described by Hugh Miller in his striking Essays.

He tells us how he once lodged in a labourer's cottage in a district where land averaged above five pounds an acre, within three hours' journey of Edinburgh, and within a hundred yards of the beautiful shrubberies and pleasure-grounds of a gentleman's estate; and he thus describes it:--"But the cottage was an exceedingly humble one. It was one of a line on the way-side inhabited chiefly by common labourers and farm servants--a cold, uncomfortable hovel, by many degrees less a dwelling to our mind, and certainly less warm and snug, than the cottage of the west coast Highlander. The tenant (our landlord) was an old farm servant, who had been found guilty of declining health and vigour about a twelvemonth before, and had been discharged in consequence. He was permitted to retain his dwelling, on the express understanding that the proprietor was not to be burdened with repairs; and the thatch, which had given way in several places, he had painfully laboured to patch against the weather by mud and turf gathered from the wayside. But he wanted both the art and the materials of Red Murouch.[8] With every heavy shower the rain found its way through, and the curtains of his two beds, otherwise so neatly kept, were stained by dark-coloured blotches. The earthen floor was damp and uneven; the walls of undressed stone had never been hard-cast; but by dint of repeated white-washing, the interstices had gradually filled up. . . . The old man's wife, still a neat and tidy woman, though turned of sixty, was a martyr to rheumatism; and her one damp and gousty room, with its mere apron breadth of partition between it and the chinky outer door, was not at all the place for her declining years. She did her best, however, to keep things in order, and to attend to the comforts of her husband and her two lodgers; but the bad roof and the single apartment were disqualifying circumstances, and they pressed upon her very severely. . . . And this was all that civilisation, in the midst of a well-nigh perfect agriculture, had done for the dwelling of the poor hind. . . . But we are building, perhaps, on a solitary instance. Would that it were so! Our description is far above the average, however exaggerated it may seem. The following account of a group of Border hovels, deemed quite good enough by the proprietary of the county for their own and their tenants' hinds, is by the Rev. Dr. W. S. Gilly, of Norham.

"Now for a more detailed description of that species of hut or hovel which prevails in this district. I have a group of five such before my mind's eye. They belong to the same property, and have all changed inhabitants within eighteen months. The property, I may add, is tenanted by one of the best and most enterprising farmers in all England. They are built of rubble loosely cemented, and from age and the badness of the materials, the walls look as if they would scarcely hold together. The chinks gap open in many places, and so widely that they freely admit every wind that blows. The chimneys have lost half their original height, and lean on the roof with fearful gravitation. The rafters are evidently rotten and displaced; and the thatch, yawning in some parts to admit the wet, and in all parts utterly unfit for its original purpose of giving protection from the weather, looks more like the top of a dunghill than a cottage. Such is the exterior; and when the hind comes to take possession he finds it no better than a shed. The wet, if it happens to rain, is making a puddle on the earth-floor. It is not only cold and wet, but contains the aggregate filth of years from the time of its being first used. The refuse and droppings of meals, decayed animal and vegetable matter of all kinds, these all mix together and exude from it. Window frame there is none. There is neither oven, nor copper, nor shelf, nor fixture of any kind. All these things the hind has to bring with him, besides his ordinary articles of furniture. Imagine the trouble, the inconvenience, and the expense which the poor fellow and his wife have to encounter before they can put this shell of a hut into anything like a habitable form. This year I saw a family of eight--husband, wife, two sons, and four daughters--who were in utter discomfort, and in despair of putting themselves into a decent condition, three or four weeks after they had come into one of these hovels. In vain did they try to stop up the crannies, and to fill up the holes in the floor, and to arrange their furniture in tolerably decent order, and to keep out the weather. Alas! what will they not suffer in winter? There will be no fireside enjoyment for them. They may huddle together for warmth, and heap coals on the fire; but they will have chilly beds and a damp hearthstone; and a cold wind will sweep through their dismal apartment; and the icicles will hang by the wall, and the snow will drift through the roof, and window, and crazy door-place, in spite of all their endeavours to exclude it."

Great as they might seem, however, these are merely

physical evils; and they are light and trivial compared with the horrors which follow. These miserable cabins consist, in by much the greater number of instances, as in the cottage of the poor old hind, of but a single room. We again quote:--"And into this apartment are crowded eight, ten, and even twelve persons. How they lie down to rest, how they sleep, how unutterable horrors are avoided, is beyond all conception. The case is aggravated when there is a young woman to be lodged in this confined space who is not a member of the family, but is hired to do the field-work, for which every hind is bound to provide a female. It shocks every feeling of propriety to think that in a room within such a space as I have been describing, civilised beings should be herding together without a decent separation of age and sex!"

Down to 1861, at all events, equally wretched cottages were found in many parts of Scotland. Mr. James Robb (general editor of *The Scottish Farmer*) thus describes those common in Aberdeenshire:--"Such cottages as are provided for ploughmen are, for the most part, of a very comfortless kind. They are simply four walls--often put together in the cheapest and roughest possible fashion, sometimes without lime or other cement even--with a vent at each gable end, two small windows, and a roof of thatch. The occupants have to depend upon their wooden box-beds or presses for making such separation between the two sexes as decency may suggest." In East Lothian, the same writer tells us:--

"The cottages generally are not good, being small, old, and ill-lighted. Many of them have but one usable room and a pantry; the garrets, where there are such, being unceiled, and, therefore, either too cold in winter or too hot in summer for sleeping purposes." And again:--"Directing our course north-east, we find in our passage to North Berwick not a few disgraceful hovels, some straw-thatched, but most with red-tiled rooms, lighted and aired (save the mark!) by a solitary and immovable pane of glass, and with a general aspect of unsanitariness and discomfort unbefitting one of the richest agricultural counties in Scotland in the nineteenth century. Inside we find the double box-bed taking up so great a portion of the space that three or four chairs, a rickety table, a dresser, and a washing-tub crowd the remainder. As occupants of the box-beds in one of these houses there were two grown-up men, two girls approaching womanhood, an elderly woman, who appeared to be their mother, and three or four children."

A considerable acquaintance with savage life in both hemispheres enables the present writer to assert that the people we term *un*civilised rarely tolerate such a state of things as that above described. The young unmarried men are always separated, often in distinct sleeping-houses, from the rest of the family or the tribe; while the dwellings are always suited to the climate and surrounding conditions. It was reserved for the wealthiest nation under the sun, and the one which prides itself on being the most religious and the most civilised, to have its peasants housed in the extreme of physical misery and social degradation. And be it noted that this state of things occurred, not only in towns and cities where the value of land and the cost of building might possibly be alleged as some excuse but over the open country, among fields and woods and mountains, where there is ample space and abundant materials ready to hand, and where such objections, therefore, could not possibly apply.

*Some Recent Improvement in the Condition of Scotch Labourers.*--Since the pictures here given of the labourers' cottages in Scotland were written, much has been done to improve them. In "A Report on the Past and Present Agriculture of the Counties of Forfar and Kincardine," by Mr. Thomas Lawson, dated 1881 (for which I am indebted to the author), it is stated that, in consequence of the exposure of the state of the bothies in 1850, an Association was formed at Edinburgh to improve them, and many model cottages and bothies were built. Wages, too, have risen considerably, in consequence of the scarcity of labour produced by the increase of factories in many districts. Mr. James W. Barclay, M.P. for Forfarshire, also informs me that wages have greatly risen in the last ten years, being about 50 per cent. higher in Scotland than in Norfolk. This he thinks is due to the fact that the men readily move from place to place and from country to town, so that the rate of wages for town work and country work is quickly equalised. Mr. Lawson speaks of "the present tidy cottages of one story, with three apartments, one room and bed-closet being floored with wood, the other room with either pavement or cement; and partitions of brick, the inside finished off with lath and plaster or cement. There is also a garret for lumber, and a small garden and pigstye." But these cottages are, he says, "not near so common as they ought to be," as many proprietors and tenant farmers do not see their way to building them, since they are not remunerative. He also says that "there is not so much payment in kind as there used to be. This applies especially to the keeping of cows, which is not nearly so common now--in fact, it is very exceptional. Some farmers even prohibit the keeping of pigs." These statements seem to show that, though wages are higher, and many cottages are fairly good, yet many remain as they were in Hugh Miller's time, and when Mr. Robb wrote his reports twenty years ago; while the movement of labourers from place to place, the "small garden" they "sometimes" have, and the occasional restriction from even keeping a pig, all seem to show that there has not been much advance towards enabling the labourer to have a permanent home, and to have land on which to employ his spare hours, which alone can truly raise his condition. The bothy-system, though it has almost disappeared from the southern counties, still prevails in Perth, Forfar, and Kincardine, where there seems to have been little change for the last twenty years.[2] The bothies are still comfortless abodes, leading to habits of uncleanliness and disorder, and giving a taste for a wandering life; and this is supposed to be one cause of the untidiness and want of comfort which prevails in the labourers' cottages of Scotland. It is remarked by Mr. Robb that the best female servants were obtained from the class of small farmers, a testimony to the beneficial influence on character of permanent occupancy of land and the household duties it necessitates, which is now almost wholly denied to the Scotch agricultural labourer. Mr. Lawson refers with dissatisfaction to the large sums spent in drink by the young men; but this is almost a necessary result of high wages when there are no home comforts or occupations, and no one great and important object, such as the acquisition of land and a permanent home, for which to accumulate savings. The result is that pauperism, though not so prevalent as in the depopulated Highlands, still abounds even in the fertile and highly-farmed Lowlands, where about one in forty of the population are returned as paupers or dependents. In all Scotland the proportion is about one in thirty-five, while in England and Wales, where the population is four times as dense, the proportion is one in twenty-five.

In Scotland the labourer is altogether dependent upon his employer for his dwelling, and is obliged to leave it whenever he changes his master. He is a mere appanage of the farm, without any of that permanence and security of tenure possessed by the villein or serf of feudal times. It is thus impossible that he can ever have a home, in the best sense of the word, and this will go far to explain the untidiness and want of thrift which all writers on the condition of the Scottish labourers so much deplore. The only way to cure the evils of the bothy-system, the inadequate housing of labourers, and all the evil consequences that arise from them, is to encourage and render possible the growth of a fixed rural population, having rights in the soil and all the interests that attach to a permanent home. If every labourer had the right to claim an acre or two of land for his dwelling-house and garden, paying only the same rent as the farmer pays for similar land, and having absolute permanence of tenure so long as he paid this fixed rent, most of the evils so forcibly depicted by the writers we have quoted would soon disappear.[10]

As will be shown in a subsequent chapter, wherever such occupying ownership of land prevails, there is comparative comfort and plenty, and the house accommodation is always fully equal to the standard demanded by the state of civilisation and social advancement of the community--not miserably below it, as it always is when the labourer is divorced from the soil. This right to share in the use of land on equal terms with his fellow citizens should be declared the indefeasible birthright of every Englishman, and in order that this right may be obtained the land must revert to the State, which ought never to have given up possession of it to individuals. These remarks somewhat anticipate the fuller discussion with which the scheme of nationalisation of the land we propose for adoption will be introduced, but it was thought necessary here to lay down clearly the points at issue, and prevent our readers from supposing that we believe that any change in the character or conduct of landlords or farmers (even if so radical a change in human nature were possible) would be an adequate remedy for the disease. So long as the labourer is absolutely *dependent* on his employer for subsistence, is without a permanent *home* of his own, and has no *land* on which he may profitably employ himself when his regular work temporarily fails--just so long will he be in a state of chronic poverty or intermittent pauperism, often dwelling in houses which it is no one's business or interest to make healthy or comfortable, living a life of physical and social degradation, and usually filling a pauper's grave. That such is the inevitable tendency and necessary result of the present system is clearly shown by the fact that, however well the system works for the landlord and capitalist, *their* advancement does little to better the condition of the labourer. A century ago the poet Burns remarked that the more highly cultivated he found a district, the more ignorant and degraded he almost always found the people, man deteriorating at least as much as the corn and cattle improved. Down to thirty years ago we have the testimony of Hugh Miller that the same state of things prevailed; and though the exposure of the evil by a number of energetic clergymen and other philanthropists, together with the increase of wages owing to the spread of manufacturing industry, have combined to ameliorate some of its worst features, there still remains the great fact of a wandering, unthrifty, and pauperised body of labourers in a region of wealthy landlords and the most advanced agriculture.

*General Results of Scotch Landlordism.*--It appears, then, that both in the barren Highlands and the fertile Lowlands, among the peaceable and contented Celts as well as among the more restless and energetic Saxons, we find the same increase in the wealth and luxury of the landlord and the capitalist, accompanied by the misery, discontent, and chronic pauperism of the labouring classes. In both districts landlordism has had its own way, and has flourished; in both it carries in its train the physical, social, and moral degradation of those by whom its wealth is created. It is not that landlords are worse than other men; perhaps it may justly be said that they are somewhat better than the average; but no amount of good intentions or good administration will suffice when the system which is administered is fundamentally wrong. No system ever had a fairer trial than pure landlordism has had in Scotland during the present century. It has had the freest liberty of action under various conditions, a peaceful, honest and contented body of labourers, a constantly increasing growth of wealth, and all the means and appliances of modern science at its command. Yet here, as always and everywhere, it has lamentably failed to produce either prosperity or contentment. It must, then, be either the conduct of the landlords or the nature of landlordism that has caused this miserable failure. We maintain that the failure has been too constant and too unvarying to be due to the acts of educated and religious men, many of whom have honestly tried to do good; that, consequently, the system alone is to blame; and that landlordism itself stands irrevocably condemned.

*Notes, Chapter Four*

1. "Reminiscences of a Highland Parish," . on

2. Most modern writers consider the croft-system a failure, and this is supposed to imply the failure of small holdings under any conditions. But there is a mass of testimony to show that the crofter of Scotland, like the cottier of Ireland, is wretched and poverty-stricken simply because he can only get poor land at exorbitant rents, and usually not enough land to live upon. Thus, in Mr. James Robb's "Enquiry into the Condition of the Agricultural Labourers of Scotland," we find the following statements, quoted with approval and confirmed by his personal observation:--"The general quality of the soil upon which crofts are now granted is vastly inferior to what it was of old. The rent is, from the increased demand and more limited supply, proportionally

greater . . . Dispassionately viewed, small crofts, *as generally let*, form merely the alembic through which is distilled into the pocket of the owner the savings of the sweat of the brow of the occupant. By holding such a croft he is literally incapacitated for performing a good day's work for a good day's wage, as, to scrape together a rent to ensure a home for a series of years, the agricultural labourer must work double hours and draw unfairly upon his stock of strength, which infallibly leads to a premature old age." Could there be a more severe condemnation of the landlord system in Scotland than this statement made by the late Secretary to the Royal Northern Agricultural Society, and endorsed by the Editor of *The Scottish Farmer*? This refers to Aberdeenshire. In Forfarshire, Mr. Robb describes the condition of some small holders on the estate of Lord Dalhousie, taking one "as a specimen of the whole." The dwelling is described as a wretched, tumble-down turf hovel, consisting of one room about ten feet square, and a division for the cow. "The occupier (an old woman) had lived all her days in the place. She had now only 2 1/2 acres of land; formerly she had some pasture land, *but that had been taken from her*. She had, therefore, to dispense with all her cows but one, and the consequence was that she had now a deficiency of manure for what little oats and potatoes she wished to raise." Mr. Robb declares that such houses are unworthy to shelter any class of humanity; and Lord Kinnaird (in the preface to

Mr. Robb's book) maintains that "the description given by the reports of the actual state of these crofters in different districts, corresponding with their state at the beginning of the century, proves how very undesirable a return to such a system would be." But neither of these writers seems to have the least perception that the facts stated are the condemnation, not of the croft system, but of the landlord system itself, which forces the poor crofter into a condition in which a reasonable amount of well-being is impossible, work as hard as he may. on p-73

3. It appears from an article on "Highland Destitution" in the *Quarterly Review*, December 1881, that Sir James Matheson bought the island of Lews or Lewis in 1844, that he at once commenced making "improvements on a great scale, with the view of giving employment to the inhabitants," spending in six years (1845-1850) more than a hundred thousand pounds, besides gratuities for purposes of education and charity. Yet the writer refers to this "princely liberality" as having been "met by the most disheartening ingratitude," and "ending in total failure." The facts given above will perhaps serve to explain both the one and the other. What the people of Lewis, as of other parts of the Highland, wanted, was sufficient land at a fixed rent, not higher than it was really worth, with perfect freedom of action, and a permanent tenure; so that all they made by their labour should be their own. This they have never had; while

they have had given them what they did not want--wages for unproductive labour on the landlord's pleasure grounds and buildings. The people have been actually taken away, by the inducement of good wages and work for their landlord, from productive labour on the soil to unproductive labour on carriage roads, bridges, shooting lodges, game preserves, and a magnificent castle and grounds, and the result has naturally been demoralisation and destitution! This is the result of benevolent landlordism. on

4. "There was a locality pointed out to us, in a barren quartz-rock district, in which the indestructible stone, that never resolves into soil, was covered by a stratum of dark peat, where the proprietors had experimented on the capabilities of the native Highlanders, by measuring out to them, amid the moor, at a low rent, several small farms, of ten or twelve acres apiece. But in a moor composed of peat and quartz-rock no rent can be low. No farmer thrives on a barren soil, let his rent be what it may; and so the speculation here had turned out a bad one. The quartz-rock and the peat proved pauper-making deposits. 'How,' we have frequently enquired of the poor people 'are you spending your strength on patches so miserably unproductive as these? You are said to be lazy. For our own part what we chiefly wonder at is your great industry.' The usual reply used to be--'Ah! there is good land in the country, but *they* will not give it to us.' And certainly we did see in the Highlands many tracts of kindly-looking

soil. Green margins, along the sides of long-withdrawing valleys, which still bore the marks of the plough, but now under natural grass, seemed much better fitted to be, as of old, scenes of human industry than the cold ungenial mosses or the barren moors. But in at least nineteen cases out of every twenty we found the green patches bound by lease to some extensive sheep-farmer, and as unavailable for the purposes of the present emergency, even to the proprietor, as if they lay in the United States or the Canadas." (Hugh Miller's Essays, .) on

5. This was the case not only in those districts where the evicted peasantry had been driven into over-populated towns and villages, but even in the very places where the population had decreased by forced deportation. Dr. Norman Macleod tells us that the "Highland Parish," which he has so well described, "which once had a population of 2,200 souls, and received only £11 per annum from public (church) funds for the support of the poor, expends now under the Poor Law upwards of £600 annually, with a population diminished by one-half, but with poverty increased in a greater ratio." Hugh Miller also tells us that "the poor-rates were heaviest in the districts from which the greatest number had emigrated." Yet in the face of these damning facts, there are still to be found men who support these "clearances" as beneficial to the community! on p-83

6. Even these deer-forest clearances find their defenders,

to whom Professor Leoni Levi thus replies:--"A comparison has been made between deer-forests and public parks. Both, it is true, comprise land kept out of cultivation for purposes of enjoyment. But while public parks greatly promote the health and enjoyment of the masses of the people, deer-forests are reserved for the sport of a few individuals. Parks are public property, purposely devoted to a great economic object--the improvement of the people. Deer-forests are private property, shut out from public use, and in many cases diverted from a fruitful to a fruitless occupation. Again, it has been represented that deer-forests employ as many persons as foresters as sheep-walks employ shepherds. But are foresters producers? The same quantity of land that will maintain 2,000 sheep will not give 300 deer. Of deer, a large number run away, many die, and very few are killed. In truth, deer-forests are exclusively intended for sport and luxury, and production enters in no manner into their economics" ("Journal of the Land Statistical Society," vol. xxviii, ). It is calculated that the loss in food by the deer-forests is equal to 200,000 sheep, besides which deer bear no wool. Deer-forests do not repay the outlay expended on them in the shape of keepers, &c., and, as far as the rest of the nation is concerned, they might as well be submerged under the ocean. on

7. "Days of the Fathers in Ross-shire," 1861, . on
8. A Highlander, whose wretched-looking, yet really

warm and comfortable, dwelling had been previously described. on

9. Communication from Mr. William Wallace, of Kinnear, Fife, through J. Boyd Kinnear, Esq. on

10. Lord Kinnaird, in his preface to the little volume of Mr. Robb's essays, says:--"A cry has been raised by those who do not understand the question for the erection of a greater number of cottages, regardless of the fact that field-labour, which cannot from its nature be constant, will not support a family." And again:--"It is a great mistake to encourage the location of families, who have no other means of support than the chance of occasional out-door work." Nothing can show more strikingly than these remarks the evil results to the entire rural population, as well as to agriculture, of that landlord system which can and does determine how and where people shall live, quite independent of their own wishes, desires, and needs, and thus brings about an unnatural division of the inhabitants of a district into capitalist farmers and a nomad population of labourers. The more natural and healthy system would be, to allow every man to have as much land as he wished either for farm or garden, with a permanent tenure, and at a just rent. Each agricultural district would then support a body of independent labourers permanently attached to the soil, and with a substantial stake in the country. The cottage which was a man's *own*, and which he intended to occupy

for his *life*, would soon be improved and even beautified. His garden or field would be cultivated with all that untiring industry which the secure possession of land always creates; poultry, pigs, or cows would furnish employment for the family, and a constant source of profit; while from the two classes of labourers and crofters, a supply of labour would be forthcoming at all seasons adequate to meet the demand. Bothies would no longer be needed, because the young men would live with their parents, or lodge with those who had small families or ample accommodation; a love of home and home-duties would be created, and with so intelligent a people as the Scotch many home industries would spring up to profitably occupy the long winter evenings, and thus tend to diminish if not to abolish pauperism.

---

# CHAPTER V.

## THE SOCIAL AND ECONOMICAL EFFECTS OF ENGLISH LANDLORDISM.

LANDLORDISM IN ENGLAND IS SEEN AT ITS BEST--DESPOTIC POWER OF LANDLORDS--LANDLORDS' INTERFERENCE WITH RELIGIOUS FREEDOM--LANDLORDS' INTERFERENCE WITH POLITICAL FREEDOM--LANDLORDS' INTERFERENCE WITH A TENANT'S AMUSEMENTS--EVICTION OF THE INHABITANTS OF AN ENTIRE VILLAGE--INJURIOUS POWER OF LANDLORDS OVER FARMERS AND OVER AGRICULTURE--LIMITATION OF THE BENEFICIAL INFLUENCE OF LANDLORDS--IT WOULD BE GREATLY INCREASED UNDER OCCUPYING OWNERSHIP--SUPPOSED IMPORTANCE OF THE LARGE FARMS WHICH LANDLORDISM FAVOURS--THE EFFECTS OF LANDLORDISM ON THE WELL-BEING OF THE LABOURING CLASSES--DETERIORATION OF THE AGRICULTURAL LABOURER DURING THE PRESENT

CENTURY--THE SOCIAL DEGRADATION OF THE AGRICULTURAL LABOURER AT THE PRESENT DAY--THIS STATE OF THINGS IS DUE TO THE SYSTEM OF LANDLORDISM, NOT TO THE BAD CONDUCT OF LANDLORDS--THE ENCLOSURE ACT AND ITS RESULTS--UNIFORM EVIDENCE AS TO THE BENEFICIAL EFFECTS OF ALLOTMENTS AND COTTAGE GARDENS--BENEFICIAL EFFECTS OF SMALL COTTAGE FARMS--THE LOGICAL BEARING OF THIS EVIDENCE--VARIOUS POWERS EXERCISED BY LANDLORDS TO THE DETRIMENT OF THE PUBLIC--FREE CHOICE OF A HOME ESSENTIAL TO SOCIAL WELL-BEING--CHARACTERISTICS OF A GOOD SYSTEM OF LAND TENURE--ENCLOSURE OF COMMONS AND MOUNTAIN WASTES AS AFFECTING THE PUBLIC--THE DESTRUCTION OF ANCIENT MONUMENTS--PUBLIC IMPROVEMENTS CHECKED BY LANDLORDISM--PERMANENT DETERIORATION OF THE COUNTRY BY THE EXPORT OF MINERALS--CONCLUDING REMARKS ON ENGLISH LANDLORDISM.

In England pure landlordism is seen at its best. Its characteristics have been determined by the great and popular class of country squires and by numerous wealthy peers owning large ancestral estates, who have usually lived among their tenants, have been accustomed to treat them liberally, and have had sympathy with their pursuits and a desire for their prosperity. The tenant-farmers, too, are usually men of some capital, of good education, and of independent spirit, who are able to understand their position and maintain their rights, and whose occupancy of the land is the result of a more or less free contract with the owner. It is impossible to imagine more favourable conditions for the trial of our actual land-system; and we may safely assume that whatever evils we find to result from it here ought not to be imputed to the misconduct of individuals, but to the essential features of the system itself. There are, no doubt, certain remediable evils due to the laws of inheritance and the power of entail. These will probably soon be cured; but their removal will have little influence on those wider and more deeply-seated effects of the system to which I shall here call attention.

*Despotic Power of Landlords.*--The Hon. George C. Brodrick, in his valuable and impartial work, "English Land and English Landlords," speaks of the large resident landowner of a parish or district as being "invested with an authority over its inhabitants which neither the Saxon chief nor the Norman lord, in the fulness of his power, ever had the right of exercising." The clergyman is usually his nominee, and often his kinsman. The farmers, who are almost the only employers of labour besides himself, are his tenants-at-will, and, possibly, his debtors. The tradespeople of the village rent under him, and, even if they do not, could be ruined by his disfavour. The labourers live in his cottages, and are absolutely at his mercy for the privilege of hiring allotments, generally of inadequate size, and at an exorbitant rent as compared with the same land occupied by farmers[1]; and they are also dependent upon him for work in winter. He is usually a magistrate, and thus has the power of the law in his hands to carry out his orders and enhance his authority. Except by his permission, merely to live upon his estate is impossible; while most of the inhabitants may have their lives rendered miserable, or may be actually ruined by his displeasure. As Mr. Brodrick says: "We are wont to look back on Saxon times as barbarous, and on the feudal system as oppressive; but the simple truth is that nine-tenths of the population in an English country parish have at this moment less share in local government than belonged to all classes of freemen for centuries before and for centuries after the Norman Conquest. Again: they have not only less share in local government than belongs to French peasants in the present day, but less than belonged to French peasants under the eighteenth century monarchy." It may be said that this could be remedied, and that local self-government could be given to our people. But this is not so. No people can be free who are dependent on others for the very right to live in their native place or wherever they have become settled. So long as a man can be evicted and banished from a local community at the will of the landlord, there can be no independence, and no possible freedom or self-government worthy of the name. It is because the French peasants are landowners, and because the Norman villeins were in the position of copy-holders, and could not be ejected by the lord of the soil, that they were really free-men, while the tenants-at-will of an English landlord to-day are really serfs. Mr. Brodrick refers to the exclusion of manufacturing industries from sites naturally adapted for them, and their excessive concentration on sites artificially limited, with the consequent evils of overcrowding in towns and depopulation in some country districts, as being due to the opposition of rural landowners who thought their interests were involved; while all who remember the early days of railway-making can call to mind instances in which landowners exercised the power of compelling a railway to be diverted from the more direct and less expensive course, to the permanent injury of the whole community. Such cases show the power to check the free development of commerce and communication given to an individual by the possession of large areas of land--a power absolutely unique of its kind, since, not only can it be exercised by subjects in no other way, but is such as no civilised government exerts except upon weighty grounds of public policy.

*Landlords' Interference with Religious Freedom.*--But even more important than these cases are those in which a great landowner exercises despotic power over individuals, such as we are accustomed to look upon with horror when occurring in the Turkish or Russian Empires. One or two illustrative examples only can be here given, but a little research through the columns of the daily press would enable any one to fill a volume with similar cases. Let us first choose an example of interference with religious freedom--a matter on which we more especially pride ourselves. In April 1879 there appeared in the *Daily News* a correspondence between Samuel McAulay, a Wesleyan Minister, and Langhorne Burton, a Lincolnshire landowner. The former asked that religious services which had been conducted for thirty years in the village of Bag-Enderby, and which the said landlord had interdicted, might be resumed, the writer urging his case forcibly, but in very respectful terms. The answer was as follows:--

"Somersby, Horncastle, 20th March. Sir,--I have to acknowledge the receipt of yours of the 17th instant, applying for permission to resume your Wesleyan services which have been for some time held in one of my cottages at Bag-Enderby, and which permission, you say at the close of your letter, you shall take for granted if you hear nothing to the contrary. Now, sir, I consider this rather an offhand way of settling the matter, and I request that you will on no account act as you propose, at any rate until you hear further from me. The result of such a step on your part would probably be the removal from Bag-Enderby of all the members of your body, *who are of little value to me as tenants.* I wish to have *as tenants none* (these italics are his own) but thorough Church people, and consider myself quite at liberty to choose such as I like, without being dictated to by anybody. Reasons apart from this for my interdict of your meetings in Bag-Enderby I do not feel called upon to enter into with you. I also forbear to remark upon your seeming disposition to dictate to me my duty as a landlord. Your letters I have placed in my rector's hands, and beg to state in conclusion that I will write to you again should occasion require it.--I am, Sir, your obedient servant,

"LANGHORNE BURTON.

"Rev. S. McAulay."

Here we note the confirmation of the interdict, and the threat of "removal of the members of your body" from the village, of which many were probably natives; as well as the claim "to have as tenants none but thorough Church people," a claim to be carried into effect only by the eviction of all Dissenters from the landlord's property. The law of England permits the free practice of their religion by any sect whatever, but it is powerless to protect the Wesleyans of Bag-Enderby from what might be to many of them a very cruel punishment if they venture to exercise their right. Mr. Burton is probably not the only landowner who acts in this manner, though few would so openly proclaim their intention of doing so; but every landowner possesses the same *power*, and since it is plainly inconsistent with religious liberty, it ought no longer to exist. Yet this power is inherent in landlordism as established by law, and the inevitable corollary is that landlordism itself is incompatible with the freedom of British subjects, and must therefore be abolished.

*Landlords' Interference with Political Freedom.*--Instances of tenant-farmers of the highest respectability being ejected from their farms for voting in opposition to their landlords' will and pleasure must be known to every reader. A few years ago the eviction of the late Mr. George Hope, of Fenton Barns, an agriculturist of world-wide reputation, startled all England. The facts, as stated in the account of his life written by his daughter, are as follows. The Hopes had had the farm (of 640 acres) for three generations, and had changed it from "a moorish waste covered with furze-bushes" to a rich and highly cultivated farm. The rent had always been regularly paid, the land kept in the highest state of cultivation, and many improvements made, so that Mr. Hope was really a model tenant, besides being, as an agriculturist, celebrated throughout Europe. He was turned out by his landlord, because he held different political opinions and took an active part in politics and in public affairs. Up to 1852 neither Mr. Hope, his father, nor his grandfather had made any profit out of the farm; since then his energy and talent had made it very profitable, but at the same time it had been vastly improved for the benefit of the landlord--Mr. Nisbet Hamilton.

Another tenant on the same estate--Mr. Saddler, of Ferrygate--was also got rid of (for political reasons it was believed), and his improvements were confiscated without the least compensation. Mr. James Howard, M.P., states that these two gentlemen were, without exception, the most enterprising farmers of his acquaintance; and he maintains that the system under which men of capital and position may, on six short months' notice, be called upon to quit their farms and to break up house and home is one worthy only of a barbarous age.[2]

*Landlords' Interference with a Tenant's Sport.*--The following is a more recent case of ejection of a well-to-do hereditary occupant of a farm, who had offended his landlord by daring to secure some sporting privileges for his private enjoyment, without first asking permission to do so.

Mr. W. R. Todd, who with his father had occupied the same Yorkshire farm for forty years, took a few fields which were let by tender, together with the right of shooting, in order to enjoy some sport, which the landlord of his farm forbade on his lands. On doing so, his landlord sent for him, and told him he must either give up the shooting or the farm, as *his* tenants were not allowed to shoot, even on land which they had taken for the express purpose. Accordingly, Mr. Todd had to quit, and stated his case in the *Daily News* of October last year. The landlord's agent thereupon wrote to explain, admitting that the facts were stated correctly by Mr. Todd, but adding that there were circumstances of aggravation, the tenant having "placed turnips to attract the hares, and shot them in the dusk when the snow was on the ground." Considering that so much damage is done by hares that the Legislature have since been obliged to give tenants the power to destroy them, whether their landlords will or no, Mr. Todd's conduct seems very natural, and was certainly neither legally nor morally wrong. Neither can we say that the landlord was wrong in using the power he possessed to preserve the hares for his own sport; but the circumstance, none the less, shows that a tenant-farmer of England lives under a hard despotism, and is liable to be expelled from the home of his childhood for the slightest interference with his landlord's fancies or privileges.

*Eviction of the Inhabitants of an Entire Village.*--In the following case, given on the authority of Mr. Froude,[3] no offence whatever appears to have been alleged against the unfortunate tenants. He says:--"Not a mile from the place where I am now writing an estate on the coast of Devonshire came into the hands of an English Duke. There was a primitive village upon it, occupied by sailors, pilots, and fishermen, which is described in Domesday Book, and was inhabited at the Conquest by the actual forefathers of the late tenants, whose names may be read there. The houses were out of repair. The Duke's predecessors had laid out nothing upon them for a century, and had been contented with exacting the rents. When the present owner entered into possession it was represented to him that if the village was to continue it must be rebuilt, but that to rebuild it would be a needless expense, for the people, living as they did on their wages as fishermen and seamen, would not cultivate his land, and were useless to him. The houses were therefore simply torn down, and nearly half the population was driven out into the world to find new homes. A few more such instances of tyranny might provoke a dangerous crisis." Here, then, for no offence whatever, a considerable village population--who, if long-continued ancestral occupancy goes for anything, had the full moral and equitable right to live on this particular portion of their native soil--were rudely driven out to what must have been to them a cruel banishment. Some grave political crime, some gross offence against law or morality, would hardly have justified such a punishment, in which old and young, women and children, were alike involved. Who can tell the mental anguish, the physical suffering involved in such an eviction; the burning sense of injury, the rending of social ties, the pain and loss of having to seek a fresh home and begin a new life at the will of an unknown and unseen despot? And the powerful Government of our free England, with its high-sounding declarations--that every man's house is his castle; that rich and poor are alike in the eye of its laws; and that there is no wrong without a remedy--was absolutely powerless to give these poor villagers any protection whatever! By recognising private property in land, the State has set up in its midst a number of petty lords more powerful than any Government; and whose decrees, whatever injustice they may do, or whatever misery bring to British subjects, no court of law or equity is able to reverse. Well may Mr. Brodrick say that neither Saxon chief nor Norman lord ever had the right of exercising such power as this; for they at all events had a superior lord over them who *could*, if he so willed, remedy such injustice, while our existing Government can *not* do so.

On the broad ground, then, that the possession of land (for other purposes than personal occupation) gives the owner powers which are inconsistent with the liberties of their fellow-subjects, we again claim the abolition of landlordism.

*Injurious Power of Landlords over Farmers and over Agriculture.*--One of the strongest points of the landlord system is supposed to be the beneficial influence of an educated and enlightened class, whose duty as well as their interest is to manage their estates on the best principles, to introduce improved methods of agriculture, and generally to set a good example in both agricultural and social economy. Admitting that the best types of landlords actually do produce these good effects, we are bound to ask what proportion these bear to the whole body, and whether in the majority of cases, a great landowner is not rather a clog upon progressive agriculture, by the antiquated regulations which he enforces on his tenants, while by inordinate game-preserving he actually destroys large quantities of the produce of the soil.

Mr. Brodrick tells us that the most profitable form of agricultural occupation is that which most resembles ownership; that "the best agriculture is found on farms whose owners are protected by leases; the next best on farms whose tenants are protected by the Lincolnshire or other customs; the worst of all on farms whose tenants are not protected at all, but rely on the honour of their landlords." Now during the present century the custom of granting leases has diminished, partly owing to the desire of landlords to secure political power by influencing their tenants' votes, and partly from the importance they attach to rights of sporting, which often induces them to accept low rents from non-improving tenants, who can be turned out at short notice if they meddle with the game; and Mr. Brodrick concludes that, "by the operation of these and other causes, it is tolerably certain that yearly tenancy has become the rule, and leasehold tenancy the exception, in most English counties;" while Mr. C. S. Read, M.P., stated, at a recent meeting of the Farmers' Club, that three-fourths of the land of England is held subject to a six months' notice to quit. Whence it follows that a system of tenure which produces "the worst agriculture of all" is that which prevails over the larger part of our country; and this result is due directly to the will and pleasure of English landlords.

But even under its best conditions--that of holding by a lease--tenant farming is essentially wasteful and imperfect. The tenant is almost always subject to covenants which restrict his freedom and keep him in a certain routine of operations, even under circumstances when a change would be advantageous to all parties. He is bound to make up a fixed amount of rent annually, and is therefore unable to carry out any operations which would diminish his profits for one or two years, to increase them largely in the future. Whatever improvements he may make at the commencement of his lease must be so calculated that he can obtain their full value before its termination; and there is great waste of capital involved in the tendency of every such tenant to exhaust the soil as much as possible towards the expiration of a lease, which has to be restored to its normal fertility in the early years of the next term.

*Limitation of the Beneficial Influence of Landlords.*--Again, whatever benefits may be due to the presence of resident landlords, these extend over comparatively a small portion of the country, owing to the number of absentees even in England. From an examination of the official New Domesday Book, Mr. Arthur Arnold has ascertained that the 525 members of the peerage own 1,593 separate estates, comprising an area of more than 15,000,000 acres; or, allowing for roads, rivers, towns, and other public property, about one-third the whole land of the United Kingdom. The Duke of Buccleugh owns 14 separate estates, and four other peers 11 each, while the whole body of peers average 3 each, often widely separated in different counties. It is evident that in all these cases the estates must be wholly managed by agents; and, although the owner may occasionally visit each of them, the supposed beneficial influence of residency must be at a minimum. The list of landowners possessing more than 5,000 acres shows that great numbers of private gentlemen also possess estates in from two to seven distinct counties; and as most of these live a considerable part of the year in London, and another part abroad, they can hardly have much time to reside even on the particular estate which they make their home. On the whole, then, it is evident that the majority of the estates of great landlords do not possess the benefit, whatever that may be, of the permanent residence of the owner among the farmers, labourers, and other people who, as we have seen, are so largely dependent on his will and pleasure.

*Whatever Beneficial Influence Landlords Exert would be Increased Under Occupying Ownership.*--It will be as well to notice here a strange misconception which pervades the ideas and arguments of those who uphold landlordism as a beneficial system. They assume that, if the nobility and educated gentry were no longer the possessors of great landed estates, beyond what they desired to occupy and maintain for their own pleasure or profit, they would not live in the country at all. But we may ask, Where, then, would they live? Is all the English love of country life a delusion? Would our wealthy classes live always in London, if they derived their income from other sources than the rents of land which they rarely or never behold? These questions really require no answer, and they serve to show the futility of the whole objection. If, as we here maintain, land ought to be owned only for personal occupation, it is as certain as anything can be that the number of wealthy resident landowners would greatly increase. The numerous fine parks and demesnes now kept up merely as show places, or let out to yearly tenants, would be each and all in the hands of a separate occupying owner. Each would be a home; and, as such, would be the object of that loving personal care and attention which, as one of half-a-dozen country houses, they never receive. For *one* resident landowner with education, wealth, and refinement, there would then be a dozen or a score; for each great estate would become the property of many owners, some owning several hundreds or even thousands of acres, others small farms; and as every one of these would be influenced by the double motive of adding to the permanent value of his own property and increasing the beauty and enjoyability of his only country home, their influence for good on each other and on the labouring classes would be certainly many times greater than that of any one half-resident landlord, even if all these were as good, and useful, and enlightened members of society as some of them really are.

*Supposed Importance of the Large Farms which Landlordism Favours.*--Another of the allegations in support of landlordism is that great landlords favour large farms, and that large farms worked by farmers of sufficient capital are more economical and produce larger profits than small ones. Admitting, for the sake of argument only, that this may possibly be sometimes true, and even that scientific farming on large farms produces larger wheat crops per acre than small ones, this only proves that such farms are better for the landlord and perhaps for the tenant, but not necessarily for the nation at large. For, since our supply of corn and cattle now comes mainly from abroad, the chief effect of a larger amount of such produce being obtained by a given amount of labour is that the landlord gets a higher rent and the farmer a larger profit, while the whole population of the country round may be positively injured. It is a well-known fact that in a district of large farms the inhabitants of the adjacent towns and villages suffer many inconveniences, especially in the difficulty of procuring new milk, fresh butter, eggs, or poultry, all of which, if produced, are sent away to London or other large cities. Families living quite in the country are thus often obliged to use Swiss milk, to eat foreign butter, or even an artificial compound of fat misnamed butter, and French eggs; while labourers and mechanics often bring up their families without the use of so wholesome and natural a food as milk.

But the question of the comparative productiveness of large and small farms is most unfairly decided by a comparison of tenant-farmers of these two classes in England. The large farmer is usually better educated and has a larger capital than the small one, and more frequently has a lease which enables him to work his land at a considerable advantage. But, as we shall show in our next chapter, when occupying owners are concerned there is no such superiority. Mr. Brodrick tells us that M. de Lavergne, writing on the Rural Economy of England, declared that no similar area of English land is cultivated so well as the Département du Nord, which is essentially a district of small farms; adding--"there is overwhelming evidence to prove that scientific English agriculturists have yet many lessons to learn from the small farms in Belgium, Switzerland, the Channel Islands, and Germany."

The great and essential point, however, is always overlooked by the apologists of landlord-and-tenant farming. This is, not which system leads to the greatest production of wealth, but, which supports the largest agricultural and rural population in comfort, decency, and reasonable well-being; which tends most to render the lowest class of workers thrifty, sober, and industrious; which will most surely abolish pauperism and diminish crime. The government of a civilised community is bound to consider the well-being of every class of its subjects, not that of capitalists only; and the experience of the last 50 years abundantly proves--as we have already shown--that the most astounding increase in the aggregate wealth of the community has no necessary tendency to diminish poverty or abolish pauperism.[4] Let us, then, proceed to inquire what are the effects of landlordism on that large mass of workers to whom the entire wealth of the country is primarily due; and whose physical, social, and moral condition is the true and final test of the success of any government or any social polity.

*The Effects of Landlordism on the Well-Being of the Labouring Classes.*--In mediæval times the villein or serf, corresponding to our agricultural labourer of to-day, could not be ejected from his land except by the judgment of a manor-court, in which the freeholders sat as jurymen.[5] However hardly he might be treated by his lord, he still had a home and a plot of land on which he could work with all the intense interest of an owner. Later on, when the villeins had become freemen, it was attempted to fix the rate of wages of labourers, who, by the continued enclosures of woods and wastes had become more dependent on daily labour for sustenance. In order to mitigate the evil results of this limitation of wages, the first Poor Law was established, and about the same time a statute of Elizabeth required four acres of land to be attached to each new cottage. If this just and far-seeing law had been strictly enforced to the present day, and the land so granted declared to be inalienable, it is probable that much of the great mass of pauperism which now exists would have been prevented. Down to a century ago, however, the position of the agricultural labourer was decidedly better than it is now. Matthews estimated that, in 1720, the wages of a labourer commanded more than at any previous or subsequent time; while a Parliamentary Report in 1868 thus forcibly sums up the advantages of his position:--"Previous to 1775 the agricultural labourer was in a most prosperous condition. His wages gave him a great command over the necessaries of life, his rent was lower, his wearing apparel cheaper, his shoes cheaper, his living cheaper, than formerly; and he had on the commons and wastes liberty of cutting furze for fuel, with the chance of getting a little land, and in time a small farm."[6] It is true that his social and moral condition was very low, but so was that of many of his superiors; and it is very doubtful whether the improvement which has taken place in this last respect is not to a great extent neutralised by the deterioration of his physical condition.

*Deterioration of the Condition of the Agricultural Labourer during the present Century.*--From that time till within the last few years the wealth of the landlords, and, in a less degree, the profits of the farmers, have been steadily increasing. The rent of even agricultural land has nearly doubled, and the price of much agricultural produce has doubled also. In the latter part of the last century meat was 4d. a pound, cheese 3 1/2d., butter 6 1/2d., and skim-milk could be had for a halfpenny a quart, or was often given away, while wages were then about 8s. a week. In 1850 all these articles of food were much dearer, while in some parts of England wages were actually lower; and whereas during the last twenty years the above articles have been usually more than double the price, wages have been less than half as high again. But the labourer has now to pay much higher house-rent, he has generally no garden, and, being usually a weekly tenant, is so dependent on his landlord that he cannot make the most of what he has; the commons and roadside wastes from which he formerly obtained fuel for winter, with food and litter for a cow, a donkey, geese or poultry, have almost all been enclosed; and the result is that he has few means of adding to his scanty wages, and is reduced to live mainly on bread and weak tea, with a little cheese or bacon and cheap artificial butter, while his children are brought up almost without knowing the taste of milk. His sole relaxation is to be found at the wayside tavern, his only prospect to end his days in the workhouse.

*The Social Degradation of the Agricultural Labourer at the Present Day.*--In a remarkable letter to the *Daily News* in 1869, Sir George Grey gave a striking picture of the social and physical degradation of the English agricultural labourer. He quotes the reports of their medical officers to the Privy Council, which tell us that--"Whether he shall find house-room on the land which he contributes to till, whether the house-room which he gets shall be human or swinish, whether he shall have the little space of garden that so vastly lessens the pressure of his poverty--all this does not depend on his willingness and ability to pay reasonable rent for the decent accommodation he requires, but depends on the use which others may see fit to make of their 'right to do as they will with their own.'" Owing to the pecuniary interest which each parish formerly had in reducing the number of its resident labourers, thus diminishing its liability to rates, the landowners had but to resolve that there should be no labourers' dwellings on their estates, and they would thenceforth be virtually free from half their responsibilities for the poor. The lord of the soil may treat its actual cultivators as aliens whom he may expel from his territory; and when it is his interest or his pleasure he often does so. The same report states:--"Besides the extreme cases where houses of a parish were pulled down in the teeth of an increasing population, there were also innumerable parishes where the demolition of houses was going on more rapidly than any diminution of the population could explain. When the process of depopulation is completed, the result is a show village, where the cottages have been reduced to a few, and where none but persons who are needful as shepherds, gardeners, or gamekeepers are allowed to live. But the land requires cultivation, and it will be found that the labourers employed upon it are not the tenants of the owner, but that they come from a neighbouring open village, perhaps three miles off, where a numerous small proprietary had received them when their cottages were destroyed in the close villages around." To the hard toil of the labourer there will then have to be added the daily need of walking six miles or more for the power of earning his daily bread. "But he suffers a still greater evil in the kind of dwelling he is obliged to inhabit. In the open village cottage speculators buy scraps of land, which they throng as densely as they can with the cheapest of all possible hovels, and into these wretched habitations (which, even if they adjoin the open country, have some of the worst features of the worst town residences) crowd the agricultural labourers of England." The habitual overcrowding of these wretched hovels leads to scenes and conditions of life too painful to dwell upon, and we need only quote the concluding statement. "To be subject to such influences is a degradation which must become deeper and deeper for those on whom it continues to work. To children who are born under its curse it must be a very baptism into infamy."

It may be supposed that these cases are the exceptions,

but the report assures us they are not so. After doing justice to the honourable instances in which landowners, even at a loss to themselves, provide decent accommodation for their labourers, it adds:--"From these brighter but *exceptional* scenes it is requisite, in the interests of justice, that attention should again be drawn to the overwhelming preponderance of facts, which are a reproach to the civilisation of England. Lamentable indeed must be the case when, notwithstanding all that is evident with regard to the quality of the present accommodation, it is the common conclusion of competent observers that even the general badness of dwellings is an evil infinitely less urgent than their numerical insufficiency."[7]

Corroborative evidence, if any be needed, is furnished by many independent authorities. Professor Fawcett, in the work already referred to, says of the British agricultural labourers--"Theirs is a life of incessant toil for wages too scanty to give them a sufficient supply of the first necessities of life. No hope cheers their monotonous career: a life of constant labour brings them no other prospect than that when their strength is exhausted, they must crave as suppliant mendicants a pittance from parish relief "; while the Bishop of Manchester states that out of 300 parishes which he visited in Norfolk, Essex, Sussex, and Gloucestershire, only two had good cottage accommodation. . . . "The majority of the cottages that exist in rural parishes are deficient in almost every requisite that should constitute a home for a

Christian family in a civilised community." Details are then given of parishes and estates of 2,000 acres with one or two cottages only and sometimes none at all; and as a result ten or eleven persons sleeping in a single bedroom.[8] And the only remedy suggested for this state of things is--not to give labourers a right to have land, the one and only possible and real remedy, but "to call upon those who own the soil to see to it that their estates are adequately provided with decent residences for those by whom they are tilled." What a weak and impotent conclusion! Call upon the landlords to build comfortable, roomy, and decent cottages at a certain loss! Truly you may call and call, but you will get no satisfactory response; and in the meantime more Commissions will inquire, more misery and horror will come to light, and no general improvement will be effected.

*This State of Things is Due to the System of Landlordism, not to the Bad Conduct of Landlords.*--Now, the great point to be noticed here is, that, except by the action of the benevolent or charitable, the labourer is, as a rule, disgracefully housed, wretchedly fed, and, however honest and industrious he may be, has rarely any other prospect than to die a pauper. The law of supply and demand has failed to give him a decent cottage. The enormous increase in the wealth of the landlord, giving him the disposal of so much larger a fund out of which to employ labourers, has in no way benefitted the tiller of the soil. And, while every one remarks that the standard of living of the tenant-farmers has been greatly raised, the foregoing evidence, no less than the glaring facts of persistent pauperism, shows that the social condition of the labourer has certainly been stationary, if it has not actually deteriorated. It is not necessary to go far to seek the cause of this apparently inexplicable state of things. Those who do not wilfully shut their eyes must see that the monopoly of the land by landlords sufficiently explains it. The land is a fixed quantity, while the population is ever increasing. The tenant-farmer with capital is in a position to make such a bargain with the landlord as will give him fair interest on his capital and adequate remuneration for his skill in superintending his farm. Between them they absorb all the profit that they extract from the soil, while the wages of the labourer are kept down by the forced competition of those who have no other means of living to that irreducible minimum which is barely sufficient to support life and health while he can work, and, as soon as his strength fails, leaves him to charity or the poorhouse.[2] It is not that the landlord or the farmer are individually to blame. Both try to make the most of the property which the law allows them to possess, and we cannot expect them to do more than pay the current rate of wages. Were all landlords without exception to devote a considerable percentage of their incomes to providing good cottages for their labourers rent-free, one of the great blots on our agricultural system would doubtless be removed. But this would be charity pure and simple; and to say that there is no way of raising the status of the labouring population except by the universal charity of the landlords is to confess that landlordism itself is an evil of the first magnitude. The labourer does not want charity, but simply justice. He wants some share in that common land which his ancestors possessed, but from which, by landlord-made law, he is now totally divorced. He claims the right to labour for his own benefit on some portion of his native soil, not doled out to him in allotments at three or four times the rent paid by the farmer, and even then considered a favour, but in plots attached to his cottage home, to which he shall have an inalienable title under a fixed quit-rent, to which he can devote those hours or days of enforced idleness now cruelly wasted, and in the cultivation of which his children may acquire habits of industry and thrift, and the simpler arts of cultivation. In our next chapter we shall show, by abundant evidence, that by conceding such a right we should soon change a pauperised into a self-supporting population and should at the same time render our country far more healthy and enjoyable to every one of its inhabitants.

*The Enclosure Act and its Results.*--Although we freely absolve landlords from blame in the matter of the wages of labourers, we cannot do the same in regard to their collective action in the enclosures of commons. By means of various Enclosure Acts, it is estimated that about seven millions of acres of land were enclosed between 1710 and 1843. The progress of enclosure has been most rapid since the time of George II, and Sir George Nicholls states that two and a half millions of acres were enclosed in thirty years between 1769 and 1799. The Royal Commissioners on the Employment of Women and Children in Agriculture remark that these enclosures were often made without any compensation to the smaller commoners, and that they have deprived agricultural labourers of ancient rights over the waste, and have disabled the occupants of new cottages from acquiring such rights. In 1845 a general Enclosure Act was passed for still further facilitating the enclosure and improvement of commons, and it empowered the Commissioners to grant portions of the land for recreation and for allotments to the labouring poor, according to population. It did not, however, allow allotments of more than *a quarter of an acre* to each labourer, and no house was in any case allowed to be erected on them. While all other persons having rights of common had allotments made to them of land in absolute property, the labourers, to whom the common rights had in many cases been of more real use and value than to most of the surrounding landowners, had nothing whatever given to them but a miserable pittance of allotment ground, for which they had *to pay a high rent*! The Commissioners, however, appear to have made little use even of these scanty powers, since, out of 7,000,000 acres enclosed since 1760, it was found in 1868 that only 2,119 acres had been reserved for allotments.[10] As examples of the more recent action of the Enclosure Commissioners, we find it stated in the report of the Commons Preservation Society that in 1869 they recommended the enclosure of 6,916 acres, of which they reserved three acres for recreation and six for field gardens! Owing to the attention drawn to these figures in Parliament and by the press, they have latterly given rather more for these purposes; yet in 1875, out of 18,600 acres enclosed only 132 acres were reserved for garden allotments.

*Uniform Evidence as to the Beneficial Effects of Allotments and Cottage Gardens.*--If we think it strange that a body of highly educated, wealthy, moral, and benevolent men saw nothing wrong in thus appropriating to themselves land which had been the birthright of the English labourers from time immemorial, we are still more astonished at the impolicy of such a course of action, in view of the evidence they possessed of the important uses this land might have been put to for the diminution of the persistent evils of pauperism and crime. So long ago as 1795, it was shown before a Select Committee of the House of Commons "that, in 1770, the lord of a manor near Tewkesbury, remarking the exceptionally good character of families holding plots of reclaimed land, set apart some twenty-five acres for cottagers' allotments, and had the satisfaction of seeing the poor-rates reduced in two years to 4d. in the pound, while they stood at 2s. 6d. in the surrounding parishes." And another Select Committee in 1843 reported that "the tenancy of land under the garden allotment system is a powerful means of bettering the condition of those classes who depend for their livelihood on manual labour, and the benefits are obtained without corresponding disadvantages." From evidence given before the "Women's and Children's Employment Commission" in 1868, it was proved that cottagers obtained a return from such allotments of £16 an acre above the ordinary farm rent, and it was estimated that, if all agricultural labourers above 20 years of age possessed half-acre or quarter-acre allotments, the annual value of the produce would be between three and four millions of pounds. If these statements are even approximately correct, it is clear that the refusal of land to labourers results in a great loss to the nation of actual food, quite independently of the enormous saving that would accrue to it by the diminution of pauperism.

The allotments that do exist (and they are far from sufficient to supply the wants of the agricultural labourers) are, however, no test whatever of the good that might accrue from a more generous system. They are almost always held from year to year, and the labourers usually pay for them double or treble the rent paid for the same land by the farmer. They are also let in far too small patches; and, what is worst of all, they are often situated a considerable distance from the dwellings of the majority of the labourers. All these conditions are adverse to their being made the most of. A garden is especially valuable because it enables a man and his family to utilise odd moments, while its progress, being constantly under his eye, gives him a new interest in his home. After a long day's labour, and a walk of perhaps two or three miles from his work, to have to walk another mile, perhaps, to his allotment must often prevent him from going there at all, except when the days are longest. But perhaps even more important is the loss which his garden sustains in not receiving the whole refuse and sewage of the house, which could be so easily applied to a cottage garden, but which involves a heavy cost in time and labour if they are to be carried to a distant allotment. Again, the temporary occupation of a field-allotment affords no scope for growing fruit, in which our country is so deficient, or in keeping poultry for the supply of eggs, which might as easily be produced by our cottagers as by those of France. It is a mere mockery to point to allotments as affording any adequate notion of the material and social benefits which our labourers directly, and the whole country indirectly, would derive from throwing open the land freely to the permanent occupation or ownership of our labouring classes.

*Beneficial Effects of Small Cottage Farms.*--As one example of the good effects produced by even an approximation to such a system is the following statement of what has been done on the Annandale estate in Dumfriesshire. "Leases of twenty-one years were offered at ordinary farm rents to deserving labourers, carefully selected for their character, who built their own cottages, at a cost to themselves varying from £21 to £40, exclusive of labour, while the landlord supplied timber, stone, &c., at a cost of about £22. These houses were not grouped in villages, but chiefly situated along roads, with plots of from two to six acres attached to each, or the addition of grass for a cow. All the work for these little farms was done at by-hours and by members of the family, the cottager buying roots from the farmer, and producing in return milk, butter, and pork, besides rearing calves. Among such peasant farmers pauperism soon ceased to exist, and many of them soon bettered themselves in life. It was also particularly observed that habits of marketing and the constant demands on thrift and forethought brought out new virtues and powers in the wives. In fact, the moral effects of the system in fostering industry, sobriety, and contentment were described as no less satisfactory than its economical success."[11]

Again, the same writer tells us that in several estates in Cheshire it is the practice to let plots of land ranging from two and a-half to three and a-half acres with each cottage at an ordinary farm rent. This practice, which is but the revival of a custom once almost universal amongst the peasantry of England, is found to be fraught with manifold advantages. The most obvious of these is an abundant supply of milk for the farm labourers' children, who in many districts grow up without tasting the natural diet of childhood. But the habits of thrift and forethought encouraged by cow-keeping and dairying, on however small a scale, constitute a moral advantage of great importance. On Lord Tollemache's estate in Cheshire, where the system has been long established and carefully managed, its results have been eminently beneficial, and attended by none of the drawbacks so often magnified into insuperable difficulties by the opponents of cottage farming. Not less satisfactory has been the experience of other landlords who have given the system a fair trial, and the Second Report of the Women and Children's Employment Commission is full of evidence in its favour. "Yet," adds Mr. Brodrick, "such is the conservatism of agriculture that it continues to be a rare feature of English rural economy, and it is quite possible that generations will elapse before it is widely extended."[12]

*The Logical Bearing of this Evidence.*--Now, when we have, on one side, a system which inevitably pauperises a large section of the labouring classes; which degrades them socially and morally; and which, through them, permanently injures the whole community--and, on the other side, one which tends *immediately* to abolish pauperism and diminish crime; to elevate this same class socially and morally; and, while doing this, to aid materially in the supply of some of the most important necessaries of life, every Englishman has a right to object to leaving this great question in the hands of any body of men, much less of those who for so long a time have shown themselves utterly incompetent to form a correct judgment upon it. We object, too, most strongly to the indefinite continuance of a system which enables any of our fellow-citizens either to withhold at their pleasure or to grant as a favour that which we maintain is the birthright of every Englishman--the freedom to enjoy and utilise some portion of his native soil, on terms to be settled by the State, in the interest of all.

*Various Powers Exercised by Landlords to the Detriment of the Public at Large.*--Having thus shown how much despotic power landlords possess over their various classes of tenants, and how much injury these tenants often suffer directly, and the community indirectly, by the exercise of these powers, we have now to consider the numerous ways in which the entire population, individually and collectively, suffer injury, by allowing the soil of the country to be monopolised by private owners and to be dealt with as mere merchandise for profit or speculation; as the means of obtaining undue political and social power; or as an exclusive possession in which the people at large have no interests and can claim no rights.

We will begin with the question of House and Home, as one which affects the interests and the happiness of a larger number of persons than any other question whatever.

*The Free Choice of a Home Essential to Well-Being.*--People have so long been accustomed to look upon land as necessarily belonging to some individual who has the right to do what he pleases with it, that to most persons the idea never occurs that, as free citizens of a free State, they ought to be able to live wherever they choose to live, so long as they do not infringe any other person's equal right to do so. As a fact, they can only live where some landlord chooses to allow them; and though hundreds and thousands who have the means would *like* to choose a spot for themselves on which to reside, paying, of course, its fair value to the actual owner, they are very frequently restricted to some building-estate, where competition and speculation have raised the price of building land to such a degree that the crowding and other inconveniences of towns are extended far into the country. Every one who has written on the subject condemns the system of building-leases, as fraught with innumerable evils, and one which ought not to be permitted. It leads to bad speculative building, in which solidity and comfort are sacrificed to ornament and show. It leads to overcrowding in the vicinity of towns, and the comparative desertion of the more remote country places. And by the large profits it gives to existing landowners, with the prospect of a still larger profit to their descendants, it leads to the crowding of houses on narrow strips of land at ground-rents altogether disproportionate to its extreme agricultural value. These leases have usually been for 99 years, but some landlords now restrict them to 80 and even to 60 years; and for the latter half of the term it is evident that the home feeling and affection which leads a man continually to improve the dwelling which he trusts will be inhabited by some portion of his family after him, and which has an important moral influence on his character, must be continually weakened and at last wholly cease. Yet, so long as absolute private property in land continues, and it is held to be a fit subject for free barter and contract, it will be practically impossible to abolish the system.

*Characteristics of a Good System of Land Tenure.*--Now, we consider it to be an indisputable axiom that that system of land-tenure is best which leads at once to the freest enjoyment of the land by the whole population, and at the same time tends to its increased cultivation and productiveness. Of all modes of enjoyment that which depends upon the *House* and its surroundings--the healthiness, beauty, convenience, and productiveness of the *Home*--is the most important, since it affects directly the bulk of the whole population, and affects them during the largest portion of their daily lives. The utmost possible freedom in the choice of a *home*, with the greatest possible facilities for procuring the necessary land at a cheap rate, would constitute perhaps the chief of all the blessings which a sound and rational system of "Nationalisation of the Land" would confer upon every individual. Under the present system the very reverse obtains, since we have the *least* possible freedom of choice, and in most cases have to pay an extravagant monopoly price for whatever we are permitted to occupy.

It will be shown further on that it is quite possible to obtain the land for the nation without confiscating the property of any existing landowner or any expectant heir; and, that being done, it will be as easy as it will be expedient to secure the right of every one to obtain land for a "house and home," in almost any spot he may choose, and at a cost only slightly exceeding its value for agricultural purposes. The quantity of land thus taken from agriculture would, it is true, be somewhat larger than at present; but, as much of this would be highly cultivated as garden ground, and would offer facilities for the rearing of poultry and pigs as well as for growing fruit and vegetables, it is probable or even certain that the general productiveness of the land would be increased rather than diminished. At all events, every one must feel that the most perfect liberty in the choice of a dwelling-place, with a sufficiency of land for garden and pleasure-grounds at a cheap rate, would be so beneficial to the health and contentment of the entire community, that a system of land-tenure which renders it possible and even easy has already much in its favour. The exact mode in which this may be effected will be explained when the scheme of Nationalisation here advocated is discussed in detail.

We may, however, at once point out that the free appropriation of land for dwellings as now proposed offers, perhaps, the only possible check to the undue growth of large towns. In all the more beautiful and healthful parts of the country land would be taken for dwellings, and these would become new centres of rural populations, forming in time country villages and small towns. All land and building speculation being abolished, the growth of towns, now mainly caused by such speculations, would be checked, and hundreds who now take houses from speculative builders merely because they have no real freedom of choice will then choose for themselves, will occupy much more land, and will thus spread themselves more generally over the country. Other checks might be applied by local authorities, which would tend greatly to the healthiness and enjoyability of our larger towns, such as the interposition of belts of park and garden at certain intervals around dense centres of population--a class of improvement which the ruinous competition prices of land held by private owners now renders impossible.[13]

*Enclosure of Commons and Mountain Wastes as Affecting the Public.*--Next in importance to the power of securing pleasant and healthy houses, the general public have most interest in the right to free passage about the country--to roam over the commons, heaths, and woods; to search out the grand and beautiful scenes afforded by our rivers, moors, and mountains; to have preserved for them the ruins which are landmarks of our written history, as well as those more ancient monuments which tell us of pre-historic ages. In each and all of these directions they suffer injury from the powers claimed and exercised by landlords. As we have already seen, enormous areas of common land have been enclosed and appropriated by the surrounding owners, often without provision even of foot-paths by which the public may enjoy any of the land they once freely roamed over. Owing to inordinate game-preservation, the woods and copses are almost always rigidly shut up, and thus the public are deprived of one of the greatest enjoyments of country life--the power to wander freely under the shade of trees, in places where the choicest wild flowers blossom, and where the living denizens of the woods may be seen in their native haunts. Were it not for the ancient foot-paths crossing the country from village to village, many parts of our land would be almost shut out from the great body of its inhabitants. Fortunately these are tolerably numerous. But however great may be the need of fresh centres of population, we rarely hear of new paths being formed, while old ones are occasionally shut up or diverted, or so enclosed by fences that all their picturesque beauty and rural enjoyability is destroyed.

Another injury to the public and deprivation of their rights is the frequent and constantly increasing enclosure of those roadside strips of green sward which add so much to the charm of rural walks. Everywhere we find roads and lanes now bounded between parallel hedges or fences at a regular distance apart, while a few yards inside the fields on either side an old bank or an irregular row of trees show the distance to which the road formerly extended. We are assured by the Commons Preservation Society "that all such absorptions are illegal, the general rule of law being that the public have a right of way over the whole space between the hedges."[14] And in a later report they repeat that such encroachments "are almost invariably illegal, and may be abated by the ordinary remedies provided in the case of the obstruction of a highway." It appears, therefore, that all over the country the public have for many years past been systematically robbed by means of these encroachments; and few more striking proofs can be given of the great evil of landlordism and the injurious power and influence of landlords than that such systematic robbery, though contrary to law, should have been almost always effected with impunity.

Equally, or perhaps even more, injurious to the interests of the public is the extensive appropriation by individual landlords of enormous areas of wild mountain country in Wales, Ireland, and especially in Scotland, whereby Englishmen are forbidden in many cases to visit and enjoy some of the most beautiful and picturesque scenery of their native land--spots where nature exhibits her full grandeur, and where alone the choicest and rarest examples of our native flora and fauna are to be met with. The right to these enormous tracts of land as private property appears to be of very recent and very doubtful origin. The Highland chiefs had certainly no such right to the land in fee, with the concomitant power to evict all the rest of the clan and sell or let the land to the highest bidder. Yet this is what the successors to those chiefs claim, and what they have in some cases actually done; and the law, ever on the side of the landlords and against the people, appears to have endorsed their claim, and has thus given to them complete and despotic power over the lives and liberties of the native inhabitants of the district. The result has been that terrible depopulation and pauperisation of the country which has been described in the last chapter, and the replacement of men and human habitations by sheep, cattle, and deer, for a parallel to which we must go back to the days of the Norman conquerors of England in the height of their despotic power. Some of the wildest and grandest mountain scenery of Scotland is now as rigidly shut up as if it were in a private pleasure ground. Hundreds of square miles of glen and rock and mountain-side are given up to deer and grouse for the pleasure and profit of a few individuals, while the public are thereby deprived of a means of enjoyment and healthful relaxation which hardly any country in Europe denies them but their own.

*The Destruction of Ancient Monuments.*--One of the

most palpable illustrations of the evil consequences of allowing land to be the absolute property of individuals is, that it has led to the destruction of a vast number of most interesting ancient monuments, while the attempt of Sir John Lubbock and others to preserve those that still remain has been for some years strenuously opposed, on the ground that it interferes with the rights of landlords. Let us cull from Sir John Lubbock's essay[15] a few examples of that destruction which several Members of Parliament have had the hardihood to deny.

One of the most remarkable and interesting of our very ancient monuments is Abury, or Avebury, in Wiltshire, which an old antiquarian declared "did as much exceed Stonehenge as a cathedral doth an ordinary parish church." The entire series of these remains presented such a colossal enigma as it would be difficult to parallel even at Karnac; but this wonderful relic of the past has been for many years undergoing destruction, the great stones of which it is composed being broken up to build cottages, to make gate-posts, and even to mend the roads. "Still, even now," says Sir John Lubbock, "there is perhaps no more remarkable monument of the kind in this country, or even in Europe." In the year 1875, the owner of the land on which this grand monument stands sold it unreservedly to a Building Society, by which it was lotted out in sites for cottages, and actually sold in small plots for this purpose. Fortunately, Sir John

Lubbock was informed of this just in time, and succeeded in purchasing the land himself, and in persuading the villagers for a small consideration to exchange their allotments for others in an adjoining field which was just as well suited to them. Abury, the wonder of antiquarians and the enigma of the learned, was thus barely saved from complete destruction by the intervention of a private gentleman living in a remote county!

As another example, the Roman camp on Hod Hill, Dorsetshire, was an unique relic of Roman military skill. Mr. Warne, a local antiquary, says:--"Nothing could be finer than its condition about ten years ago; until then it might be seen as in its pristine state, and, making due allowance for the lapse of ages, as perfect as when excavated by the Roman cohorts. . . . It was indeed so perfect as to render it a model of Roman castramentation." Yet since that time, this magnificent camp has been almost entirely destroyed.

Sir John Lubbock mentions scores of similar cases, which have occurred and are occurring all over the country. No less than forty of the Irish round towers have perished during the present century; and quite recently, when Mr. Payne went to see the Long Stone, a remarkable monolithic monument described in the "History of Gloucestershire," he found that it had just been blown up with gunpowder by the farmer "because it cumbered the ground." It may be said that the landowners erred through ignorance of the value and interest of these monuments, but that cannot be said now; for after repeated discussions in Parliament, and after an overwhelming body of facts of the character of those here presented has been laid before them, the great landlords still refuse to give up their right to "do what they like with their own." and have strenuously opposed, and hitherto prevented from passing, the very moderate measure of Sir John Lubbock for the purchase and preservation of the most important of these ancient monuments which still remain to us.

*Public Improvements Checked by Landlordism.*--Another mode in which private property in land operates to the serious injury of the public at large is the power which landlords possess, and very often use, of demanding enormous sums for the land required for public improvements. Whether it is the formation of new streets in the Metropolis, or the construction of railways or docks, or the securing of land for public recreation, the claims of landlords invariably stand in the way, sometimes preventing the desired improvements from being carried into effect, sometimes burthening them with a heavy load of debt and so diminishing their usefulness. Instances of this will occur to every one who takes note of passing events. I will only here quote the following statement of Mr. Brodrick:--"The landed interest of England is estimated to have received a sum exceeding the national revenue from railway companies alone *over and above the market price of the land thus sold.*" The italics are mine, to call attention to the fact that this sum of 70 or 80 millions paid to the landlords is a permanent injury to the community, by increasing to that extent the unproductive capital expenditure of the railway companies of the kingdom; while no class has received so much benefit from railways as the landlords, in the enormous increase given thereby to the value of their estates, so that if they had freely given the land required to construct the lines, they would still have been gainers. As another example:--"One nobleman is known to have received three quarters of a million sterling for the mere sites of docks constructed by the enterprise of others." Here again no doubt his other land in the neighbourhood would be greatly increased in value by these very docks, and, equitably, all this increase of value should go to those whose expenditure caused it, or at least to the community at large. But the public and the Government are alike powerless, and must submit to pay whatever landlords choose to demand for permission to make public improvements; and this state of things will continue so long as private property in land is allowed.

*Permanent Deterioration of the Country by the Export of Minerals.*--I have already given an example of a landlord denying the free exercise of their religion to his tenants, and cases in which sites for chapels have been refused are not uncommon; but I shall pass on to an example of the power of landlords which appears to me to go far beyond what should be allowed to any citizens of a densely populated country. I allude to the possession as private property of the minerals beneath its surface, and the power to work, sell, export, and totally exhaust them for their individual benefit.

It has not been sufficiently considered that the minerals of a country are in a totally different category from its agricultural products or even the agricultural land, inasmuch as man can neither produce them nor hasten their production by nature, while in the process of use they are completely destroyed. They are, besides, a portion of the very land itself; and their export to such an extent as to render the remainder more difficult of access, and therefore more costly, is *a permanent and irretrievable deterioration of the country*, rendering it less valuable to its future inhabitants. The power of doing this injury to the community should never have been permitted to individuals (any more than the right to sell their estates to a foreign Government), but it has become so great a source of wealth and is so firmly established as one of the "sacred rights of property" that only by the complete nationalisation of the land does it seem possible to abolish it.

It must be remembered that almost every extensive country in the world possesses coal and iron, besides many other minerals, and there is therefore no adequate reason for permanently impoverishing our country by sending its minerals all over the world and thus robbing future generations; and this, *not* for the benefit of the whole community, but for that of the few individuals who have been allowed to monopolise the land.

It may be said that the price of coal and iron has not yet been raised by the exhaustion of our supplies; but this is very doubtful. It is an admitted fact that the enormous consumption of coal, both for export and in the manufacture of exported iron, has led to coal being now worked at much greater depths than formerly, and this necessarily implies greater cost of working, and consequently a higher price than would be necessary at less depths; and this extra cost must go on increasing as more and more of the coal at moderate depths is worked out. But there is another way in which the community suffers by this excessive export of minerals. The areas devoted to mining and smelting are thereby increased far beyond what is necessary for supplying our own wants, and this leads directly to the sterilising of large tracts of land, and besides renders whole districts hideous and unfit for any enjoyable human habitation. Many thousands of acres of good land are covered up with the "waste" from mines and the "slag" from furnaces, and are thus rendered permanently barren; while the extent of black country over which all natural beauty is destroyed must be reckoned by hundreds or even by thousands of square miles. Whatever part of this destruction and disfigurement is absolutely needed to supply our own wants we must submit to; but that more extensive portion which owes its origin to the excessive export of the very vitals of our land for the aggrandisement of landlords and speculators is a serious loss which should be checked, and a public nuisance which should be abated.

*Concluding Remarks on English Landlordism.*--I have now shown by a series of brief but illustrative cases that landlordism as it exists in England--that is, under perhaps the most favourable conditions possible to it--has produced, and is daily producing, evil results to every class of the community of the most alarming magnitude. It has also been made clear that these evil results do not in any way depend upon the absence of free trade in land, but that they depend essentially on the relation of landlord and tenant--a relation which gives a power to one citizen over the liberty and well-being of others which is incompatible with freedom, while it denies the right of Englishmen to occupy any portion of their native land except at the will and pleasure of its comparatively few owners. Further, it has been shown that the divorce of the working classes from the soil is the prolific parent of pauperism, vice, and crime; and that, as a mere question of national policy, it is essential that some means should be adopted to give every labourer, as well as every Englishman, a *right* to a portion of land at a fixed rent, for cultivation and home occupation. This can only be done by the abolition of private property in land and its complete nationalisation--undoubtedly a measure of a radical if not of a revolutionary character, but the evils to be cured are so gigantic and so deeply rooted that any less searching remedy would be powerless to effect a cure of the disease.

*Notes, Chapter Five*

1. A labourer on the estate of the Duke of Bedford, writing to the *Bedford Record*, states that he can only get an allotment of 20 poles of the worst land in the parish, at double the rent paid by the farmers. In other parishes fair land is let at three times the agricultural rate; and I am informed that in some parts of the New Forest allotments are paid for at rates up to as high as £16 an acre.

2. "The Tenant-Farmer" (1879).

3. *Nineteenth Century*, September, 1880.

4. See , Footnote.

5. Prof. Thorold Rogers in *Contemporary Review*, April, 1880.

6. First Report of the Women's and Children's Employment Commission (1868), Par. 251.

7. This depopulation of estates and parishes has been going on for more than a century. Arthur Young described the operation of the old Poor Law in his time as causing universally "an open war against cottages." Gentlemen bought them up whenever they had an opportunity, and immediately levelled them with the ground, lest they should

become "a nest of beggars' brats." The removal of a cottage often drove the industrious labourer from a parish where he could earn 15s. a week to one where he could earn but 10s. Thus, as among the Scotch labourers of the present day, marriage was discouraged; the peasantry were cleared off the land, and increasing immorality was the necessary consequence. The effect of this system was actually to depopulate many parishes. The author of a pamphlet on the subject, Mr. Alcock, stated that the gentlemen were led by this system to adopt all sorts of expedients to hinder the poor from marrying, to discharge servants in their last quarter, to evict small-tenants, and pull down cottages. The duties of an overseer under the old Poor Law system in England are described by Dr. Burn to be--"Not to let anyone have a farm of £10 a year. . . . To bind out poor children apprentices, no matter to whom or to what trade; but to take special care that the master live in another parish. . . . To pull down cottages; to drive out as many inhabitants and admit as few as they possibly can: that is to depopulate the parish, in order to lessen the poor rate." (Godkin's "Land War in Ireland," .)

8. Appendix to First Report of the Commission appointed to inquire into the condition of women and children employed in agriculture.

9. That this is a necessary consequence of private property in land has been demonstrated with great force in Mr. George's remarkable work, "Progress and Poverty,"

of which some account is given in a later chapter. It has also been seen by some of our recent political economists, especially by Professor Cairnes, who writes as follows:--"A given exertion of labour and capital will now produce in a great many directions five, ten, or twenty times--in some instances, perhaps, a hundred times--the result which an equal exertion would have produced a hundred years ago; yet the rate of wages . . . has certainly not advanced in anything like a corresponding degree, whilst it may be doubted if the rate of profit has advanced at all. . . . We should be inclined to say it had even positively fallen. . . . Someone, no doubt, has benefited by the enlarged power of man over material nature; the world is, without question, the richer for it. . . . The large addition to the wealth of the country has gone neither to profits nor to wages, nor yet to the public at large, but to swell a fund ever growing, even while its proprietors sleep--the rent-roll of the owners of the soil." ("Some Leading Questions of Political Economy Newly Expounded," p-333).

10. Brodrick, "English Land and English Landlords," .

11. "English Land and English Landlords," .

12. "English Land and English Landlords," .

13. That the evils of landlord-made law are still rampant among us is well shown by the manner in which the late Government dealt with the owners of house-property by means of their "Artisans' Dwellings Act." Professor Fawcett,

speaking at Hackney on December 14th, 1880, said of this Act "that a more unfortunate measure, or one based on more radically unsound principles, has seldom been brought forward in Parliament. Under its provisions the owners of houses unfit for human habitation, instead of being punished for their neglect, have been compensated at such an extravagant rate that on six of the sites which have been already cleared the loss to the metropolitan ratepayers has been £643,000, and if the Act is permitted to remain in operation in its present form the loss will soon be more than £2,000,000. Many sites which have been cleared under this Act remain unoccupied because houses cannot be built under the conditions imposed by the Act. The people who have been driven out must find refuge somewhere, and districts which were before overcrowded become more overcrowded still. Difficult as it has been for the poor of London to provide themselves with suitable homes, the money which the carrying out of this Act has caused to be lost will have to be supplied by increased rates, and each addition to the rates makes the payment of rent more difficult for those of humble means." This is a fine example of the difficulty of curing evils arising from the radically unsound principles that now prevail. With the land of the country in the possession of the State, and with free choice of sites at a cheap rate, as here proposed, no such overcrowding could ever have arisen; and even now, if true principles were adopted, the evil would soon cure itself.

14. Report of Proceedings, 1870-1876--.
15. *Nineteenth Century*, March, 1877.

# CHAPTER VI.

## THE RESULTS OF OCCUPYING OWNERSHIP AS OPPOSED TO THOSE OF LANDLORDISM.

SUMMARY OF THE EVILS OF THE LANDLORD SYSTEM--OCCUPYING OWNERSHIP DEFINED--THE ADVANTAGES OF OCCUPYING OWNERSHIP--RESULTS OF OCCUPYING OWNERSHIP IN SWITZERLAND--CO-OPERATION OF OCCUPYING OWNERS IN NORWAY--OCCUPYING OWNERSHIP IN GERMANY--IMPROVEMENT OF THE SOIL UNDER OCCUPYING OWNERSHIP IN BELGIUM--EFFECTS OF OCCUPYING OWNERSHIP IN FRANCE--THE LABOURERS OF FRANCE UNDER OCCUPYING OWNERSHIP--RESULTS OF OCCUPYING OWNERSHIP IN THE CHANNEL ISLANDS--GENERAL RESULTS OF OCCUPYING OWNERSHIP AND THOSE OF LANDLORDISM COMPARED--RESULTS OF LANDLORDISM IN ITALY--RESULTS OF LANDLORDISM IN SPAIN AND

SARDINIA--THE OCCUPYING OWNER UNDER EXTREMELY UNFAVOURABLE CONDITIONS--LARGE FARMS *versus* SMALL NOT THE QUESTION AT ISSUE--VARIOUS OBJECTIONS TO PEASANT-PROPRIETORSHIP ANSWERED BY FACTS--THE FINAL ARGUMENT IN FAVOUR OF LANDLORDISM SHOWN TO BE UNSOUND--BENEFICIAL INFLUENCE OF OWNERSHIP ON AGRICULTURE--THE CONCLUSION FROM THE EVIDENCE.

In the preceding chapters the many, and serious, and widespread evils resulting from the divided interest in land of landlord and tenant have been illustrated by some typical cases; and these evils have been shown to result, not from any special ignorance or ill-conduct of individuals, but to be inherent in the system itself. The great landlord is necessarily a monopolist and a despot. The land is his own to be dealt with as he pleases; and the greater the income he can derive from it, the greater share he can secure to himself of the produce of others' labour upon it, the more respect and admiration he usually receives. In every step he takes to secure this end he is supported by the power and majesty of the law. His tenants have no rights on the soil but such as he allows them. Whatever added value their labour has given to the land, in the absence of special agreement becomes his and not theirs. If they offend him in any way, if they refuse to act against their political convictions, if they are too demonstrative in their claims for religious equality, he may--and not unfrequently does--eject them from the house in which they and their fathers were born, and from the land which they have industriously tilled for generations--more for his benefit than for their own.

To the entire system may be applied the severe judgment which Mr. Charles Russell passed upon it as regards Ireland:--"It may as a whole be truly said that it seems to have been contrived, as if by a malevolent genius, to develope the worst qualities in the national character, and to repress the best--contrived to encourage idleness, thriftlessness, insincerity, and untruthfulness. To me the wonder is, not that the faults of the Irish (English) people exist as they are, but that they have managed to retain so much that is estimable, so much that is kindly in their nature, so much befitting the natural dignity of men."

*Occupying Ownership Defined.*--Let us now turn from this radically vicious and unjust system to its opposite and correlative--occupying ownership.[1] It is often alleged that if you abolish landlords you must revert to one dead level of peasant-proprietorship; but this is not the case. The essential evils of landlordism do not in any way arise from large farms as opposed to small ones--from cultivators possessed of large capital as opposed to those who have little or none; but they arise solely from the relation of landlord and tenant--from one man *letting* land in order to get the largest income he can from it, and another *hiring it temporarily* to extract what he can from it before the time comes when he may be called to give it up. The evil is of the same nature, and often of the same degree, whether the landlord owns ten thousand acres or only a hundred, whether he lets it out in farms of five hundred acres each or in allotments of an acre or less. The true opposite of landlord and tenant--two persons with conflicting interests--is owner and occupier combined in the same person, or "occupying ownership." This ownership may be of the nature of freehold or of copyhold; but, in order that all the evils of landlordism be avoided, it must be secure and permanent; it must be transmissible to a man's children or heirs; and it must be freely saleable or otherwise transferable. The one thing to be aimed at is, that the occupier and cultivator of the land be also the virtual owner; that all the fruits of his labour shall be secure to him; that the increased value of the land given by permanent improvements shall be all his own. To ensure this, subletting under any form or disguise must be prevented, or it is evident that many of the evils of landlordism will again spring up. Mortgages or other encumbrances on the land (except to a limited proportion of its value and repayable by instalments in a moderate term of years) must also be forbidden, because a farmer whose land is heavily encumbered, and who, on failure to pay interest in a bad year, may have his land taken from him, has little more power or inducement to make permanent improvements or cultivate in the best manner than the mere tenant-at-will under a landlord. These conditions are, as yet, not fulfilled in their entirety anywhere; but there is a large body of evidence to show what good effects are produced by that portion of them involved in ordinary occupying ownership; and these effects are so striking and so instructive, and form so remarkable a contrast to the evil results of the opposite system, that they need to be carefully considered. Having done so, we shall be in a position to explain the mode by which our existing system of landlordism may be best abolished, and a sound and well-guarded system of occupying ownership be established in its place.

*The Advantages of Occupying Ownership.*--The advantages of peasant proprietorship (or the occupying ownership of small farms) are of two kinds, economical and moral. These have been dwelt upon by many writers, both English and foreign, and have been the subject of several important works. It will be here only necessary to give a few of the illustrations and conclusions of these writers, many of which are admirably summarised in "Mill's Political Economy," Book II, Chap. VI; and from this work, and the more recent volume of Mr. Brodrick, many of our facts and quotations will be taken.

Of all countries in Europe Switzerland affords, perhaps, the best example of a good land-system, in which almost every farmer owns the land he cultivates; and the result is well shown in the following extract from Sismondi's "Studies in Political Economy."

*Results of Occupying Ownership in Switzerland.*--"It is from Switzerland we learn that agriculture practised by the very persons who enjoy its fruits suffices to procure great comfort for a very numerous population; a great independence of character, arising from independence of position; a great commerce of consumption, the result of the easy circumstances of all the inhabitants, even in a country whose climate is rude, whose soil is but moderately fertile, and where late frosts and inconstancy of seasons often blight the hopes of the cultivator. It is impossible to see without admiration those timber houses of the poorest peasant, so vast, so well closed in, so covered with carvings. In the interior spacious corridors separate the different chambers of the numerous family; each chamber has but one bed, which is abundantly furnished with curtains, bedclothes, and the whitest linen; carefully kept furniture surrounds it; the wardrobes are filled with linen; the dairy is vast, well aired, and of exquisite cleanness; under the same roof is a great provision of corn, salt meat, cheese, and wood; in the cow-houses are the finest and most carefully tended cattle in Europe; the garden is planted with flowers; both men and women are cleanly and warmly clad; all carry in their faces the impress of health and strength. Let other nations boast of their opulence. Switzerland may always point with pride to her peasants."

In case we may think that this delightful picture is exaggerated by national pride, let us compare with it the following account by an observant English traveller--Mr. Inglis:--

"In walking anywhere in the neighbourhood of Zurich one is struck with the extraordinary industry of the inhabitants in the cultivation of their land. When I used to open my casement between four and five in the morning to look out upon the lake and the distant Alps, I saw the labourer in the fields; and when I returned from an evening walk, long after sunset, as late perhaps as half-past eight, there was the labourer mowing his grass, or tying up his vines. . . . It is impossible to look at a field, a garden, a hedging, scarcely even a tree, a flower, or a vegetable, without perceiving proofs of the extreme care and industry that are bestowed upon the cultivation of the soil." And again, describing a district now well known to English tourists, he says:--"In the whole of the Engadine the land belongs to the peasantry, who, like the inhabitants of every other place where this state of things exists, vary greatly in the extent of their possessions. . . . Generally speaking, an Engadine peasant lives entirely upon the produce of his land, with the exception of the few articles of foreign growth required in his family, such as coffee, sugar, and wine. Flax is grown, prepared, spun, and woven without ever leaving the house.

He has also his own wool, which is converted into a blue coat without passing through the hands of either the dyer or the tailor. The country is incapable of greater cultivation than it has received. All has been done for it that industry and an extreme love of gain can devise. There is not a foot of waste land in the Engadine, the lowest part of which is not much lower than the top of Snowdon. Wherever grass will grow there it is; wherever an ear of rye will ripen there it is to be found. Barley and oats have also their appropriate spots, and wherever it is possible to ripen a little patch of wheat the cultivation of it is attempted. In no country in Europe will be found so few poor as in the Engadine. In the village of Suss, which contains about 600 inhabitants, there is not a single individual who is indebted to others for what he eats." It is true that in other parts of Switzerland there is abundance of pauperism, but the fact remains that wherever the land is occupied by peasant proprietors, there industry, ease, and comfort prevail.

*Co-operation of Occupying Owners in Norway.*--Equally conclusive is the testimony of Mr. Laing as to the occupying owners of Norway. He says:--"If small proprietors are not good farmers, it is not from the same cause here which we are told makes them so in Scotland--indolence and want of exertion. The extent to which irrigation is carried on in these glens and valleys shows a spirit of exertion and co-operation to which the latter can show nothing similar." And after giving details of the miles of wooden troughs to carry water to the small fields on the mountain-side, he adds:--"Those may be bad farmers who do such things; but they are not indolent, or ignorant of the principle of working in concert and keeping up establishments for common benefit. They are, undoubtedly, in these respects, far in advance of any community of cottars in our Highland glens. They feel as proprietors, who receive the advantage of their own exertions. The excellent state of the roads and bridges is another proof that the country is inhabited by people who have a common interest to keep them in repair. There are no tolls."

*Occupying Ownership in Germany.*--We will now turn to Germany, and here we have the testimony of another well-known English writer and traveller, the late William Howitt. Speaking of the Rhenish peasantry, in his "Rural and Domestic Life of Germany," he says:--"The peasants are the great and ever-present objects of country life. They are the great population of the country because they are themselves the possessors. . . . The peasants are not as with us, for the most part, totally cut off from property in the soil they cultivate--they are themselves the proprietors. It is, perhaps, from this cause that they are probably the most industrious peasantry in the world. They labour early and late, because they feel that they are labouring for themselves. . . . The German peasants work hard, but they have no actual want. Every man has his house, his orchard, his roadside trees, commonly so heavy with fruit that he is obliged to prop and secure them all ways, or they would be torn in pieces. He has his corn plot, his plots for mangel wurzel, for hemp, and so on. He is his own master; and he and every member of his family have the strongest motives to labour. You see the effect of this in that unremitting diligence which is beyond that of the whole world besides, and his economy, which is still greater. . . . The English peasant is so cut off from the idea of property that he comes habitually to look upon it as a thing from which he is warned by the laws of the large proprietors, and becomes in consequence spiritless and purposeless. . . . The German bauer, on the contrary, looks on the country as made for him and his fellow men. He feels himself a man; he has a stake in the country as good as that of the bulk of his neighbours; no man can threaten him with ejection or the workhouse so long as he is active and economical. He walks, therefore, with a bold step; he looks you in the face with the air of a free man, but a respectful air."

*Admirable Cultivation Under Occupying Ownership.*--Now let us call another witness to the condition of another part of Germany. Mr. Kay, well known for his long study, from personal observation, of the condition of the various populations of Europe, says of Saxony:--"It is a notorious fact that during the last 30 years, and since the peasants became the proprietors of the land, there has been a rapid and continual improvement in the condition of the houses, in the manner of living, in the dress of the peasants, and particularly in the culture of the land. I have walked twice through that part of Saxony called Saxon Switzerland, in company with a German guide, on purpose to see the state of the villages and of the farming, and I can safely challenge contradiction when I affirm that there is no farming in all Europe superior to the laboriously careful cultivation of the valleys of that part of Saxony." And after giving a picture of the perfect condition of the crops, the total absence of weeds, the excessive care of manure, and other details, he goes on:--"The peasants endeavour to outstrip one another in the quantity and quality of the produce, in the preparation of the ground, and in the general cultivation of their respective portions. All the little proprietors are eager to find out how to farm so as to produce the greatest results; they diligently seek after improvements; they send their children to agricultural schools in order to fit them to assist their fathers; and each proprietor soon adopts a new improvement introduced by any of his neighbours." And the general result of Mr. Kay's observations is thus summed up:--"The present farming of Prussia, Saxony, Holland, and Switzerland is the most perfect and economical farming I have ever witnessed in any country."

*Improvement of the Soil Under Occupying Ownership in Belgium.*--Belgium is another striking example of what can be done, under the most adverse circumstances, under the influence of property in the soil. Much of the country consists of loose white sand just like the sands of a sea-shore. This sand has been so greatly improved by laborious cultivation and manure that it cannot be distinguished from soil naturally of good quality. The most highly cultivated part of this country consists of peasant properties managed by the proprietors either wholly or partly by spade industry; and Mr. M'Culloch says that--"The cultivation of a poor light soil, or a moderate soil, is generally superior in Flanders to that of the most improved farms in Britain. . . . In the minute attention to the qualities of the soil, in the management and application of manures of different kinds, in the judicious succession of crops, and especially in the economy of land, so that every part of it shall be in a constant state of production, we have still something to learn from the Flemings." And he shows by minute calculations and estimates how it is that a man and his family can live and thrive on the produce of six acres of land.

*Effects of Occupying Ownership in France.*--France is often referred to as an example of the ill-success of small farms, even when owned by the farmers themselves, owing to the extreme subdivision of property enforced by the French laws. Mr. M'Culloch, writing in 1823, predicted that within fifty years France would become "the greatest pauper warren in the world," and share with Ireland the honour of furnishing hewers of wood and drawers of water to other countries. Yet almost exactly at the end of the fifty years France suffered devastation by war and had to pay a war-indemnity of unparalleled magnitude. And it was the savings of her peasant-proprietors that enabled her to do this with marvellous ease, and to recover from a state of collapse with a celerity and completeness which astonished Europe. The celebrated Arthur Young, a strong advocate of large farms, who travelled in France in 1787-89, whenever he finds remarkable excellence of cultivation, never hesitates to ascribe it to peasant property. Speaking of a district near Dunkirk, he says:--"Between the town and Rosendal is a great number of neat little houses, built each with its garden, and one or two fields enclosed of most wretched blowing dune sands, naturally as white as snow, but improved by industry. *The magic of property turns sand to gold.*" And again:--"Going out of Gange, I was surprised to find by far the greatest exertion in irrigation which I had yet seen in France. . . . An activity has been here that has swept away all difficulties before it, and has clothed the very rocks with verdure. It would be a disgrace to common sense to ask the cause; the enjoyment of property *must* have done it. Give a man the secure possession of a bleak rock, and he will turn it into a garden; give him a nine years lease of a garden, and he will convert it into a desert."

Again, take his description of the country at the foot

of the Western Pyrenees:--"A succession of many well-built, comfortable farming cottages, built of stone and covered with tiles; each having its little garden, enclosed by clipt thorn hedges, with plenty of peach and other fruit trees, some fine oaks scattered in the hedges, and young trees nursed up with so much care that nothing but the fostering attention of the owner could effect anything like it. To every house belongs a farm, perfectly well enclosed, with grass borders mown and neatly kept round the corn-fields, with gates to pass from one enclosure to another. There are some parts of England (where small yeomen still remain) that resemble this country of Béarn; but we have very little that is equal to what I have seen in this ride of twelve miles from Pau to Moneng. It is all in the hands of little proprietors, without the farms being so small as to occasion a vicious and miserable population. An air of neatness, warmth, and comfort breathes over the whole. It is visible in their new-built houses and stables; in their little gardens; in their hedges; in the courts before their doors; even in the coops for their poultry and the sties for their hogs. A peasant does not think of making his pig comfortable if his own happiness hangs by the thread of a nine years' lease."

This same author is often quoted on the other side, as an opponent of small farms, even when in the hands of peasant-proprietors; though what he really says is, that the farming in many of these small farms in France is exceedingly bad. But this is owing to ignorance only, which may be easily amended, not to want of industry; and we must remember that the time he speaks of was just before the French Revolution, when the people were subject to the most oppressive taxes, restrictions, and exactions, and were kept in profound ignorance.[2] Yet, note what he says of the farms he is supposed to be condemning:--"It is necessary to impress on the reader's mind that though the husbandry I met with, in a great variety of instances on little properties, was as bad as can be well conceived, yet the industry of the possessors was so conspicuous and so meritorious that no commendations would be too great for it. It was sufficient to prove that property in land is, of all others, the most active instigator to severe and incessant labour. And this truth is of such force and extent that I know of no way so sure of carrying tillage to a mountain top as by permitting the adjoining villagers to acquire it in property; in fact, we see that in the mountains of Languedoc, &c., they have conveyed earth in baskets, on their backs, to form a soil where nature had denied it." These extracts are surely sufficient to prove that the celebrated Arthur Young, like the other writers whose opinions and observations have been adduced, gives his testimony in the most forcible manner in favour of *ownership* as against*tenancy*, on every ground of economical, social, and moral superiority.

*The Labourers of France under Occupying Ownership.--*

That the labourer no less than the farmer is elevated and improved by the possession of land is shown by a more recent writer. Dr. Ireland, in his "Studies of a Wandering Observer" tells us, that--"At Die, a town of 4,000 inhabitants, there are about 500 proprietors of land, the properties being of all sizes, from two-and-a-half acres upwards, but generally small. The peasant-labourers have been generally improving since the Revolution in wealth, comfort, and intelligence. They ate black bread, and now they eat brown; they wore rags, and now everybody is decently clad. Their wages have doubled, while the price of corn has only risen one-fifth. The peasant proprietors are gradually becoming richer. A frugal and sober family in fifteen or twenty years generally manages to put by £600."[3]

*Result of Occupying Ownership in the Channel Islands.*--One more example we must give, and one especially valuable because it is nearer to our shores, and actually under our own government--that of the Channel Islands. Mr. William Thornton, in his "Plea for Peasant Proprietors," speaks thus of the island of Guernsey: "Not even in England is nearly so large a quantity of produce sent to market from a tract of such limited extent. This of itself might prove that the cultivators must be far removed above poverty, for being absolute owners of all the produce raised by them, they, of course, sell only what they do not themselves require. But the satisfactoriness of their condition is apparent to every observer. 'The happiest community,' says Mr. Hill, 'which it has ever been my lot to fall in with is to be found in this little island of Guernsey.' 'No matter,' says Sir George Head, 'to what point the traveller may choose to wend his way, comfort everywhere prevails'. . . . In the whole island, with the exception of a few fishermen's huts, there is not one house so mean as to be likened to the ordinary habitation of an English farm labourer. . . . Beggars are utterly unknown. . . . Pauperism, able-bodied pauperism at least, is nearly as rare as mendicancy."

Mr. Brodrick, writing on the subject only last year, with all the latest information at his command, shows how economically successful is the agriculture. He says:--"If we judge of success in cultivation by the produce, we find that a much larger quantity of human food is raised in Jersey than is raised on an equal area, by the same number of cultivators, in any part of the United Kingdom. Not only does it support its own crowded population in much greater comfort than is enjoyed by the mass of Englishmen, but it supplies the London market, out of its surplus production, with shiploads of vegetables, fruit, butter, and cattle for breeding. Even wheat, for the growth of which the climate is not very suitable, is so cultivated that it yields much heavier crops per acre than in England; and the number of live-stock kept on a given area astonishes travellers accustomed only to English farming. Nor are these only the results of spade-husbandry, for machinery is largely employed by the yeomen and peasant-proprietors of the Channel Islands, who have no difficulty in arranging among themselves to hire it by turns." Mr. Brodrick, like every one else, traces this wonderful success and prosperity to the land-system of the country. The soil is naturally rather poor and the climate is no better than on our own southern coasts, yet, he tells us, the land "yields an amount and variety of produce which seems fabulous to persons conversant only with tenant-farming on the grand scale, not merely because it is more liberally manured, but also because it is studded with orchards, vineries, and other profitable *hors d'œuvres* of agriculture, which nothing but the magic of property will call into existence. The same lesson is taught by the abundance of markets, the substantial character of the dwellings, even down to the humblest cottages, the magnitude of the public works, the dress and diet of the labouring classes, the comparative rarity of pauperism, and other signs which betoken a happy and thriving community."

*General Results of Occupying Ownership and those of Landlordism Compared.*--Now, when we consider and weigh carefully this unvarying mass of testimony as to the happiness and well-being that everywhere prevail among peasant-proprietors or occupying-owners, and compare it with the facts already adduced as to the condition of our own agricultural labourers, and our wide-spread pauperism; with the chronic starvation of Ireland, and the landlord-made deserts of the Highlands; with our wretched building-lease houses; with the scarcity of milk, butter, fruit, and vegetables in all our country towns and villages; and add to this the difficulty that any Englishman of moderate means finds in getting a small plot of land for his personal occupation and enjoyment,--the only conclusion any rational and unbiassed thinker can arrive at is, that modern landlordism is the greatest curse that any country can groan under; that it is utterly incompatible with freedom; that it takes away the chief incentives to industry and thrift; that it creates poverty, pauperism, and crime, and checks all real progress in civilisation or in national prosperity.

Will it be said that Englishmen alone are not fitted for a system which succeeds alike in Norway, in Belgium, in Germany, and in France? The equal success of the yeomen of Cumberland and Devonshire, and of Englishmen, Scotchmen, and Irishmen alike, in every colony where they can obtain land, contradicts the absurd and libellous statement; while the industry and thrift our labourers display whenever a little land is granted them, even as tenants at fair rents and very imperfect security, shows what they would do under the more favourable conditions of an absolutely secure and permanent tenure. Even the much abused Irish themselves, who are supposed to be lazy because they are Celts, at once become industrious when they see a fair prospect of being allowed to retain the produce of their labour. Mr. Jonathan Pim gives the following illustration on the personal testimony of a friend:--"Within a few miles of the town of Wexford is a range of rocky hills, called the Mountain of Forth. They are about seven hundred feet above the sea, are exceedingly rugged, bleak, and sterile, and are naturally almost destitute of soil or vegetation. It was probably for this reason that the district remained in a state of commonage until within the last thirty or forty years. It is now sprinkled with little patches of land, many of them on the highest part of the mountain, reclaimed and enclosed at a vast expense of labour by the peasant-proprietors, who have been induced to overcome extraordinary difficulties in the hope of at length making a little spot of land their own. The surface was thickly covered with large masses of rock of various sizes, and intersected by the gullies formed by winter torrents. These rocks have been broken, buried, rolled away or heaped into the form of fences. The land when thus cleared has been carefully enriched with soil, manured, and tilled. These little holdings vary from half an acre to ten or fifteen acres. The occupiers hold by the right of possession; they are generally poor; but they are peaceable, well-conducted, independent, and industrious; and the district is absolutely free from agrarian outrage."[4]

In another part of his work Mr. Pim says: "It is well known that much waste land has been brought under culture for several years past. This has been effected chiefly by allowing cottiers to take in a portion of the mountain side; and when they had tilled it for a few years, and partially reclaimed it, calling on them either to give it up to the landlord, or to pay a rent. In some cases they probably retained it, and became permanent tenants; but in others, they gave it up, and commenced anew, not unfrequently ending near the top of the mountain, at the bottom of which they commenced many years before. Thus cultivation crept up the mountain sides, or encroached on the secluded valleys heretofore untilled. This mode of reclamation required no capital on the part of the landlord. The cottier or tenant was the sole agent. He obtained a bare subsistence by very severe labour, and rarely effected any improvement in his own condition."

Here are facts, coldly stated as if they were of the most ordinary nature, which are yet sufficient to make one's blood boil, in view of the actual condition of Ireland and the reckless accusations against its people. Is it not truly pitiable to think of these poor people, working all their lives at the endless task of reclaiming mountain land, with no other prospect than to have the fruits of their labour taken from them the moment it becomes worth the taking? What would not these people effect, if they had that legal security for the products of their own labour to give which is held to be the *first* duty of even the most rudimentary government, the *first* condition of any social or material progress? Can we have any doubt that they would soon rise to that state of well-being, order and contentment that everywhere else prevails when the tillers of the soil have full and complete security in its possession?[5]

*Results of Landlordism in Italy.*--Lest, however, it be supposed that there is something specially favourable in the soil, or the climate, or the character of the people in the countries we have referred to as examples of the admirable results of occupying ownership, let us take a glance at the other side of the picture; for it must not be supposed that over the whole Continent peasant-proprietorship prevails. Landlordism, as with us, is often predominant, and wherever it is so *there* is misery and discontent in the place of happiness and peace. Over large portions of Italy there are still, as in the times of the Romans, *latifundia*, or large estates farmed by middlemen and cultivated by labourers and tenants-at-will. In a recent work on Italy, by M. de Laveleye, he speaks of--"Naked and desolate fields, where the cultivator dies of famine in the fairest climate and on the most fertile soil, such is the result of the *latifundia*. Economists who defend the system of huge properties, visit the interior of the Basilicata and Sicily if you want to see the degree of misery to which your huge properties reduce the earth and its inhabitants."

Their condition is further shown by the following extract from a petition of the peasants of Lombardy, in reply to a Ministerial circular warning them against the dangers of emigration:--

"What do you mean by the nation, Signor Minister? Is it the multitude of the miserable? Then we, indeed, are the nation. Look at our pale and emaciated faces, at our bodies exhausted by excessive labour and insufficient food. We sow and reap the wheat, but never eat white bread. We cultivate the grape, but never drink its wine. We raise the cattle, but never taste meat. We are clad in rags. We dwell in dens of infection. We freeze in winter, and in summer we starve. Our only nourishment on Italian soil is a handful of maize, made costly by the tax. The burning fever devours us in the dry regions, and in the wet ones we are the prey of the fever of the marsh. Our end is a premature death in the hospital, or in our miserable cabins. And, in spite of all this, Signor Minister, you recommend us not to expatriate ourselves! But can the land, where even the hardest labour cannot earn food, be called a native country?"

That this is not exaggeration is proved by the prevalence of *pellagra*, a frightful form of leprosy brought on by unwholesome food. M. de Laveleye says:--

"Twelve and eleven per cent. of the Lombard and Venetian population are smitten, and those who are not actually struck by the plague are debilitated by the bad nourishment. The statistics of the conscription for the Army give horrifying results. In 1878 the report of General Torre shows that the number of conscripts excused for constitutional infirmity was 20 per cent. in Lombardy and 18 per cent. in Venetia. . . . Thus, in the fairest country in the world a fifth of the population, in the flower of their life, are incapable of military service, in consequence of extreme poverty. . . . The Commission of Inquiry on the subject of the *pellagra* says, 'The cause of this malady is extreme misery, so that under the medical question we find the social question.'"

And in a recent report to the Italian Government by Dr. Ruseri (as quoted in the *Daily News*, April 16th, 1881) we have the following statement:--

"Since 1856 the condition of the agricultural population, in spite of the improvement in other respects that has taken place, has remained much the same. In the neighbourhood of the thriving city of Milan are to be found the poorest labourers of Lombardy, for many of whom even polenta is a luxury. In Puglia the agricultural labourers live in small cottages of one room, and sleep in the clothes they have worn the whole day, for they never undress, on a bare mattress in a niche left in the wall. They are put under an overseer, who furnishes them daily, at the expense of the proprietor, with about two pounds of bad black bread each. They work from dawn to sunset, and have no other food, except during harvest, when about two quarts of small wine is added to their fare, in order to enable them to undergo the extra fatigue. The condition of the peasants in the Basilicata is no better.

There they collect at evening in the towns or villages, living in damp cellars or caves. Often a whole family possesses but one bed, upon which men, women, children, and old people sleep pell-mell."

Yet wherever fixity of tenure, or peasant-properties exist, *there*, in Italy as elsewhere, the utmost prosperity prevails. M. de Laveleye says:--"I know of no more striking lesson in political economy than is taught at Capri. Whence come the perfection of cultivation and the comfort of the population? Certainly not from the fertility of the soil, which is an arid rock. . . . Before obtaining the crops, it was necessary, so to speak, to create the soil. It is the magic of ownership which has produced this prodigy."

From the facts presented in different parts of Italy alone M. de Laveleye arrives at the very same conclusion as we have reached from examination of similar facts in the British Isles, that the prosperity of the country is a question of the establishment of a body of independent cultivators of their own land instead of a population of dependent, and therefore improvident and wretched, peasants, who have no security for the enjoyment of the fruits of their labour.

*Results of Landlordism in Spain and Sardinia.*--In Spain also the greater part of the land is held in large estates strictly entailed, so that the great mass of the people are deprived of all interest in the soil. These vast estates are generally managed by stewards, anxious only to remit money to their masters.

The land is ill cultivated, and the peasantry are indolent and poor.[6] In Sardinia the same causes are followed by the same results. Arthur Young says:--"What keeps it in its present unimproved situation is chiefly the extent of estates, the absence of some very great proprietors, and the inattention of all. . . . The peasants are a miserable set, that live in poor cabins without other chimneys than a hole in the roof to let the smoke out." And at a much later period M'Culloch still writes: "The division of the island into immense estates, most of which were acquired by Spanish grandees, the want of leases, and the restrictions on industry, have paralysed the industry of the inhabitants, and sunk them to the lowest point in the scale of civilisation."

*The Occupying Owner under Extremely Unfavourable Conditions.*--The evidence, therefore, on this point appears to be absolutely conclusive: wherever we find large estates cultivated by tenants-at-will, *there* is bad farming, discontent, and pauperism; wherever we find the land cultivated by its owners or permanent occupiers, *there* we find industry, economy, great productiveness, content, and comfort. Climate, soil, civilisation, government may vary, but the results of these two systems of land-tenure never vary in *kind* but only in *degree*. And we must remember that in no country are the conditions so favourable to the complete success of occupying ownership as they might easily be made. Bad fiscal regulations, compulsory division of inheritance, and oppressive taxation often interfere; while nowhere is the mortgaging of the land forbidden; and thus the cultivator of his own farm may often be hampered by want of capital, cramped by having to pay interest equal to a high rent, and be living under a sense of insecurity hardly inferior to that of a tenant-at-will. Yet with all these disadvantages, the difference of the two systems stands out in prominent relief--on the one hand insecurity, with idleness, poverty, and discontent; on the other hand "the magic of property which turns sand into gold."

It is true that even the peasant proprietor is often miserably poor, but when this is the case it is invariably due to the bad conditions and unnatural restrictions under which he labours. This is strikingly shown over a large part of North Germany, where the old common-field system of culture has led to each farm or holding consisting of a vast number of distinct plots or strips, which are scattered about over the whole parish and no two of them contiguous. Mr. Baring Gould, in his valuable work "Germany Past and Present," states that sometimes a farm of about 50 acres will consist of 1,000 bits of land, distributed over the whole surface of the parish. This is an extreme case, but the strips are often only seven yards wide, sometimes only three or even one yard! None of these are fenced, so that all domestic animals, even sheep, have to be stall fed, and then the sheep produce no wool and very poor mutton. These farms are transmitted from a father to his sons, and their frequent division has led to the minute division of the separate plots, so that each heir may have a share of each quality of land. In addition to this the individual farms are too small, while they are often heavily mortgaged to Jews, who advance funds for the portions of some members of the family when the owner dies. Mr. Baring Gould thus describes these farms:--"In almost every parish are a large number of small proprietors, existing on the fragments of a parcelled farm. They have too little land to allow of their keeping a horse or oxen, consequently they have to depend on the great bauers for the tilling of their land and the carting of their harvests. These little holders have to pay dear for this hire, and they can often only obtain it too late in the season. They are behindhand with their ploughing, and their crops are not carried till bad weather sets in. An English labourer lives in luxury compared to these small farmers, who drag on in squalor and misery, bowed under debt to the Jew who waits to sell them up."

It is clear enough that this want of success is due to the utterly abominable conditions under which these poor people live--conditions handed down to them from the past and from which they are unable to escape. Yet even here they have advantages which neither our agricultural labourers nor our factory-workers possess--that of independence and personal interest in their work. Mr. Baring Gould says:--

"The artisan is restless and dissatisfied. He is mechanised. He finds no interest in his work, and his soul frets at the routine. He is miserable, and he knows not why. But the man who toils on his own plot of ground is morally and physically healthy. He is a freeman; the sense he has of independence gives him his upright carriage, his fearless brow, and his joyous laugh."

These cases in which occupying ownership is a comparative failure are therefore instructive, because we find that the failure depends wholly on adverse conditions of custom or law--conditions which no sane man would adopt in establishing a system of land tenure, but which would necessarily lead to adverse results under any system. This is pre-eminently a case in which the exception proves the rule. For it *is* an exception, the rule being that wherever the conditions are only in a very moderate degree favourable, we find those striking results of prosperity, contentment, order, and general well-being which we have already set forth on the unimpeachable and consistent testimony of a large body of competent observers.[7]

*Large Farms* versus *Small Not the Question at Issue*.--The opponents of any alteration of our system of land-tenure in the direction indicated by the evidence here adduced usually evade the real point at issue by treating it as if it were solely a question between small and large farms. They endeavour to show that large farms can be cultivated more economically and produce larger returns than small ones, and that therefore "peasant-proprietorship" is wasteful, and should be discouraged. To this there are two valid replies. In the first place, the objection is not applicable to the proposals here advocated, which are, to secure occupying ownership in farms of any and all sizes that there may be a demand for, not in small farms for peasants only; and, in the next place, the allegation of the inferior productiveness of small farms under equally favourable conditions with large ones is not only not proved, but is directly opposed to all the evidence. The small farms of the Channel Islands, of Belgium, and of the Palatinate surpass in productiveness those of equal areas in the best examples of large English farms; while the political, moral, and social superiority of peasant proprietors to mere agricultural labourers is so overwhelming, that even if the produce were in some cases smaller, there could be not a moment's hesitation in preferring the well-being of the whole rural population to the increased wealth of a few capitalist farmers and great landowners.[8]

*Various Objections to Peasant-Proprietorship Answered by Facts.*--Another objection sometimes made is that land cannot be efficiently cultivated and permanently improved without capital, and that peasant-proprietors have usually no capital. Here again the facts are against the objectors. In several countries, notably in Norway, in Jersey, and in Switzerland, co-operation has effected quite as much in these respects as the most lavish expenditure of capital in a country of large estates.[9] Moreover, occupying owners need not necessarily be without capital, and most certainly they will expend it with more judgment and more confidence, than either a landlord ignorant of practical agriculture or a tenant without any permanent interest in the soil. The scheme of land-tenure here advocated (as will be seen further on), owing to the prohibition of mortgages, renders the application of capital to the land far more easy and more likely to be general than under any existing system.

It has also been objected that peasant-proprietorship leads to too rapid increase of the population, and must thus soon produce over-crowding and pauperism. But here again the facts are all the other way. Nothing is such a powerful check to early marriages as the need of first obtaining a farm sufficient to support a family; and in every country where peasant-properties largely prevail the age of marriage is higher than among our agricultural labourers. John Stuart Mill has brought a mass of interesting evidence to bear upon this question, and the reader who desires to become acquainted with it is referred to his "Political Economy," Chap. VII, or to Mr. Thornton's "Plea for Peasant Proprietors," Chap. II, where the subject is fully examined by the light of history and experience.[10]

*The Last Argument in Favour of Landlordism Shown to be Unsound.*--Yet one more objection must be noted, and this is perhaps the weakest of all, though it is made much of by the advocates of landlordism. It is said that by abolishing landlords and transferring all the land to peasant-proprietors the great advantage will be lost of a wealthy and educated man in every parish, whose interest it is to promote good feeling no less than good agriculture, and whose refinement and talents tend to elevate and improve the whole population. Now, waiving all objection to this as a true picture of the average landowner and country gentleman, we must first note that, according to the corrected returns given in Mr. Brodrick's work, there are only about 4,200 great landowners and squires in England and Wales (owning considerably more than half the total area of the country), while there are 10,000 parishes; so that, allowing for the number of non-resident landowners, and the still larger number of those who, being only occasionally resident, leave the management of their estates to their agents, it is evident that only one parish in four or five can now enjoy the supposed advantages of the resident influential landowner. In the next place, what reason have we to suppose that all (or the greater part of) these country gentlemen would quit their ancestral houses and lands if they no longer derived their income mainly from the rents of farms? They could still have their own houses and grounds and home-farms, which, if they were really fond of agriculture and had no other estate to manage, they would probably make larger than at present and cultivate with more care and personal attention. Would such a man be of less value in a district because he had lost the despotic power he formerly possessed over his tenants and labourers? Would not his advice carry more weight and his example have more influence, as the best educated, the most gentlemanly, and the richest man in his parish, when his advice would be wholly disinterested and his neighbours would be influenced by genuine respect for his abilities and his character? Then again, if we look at the number of separate mansions now belonging to the same owner, and, except perhaps for a few weeks in the year, occupied only by servants, and remember that each of these would almost certainly be occupied by a resident gentleman owning and cultivating a greater or less extent of land, we should here have a decided increase of that beneficial influence in country life which our actual landlordism sometimes, but by no means always, exerts.

*Beneficial Influence of Ownership on Agriculture.*--Yet more important is the consideration that the class of English farmers would itself be greatly improved, and would perhaps exert an influence quite as beneficial as that of the existing squire. For each of these would be the potential owner of the land he cultivated, and every improvement in its value or enjoyability would be his own. The same land would then, as a rule, be cultivated by the same family generation after generation, and this would certainly lead to improvements such as none but a permanent occupying owner would ever think of making. The poorer land would be planted for timber, the more sheltered and otherwise suitable with fruit trees. The farm houses would be improved and beautified; and the whole character of many parts of our country would thus be altered for the better. Farmers of this class, unhampered by any tenancy restrictions, with a good knowledge of agricultural chemistry, and often with the experience gained by visits to the United States, to European countries, or Australia, would introduce new modes of culture, would make experiments with new crops, and thus do more to develope the capabilities and increase the production of our land than has been or ever can be possible under the old system of landlord and tenant, with its conflicting interests, its divided responsibility, and its mutual jealousy, which throw obstacles in the way of all advances in cultivation and render many of the most important kinds of permanent improvement all but impossible.

This is well shown in the contrast between the Eastern States of America and England. The former have felt the pressure of competition by the Western States almost as much as we have; but wherever the farmer cultivates his own land he has adapted himself to the circumstances by a more varied system of cultivation, leading to a considerable increase in the total value of farm produce. Mr. Brodrick tells us that, though only half as much barley was grown by Massachusetts farmers in 1875 as in 1865, and only one-third as much as in 1855, the yield per acre rose during this period from nineteen and a half bushels to twenty-five and a half bushels, and a similar increase was realised in wheat, oats, Indian corn, beet-root, and potatoes. In the meantime the production of milk was far more than trebled. The total value of the farm products of Massachusetts in 1875 exceeded their value in 1865 by 8,000,000 dollars, notwithstanding the stress of western competition and the general reduction of prices. No such power of adapting our agriculture to new conditions has been exhibited in England, nor was it possible to tenant farmers hampered by restrictive covenants and with no permanent interest in the soil.

That English farmers, however, are equally capable and energetic when they have the inducement and the means of being so, is shown by the example of Mr. John Prout, who, nearly twenty years ago, purchased a farm near Sawbridgeworth, in Hertfordshire, and has since cultivated it himself so as to compete successfully in wheat-growing with America, obtaining during the whole of that period fair interest on his capital and a good profit besides. This has been effected by a system of cultivation which no landlord would ever have permitted; and though there is some difference of opinion as to whether this can be carried on indefinitely, the fact seems to be admitted that his later crops are even better than his earlier ones, and that the cleanliness and general character of the soil has been greatly improved.

The great fact to be noted is, that while tenant farmers are being everywhere ruined and hundreds of farms are going out of cultivation, an occupying owner has been able to pay the equivalent of rent in interest on capital, and to obtain a handsome average return for his agricultural skill and personal supervision.[11]

*The Conclusion from the Evidence.*--We thus see, not only that an overwhelming mass of evidence, afforded by the chief civilised countries in the world, proves the vast superiority of occupying ownership to landlordism as it exists with us; but, further, that every objection urged on behalf of landlordism only serves more clearly to bring out the numerous advantages--political, social, and moral, as well as merely economical--of occupying ownership, whether exhibited in small, in moderate, or in large farms.

*Notes, Chapter Six*

1. "Occupying ownership is treated of in this chapter, not as a system to be generally adopted, for it has many evils, but as the only existing system which affords us actual examples of the advantages of that permanence of tenure and secure possession of the increased value due to the occupier's labour and expenditure, which would be universal under Land Nationalisation." on

2. The French peasants were heavily taxed on the profits of their farms, which profits were assessed by the collectors

at their pleasure; and as the taxes were farmed out, the condition of the peasant was exactly analogous to that of the subjects of Turkey at the present day, and in both cases it was necessary to conceal all signs of wealth or even of comfort. There were also edicts against weeding and hoeing, lest the young partridges should be disturbed, and the very best of all manures was prohibited lest it should give a flavour to the game which fed upon the peasants' corn! The peasants were also subjected to forced labour both for the Government and for the lords of the manor; and because, under these conditions, the peasant proprietors of France were not prosperous, peasant-proprietorship itself was alleged to be a failure! (See Thornton's "Plea for Peasant Proprietors," .) on

3. Corroborative evidence in the same direction is afforded by the following statements given in Mr. Thornton's "Plea for Peasant Proprietors":--

" Mr. Henry Bulwer remarks that by far the greatest number of indigent is to be found in the northern departments, where land is less divided than elsewhere and cultivated with larger capitals" (). " Mr. Birkbeck (in his tour in France) noticing that on the road from St. Pierre to Moulins the lower class appeared less comfortable, found on inquiry that few of the peasantry thereabouts were proprietors" ().

" Mr. LeQuesne, who, when asking the causes of the smiling productiveness of Anjou and Touraine, received for answer that the land was divided into small parcels, noticed that the houses of the country people there were remarkable for their neatness, and indicative of the ease and comfort of their possessors" ().

4. "Condition and Prospects of Ireland" .

5. The example above referred to is especially valuable as showing that large areas of mountain land may be reclaimed by the simple process of allowing peasants to reclaim it; and if they are secured in the *whole* increased value they give to it, it seems difficult to place limits to what may be done. The usual proposal is that land should be *first* reclaimed at the expense of the landlord or of Government, and that *then* peasants should be settled on it at rents proportioned to the money expended. But this is both unnecessary, wasteful, and unfair to the peasants themselves. The cost of reclamation by hired labour would be far greater than when it is effected by the occupying owner, who can do it bit by bit, at times when he would otherwise be idle, and therefore at a minimum of cost. Moreover, he knows best exactly what and how much to do; whereas large schemes of reclamation on the plans of engineers or agriculturists are sure to involve much work which is needless, and much that will be done in a needlessly expensive fashion--and for all this the poor peasant will be saddled with a needless amount of perpetual rent! It is a most

essential principle that all reclamation and improvement on land let to a peasant on a permanent tenure should be done by himself, not for him by others. If he wants help, a small loan, at fair interest and repayable by instalments, would be the only proper mode of giving it.

6. M'Culloch's Geographical Dictionary, art. Spain.

7. An article has recently appeared in the "Contemporary Review" on "Peasant Proprietors in France," in which a very discouraging account is given of the peasants in some parts of Savoy, more especially as regards the discomfort and dirt of their dwellings. The adjacent Departments of France are also remarkable for the dirty habits of the people, but this depends more on custom than on want, and is often no indication whatever of poverty. It must be remembered that Savoy has been till recently very isolated, being cut off by the Alps from Piedmont, to which it formerly belonged; and the ignorance which even now widely prevails in Italy was perhaps there exaggerated, and may have checked the outflow of the surplus population and the influence of new ideas and habits. It is clear from the article itself that the properties are often too small, and also that they are in some cases let out to tenants on the metayer system; while there is a total absence of details as to the average size and character of the tenures and the political and social surroundings, present and past, which renders it impossible to form an accurate judgment as to the real condition of the population.

8. The evidence on this point is conclusive. Mr. C. Wren Hoskyns, M. P., in his work on "The Land Laws of England," says: "It is obvious, almost to a truism, that the occupation which most resembles ownership itself must, by the imperative laws equally of the soil and of human instinct, be the most profitable to both parties by the uninterrupted progress of improvement and addition to the land." Dr. Ireland, in his "Studies of a Wandering Observer," says:--"People find that a man who puts his own work into his land, or employs his whole attention in directing a few workmen, can make a great deal more out of it than the scientific farmer, who has to struggle with the weary negligence of bands of day-labourers." M. Passy, in his "Systems of Cultivation in France and their Influence on Social Economy," gives the following as the result of his investigations:--"1. That in the present state of agricultural knowledge and practice it is the small farms, owned by the farmers, which, after deducting the cost of production, yield, from a given surface, and on equal conditions, the greatest net produce; and, 2. That the same system of cultivation, by maintaining a larger rural population, not only thereby adds to the strength of a State, but affords a better market for those commodities the production and exchange of which stimulate the prosperity of the manufacturing districts." And of the character of the cultivation by peasant-proprietors, M. Passy says: "They carry into the least details of their

undertaking an attention and care which are productive of the most important advantages. There is not a corner of their land of which they do not know the special qualities and capabilities, and to which they do not know how to give the peculiar treatment and care it requires," and after comparing some of the best English agricultural counties with an extensive area of the north of France, he states that the net produce of the latter is the larger of the two. M. de Laveleye, in his Essay on Systems of Land Tenure, shows that the small peasant-proprietors of Belgium and Flanders use an enormous quantity of manure, and obtain crops far surpassing those of the best large farms in any part of the world. In Switzerland, wherever the Government have sold to peasants the land which formerly belonged to the State, "very often a third or a fourth part of the land which was before let out to farmers produces at present as much corn, and supports as many head of cattle, as the whole estate formerly did when it was cultivated by leasehold tenants." Mr. Thornton's "Plea for Peasant-Proprietors," and Mr. Kay's "Free Trade in Land," are literally crowded with facts of the same character as these and leading irresistibly to the same conclusion. Notwithstanding this mass of evidence, English writers still maintain that English agriculture is more advanced and more productive than that of France, grounding their conclusions solely on the average crop of wheat. To one such writer the following letter, which appeared in the *Daily News*

(Dec. 28th, 1881), is a complete reply and full explanation:--"Mr. Caird and other writers have recently asserted that 'the average wheat crop in England yields 28, as opposed to 18 bushels to the acre in France;' thus attempting to prove that the English system is the most productive in a national point of view. I submit that if we examine the effect of the English and French systems of land tenure on an entire province, consisting of good, indifferent, and waste soil, we shall arrive at a very different conclusion. In France the peasant proprietor (aided by his family, and thus commanding the cheapest possible labour) will successfully attack land of the very poorest description and bring it into cultivation. It may possibly produce but five bushels to the acre, but it repays the 'owner.' In the French official returns of cultivated land the average is thus brought down to a very low figure. In England such poor soil is as a rule left waste, simply because it will not repay cultivation--i.e., it will not produce rent after maintaining the farmer and labourer, and, as the English proprietor cannot command either cheap labour or apply the stubborn energy and minute attention and thrifty habits of the French peasant proprietor, we see immense tracts in England left in a state of nature which in France would be gradually but surely reclaimed. The French peasant cannot afford hedgerows, waste land, and game preserves, but he is the owner of his own farm, and devotes all his energies to its improvement. He is consequently the backbone of France in more than one sense.--I am, Sir, yours truly, French Resident." A further demonstration of the superiority of the French to the English system of land-tenure is afforded by one whose facts at all events will not be disputed--Mr. Gladstone. In his speech at West Calder he makes the following important remarks:--"A peasant proprietary is an excellent thing to be had, if it can be had, in many points of view. It interests an enormous number of the people in the soil of the country and in the stability of its institutions and its laws. But now look on the effect it has on the progressive value of the land. What will you think when I tell you that the agricultural value of France--the taxable income derived from the land, and therefore the income to the proprietors of that land--has advanced during our life-time far more rapidly than that of England? . . . While the agricultural income of France increased 40 per cent. in thirteen years from 1851 to 1864, the agricultural income of England only increased 20 per cent. in thirty-four years from 1842 to 1876. . . . What I do wish very respectfully to submit to you is this--this vast increase in the agricultural value of France is not upon the large properties, which, if anything, are inferior to the cultivation of the large properties in England, but it is upon these very peasant properties which some people are so ready to decry."

9. See on this point the evidence adduced by Mill and Fawcett in their works on "Political Economy."

10. In Prof. Fawcett's "Political Economy," the same view is strongly maintained.

11. "English Land and English Landlords," ; *Daily News*, Feb. 9th, 1881, where an excellent account of Mr. Prout's farm and its results is given.

---

# CHAPTER VII.

## LOW WAGES AND PAUPERISM THE DIRECT CONSEQUENCES OF UNRESTRICTED PRIVATE PROPERTY IN LAND.

PROGRESS AND POVERTY--LABOUR, NOT CAPITAL, THE FIRST MOVER IN PRODUCTION--INDUSTRY NOT LIMITED BY CAPITAL BUT BY RESTRICTED ACCESS TO THE LAND--INTEREST DETERMINED BY LAND MONOPOLY AND RENT--CAPITAL AND LABOUR NOT ANTAGONISTIC--PROGRESS OF SOCIETY CAUSES A RISE OF RENTS--PRIVATE PROPERTY IN LAND LEADS TO AN INEQUITABLE DIVISION OF WEALTH--SPECULATIVE INCREASE IN LAND VALUES--MR. GEORGE'S WORK SUPPLEMENTS AND ENFORCES THE CONCLUSIONS ARRIVED AT IN THE PRESENT VOLUME.

Since the greater part of this volume was in MSS., the writer has become acquainted with the remarkable work of Mr. Henry George--"Progress and Poverty"--in which, among other valuable matter, the statement at the head of this chapter is demonstrated by an irresistible appeal to logic and to facts. This demonstration, as a part of the science of political economy, so well supplements and supports the conclusions here arrived at that a short account of Mr. George's treatment of the subject may be appropriately given.

Mr. George first shows that political economists, from Adam Smith downwards, have adopted an erroneous starting-point, through making their observations in a state of society in which a capitalist generally rents land and hires labour. The capitalist therefore appears to be the first mover in production, and *capital* a necessity before *labour* can be employed. Our author points out that this is not the natural sequence of the three essentials to the production of wealth. He says:--"There must be land before labour can be exerted, and labour must be exerted before capital can be produced. Capital is a result of labour, and is used by labour to assist it in further production. Labour is the active and initial force, and labour is therefore the employer of capital. Labour can only be exerted upon land, and it is from land that the matter which it transmutes into wealth must be drawn. Land, therefore, is the condition precedent, the field and material of labour. The natural order is land, labour, capital; and instead of starting from capital as our initial point, we should start from land. There is another thing to be observed. Capital is not a necessary factor in production. Labour can produce wealth without the aid of capital, and in the necessary genesis of things must so produce wealth before capital can exist."

*Capital*, therefore, in the hands of a *capitalist*, is not necessary before labour can reap its reward, in other words, earn wages, for "where land is free, and labour is unassisted by capital, the whole produce will go to the labourer as wages." Thus the natural wages of labour is the whole of the produce of that labour. But, "where land is free and labour is assisted by capital, wages will consist of the whole produce, less that part necessary to induce the storing up of labour as capital." Here again there is no need for the labourer to be employed by the capitalist for wages, for the labourer will employ the capital himself, paying interest for it. It is only when land is all monopolised and rent has to be paid for the use of it that the labourer, unable to obtain land to exert his labour upon, is forced to work for wages for the capitalist who hires the land; and then "wages may be forced by the competition among labourers to the minimum at which labourers will consent to live."

This important conclusion becomes clear if we consider that, were the monopoly not complete, and any considerable quantity of land left open for labourers to work on for themselves, wages would certainly rise, since no man would consent to work for another unless he could get considerably more than he could earn when working for himself. It is when all natural opportunities are taken away from him, that he is compelled to labour for whatever wages he can obtain, and thus, when labourers are superabundant, wages are always kept down to the minimum at which life can be supported.

An elaborate enquiry as to the true use and function of capital leads Mr. George to the conclusion that it does not limit industry, as is erroneously taught; the only limit to industry being the access to natural material. But capital may limit the form of industry and the productiveness of industry, by limiting the use of tools and the division of labour. As illustrative of this important conclusion, he observes:--"But whether the amount of capital ever does limit the productiveness of industry, and fix a maximum which wages cannot exceed, it is evident that it is not from any scarcity of capital that the poverty of the masses in civilised countries proceeds. For, not only do wages nowhere reach the limit fixed by the productiveness of industry, but wages are relatively the lowest where capital is most abundant. The tools and machinery of production are in all the most progressive countries evidently in excess of the use made of them, and any prospect of remunerative employment brings out more than the capital needed. The bucket is not only full; it is overflowing. So evident is this that, not only among the ignorant, but by men of high economic reputation, is industrial depression attributed to the abundance of machinery and the accumulation of capital; and war, which is the destruction of capital, is looked upon as the cause of brisk trade and high wages--an idea, strangely enough, so great is the confusion of thought on such matters, countenanced by many who hold that capital employs labour and pays wages."

Exactly the same thing happens with interest. Its variations in different countries, and at different times, depend, primarily, on the average profits that can be made by labour, when applied to land or other natural opportunities which can be had free of rent. When, however, land is monopolised and rent has to be paid for the use of even the poorest land, then interest, like wages, is kept down to the lowest point which will tempt its investment; and this point becomes lower and lower, in proportion as rent, ever growing higher and higher, absorbs a larger proportion of the joint produce of labour and capital.

As Mr. George well puts it:--"Wages and interest do not depend upon the produce of labour and capital, but upon what is left after rent is taken out; or, upon the produce which they could obtain without paying rent--that is, from the poorest land in use. And hence, no matter what would be the increase in productive power, if the increase of rent keeps pace with it, neither wages nor interest can increase. The moment this simple relation is recognised, a flood of light streams in upon what was before inexplicable, and seemingly discordant facts range themselves under an obvious law. The increase of rent which goes on in progressive countries is at once seen to be the key which explains why wages and interest fail to increase with increase of productive power. For the wealth produced in every community is divided into two parts by what may be called the rent line, which is fixed by the margin of cultivation, or the return which labour and capital could obtain from such natural opportunities as are free to them without the payment of rent. From the part of the produce below this line wages and interest must be paid. All that is above goes to the owners of land. Thus, where the value of land is low, there may be a small production of wealth, and yet a high rate of wages and interest, as we see in new countries. And when the value of land is high, there may be a very large production of wealth, and yet a low rate of wages and interest, as we see in old countries. And when productive power increases, as it is increasing in all progressive countries, wages and interest will be affected, not by the increase, but by the manner in which rent is affected. If the value of land increases proportionally, the increased production will be swallowed up by rent, and wages and interest will remain as before. If the value of land increases in greater ratio than productive power, rents will swallow up even more than the increase; and while the produce of labour and capital will be much larger, wages and interest will fall. It is only when the value of land fails to increase as rapidly as productive power that wages and interest can increase with the increase of productive power."

It follows that the old idea, so prevalent still among workmen, that capital and labour are antagonistic, is a mistake. Both alike suffer from the common enemy--the landlord; and rent absorbs the profits which the steady increase of productive power in all civilised countries should give to labour and capital. And the facts strictly agree with this conclusion. For, though neither wages nor interest anywhere increase as material progress goes on, yet the invariable accompaniment and mark of material progress is the increase of rent--the rise of land values. "It is the general fact, observable everywhere, that as the value of land increases, so does the contrast between wealth and want appear. It is the universal fact that, where the value of land is highest, civilisation exhibits the greatest luxury side by side with the most piteous destitution. To see human beings in the most abject, the most helpless and hopeless condition, you must go, not to the unfenced prairies and the log cabins of new clearings in the backwoods, where man single-handed is commencing the struggle with Nature, and land is yet worth nothing, but to the great cities, where the ownership of a little patch of ground is a fortune."

Mr. George then goes on to show that increase of

population and improvements in the arts necessarily cause a steady increase of the rent of land; and that this is so is shown both by fact and by reasoning. It is a fact that Free Trade has enormously increased the wealth of England; and this increase of wealth has not diminished pauperism, but has simply increased rent. This same result may be arrived at logically, by supposing that the labour-saving machinery which has had so large a share in increasing the wealth of all civilised countries arrives at such absolute perfection that the necessity for labour in the production of wealth is entirely done away with, so that everything the earth can yield may be obtained without labour. "Wages then would be nothing, and interest would be nothing, while rent would take everything. For the owners of land being enabled without labour to obtain all the wealth that could be procured from nature, there would be no use for either labour or capital, and no possible way in which either could compel any share of the wealth produced. And no matter how small population might be, if anybody but the landowners continued to exist, it would be at the whim or by the mercy of the landowners--they would be maintained either for the amusement of the landowners, or, as paupers, by their bounty." Now as labour-saving machinery is ever improving, and man's power over nature ever increasing, the *tendency* is towards this state of things, that is, to the greater wealth and greater power of the landowners, to the more complete dependence or the more abject poverty of the rest of the community.

One more quotation still further to elucidate this point:--"The recognition of individual proprietorship of land is the denial of the natural rights of other individuals--it is a wrong which *must* show itself in the inequitable division of wealth. For, as labour cannot produce without the use of land, the denial of the equal right to the use of land is necessarily the denial of the right of labour to its own produce. If one man can command the land upon which others must labour, he can appropriate the produce of their labour as the price of his permission to labour. The fundamental law of nature, that her enjoyment by man shall be consequent upon his exertion, is thus violated. The one receives without producing; the others produce without receiving. The one is unjustly enriched; the others are robbed. To this fundamental wrong we have traced the unjust distribution of wealth which is separating modern society into the very rich and the very poor. It is the continuous increase of rent--the price that labour is compelled to pay for the use of land, which strips the many of the wealth they justly earn, to pile it up in the hands of the few who do nothing to earn it."

The only political economist who, so far as I know, has independently arrived at these results is the late Professor Cairnes. He says:--

"The soil is, over the greater portion of the inhabited globe, cultivated by very humble men, with very little disposable wealth, and whose career is practically marked out for them by irresistible circumstances as tillers of the ground. In a contest between vast bodies of people so circumstanced and the owners of the soil--between the purchasers without reserve, constantly increasing in numbers, of an indispensable commodity, and the monopolist dealers in that commodity--the negotiation could have but one issue, that of transferring to the owners of the soil the whole produce, *minus* what was sufficient to maintain in the lowest state of existence the race of cultivators. This is what has happened wherever the owners of the soil, discarding all considerations but those dictated by self-interest, have really availed themselves of the full strength of their position. It is what has happened under rapacious Governments in Asia; it is what has happened under rapacious landlords in Ireland; it is what now happens under the bourgeois proprietors of Flanders; it is, in short, the inevitable result which cannot but happen in the great majority of all societies now existing on earth where land is given up to be dealt with on commercial principles, unqualified by public opinion, custom, or law" (J. E. Cairnes, *Fortnightly Review*, Jan., 1870).

Again, in a later work, "Some Leading Principles of Political Economy Newly Expounded," published in 1874, he still further illustrates the same views, distinctly laying down the proposition that neither profits nor wages have advanced with the increasing wealth of the community due to advancing civilisation and increased power over the forces of nature:--

"Not indeed that the introduction of improved processes into agriculture has been for nought: it has resulted in a large augmentation of the aggregate return obtained from the soil, but without permanently lowering its price, and, therefore, without permanent advantage to either capitalist or labourer, or to other consumers. The large addition to the wealth of the country has gone neither to profits nor to wages, nor yet to the public at large, but to swell a fund ever growing, even while its proprietors sleep--the rent-roll of the owners of the soil. Accordingly we find that, notwithstanding the vast progress of agricultural industry effected within a century, there is scarcely an important agricultural product that is not at least as dear now as it was a hundred years ago--as dear not merely in money price but in real cost. The aggregate return from the land has immensely increased; but the cost of the costliest portion of the produce, which is that which determines the price of the whole, remains pretty nearly as it was. Profits, therefore, have not risen at all, and the real remuneration of the labourer, taking the whole field of labour, in but a slight degree--at all events in a degree very far from commensurate with the general progress of industry" ().

In these passages from the works of an English writer of established reputation we have a very remarkable and quite independent accordance with the special views of Mr. George--an accordance which must add greatly to the weight of their teaching.

There is, however, another important consideration, which tends still further to intensify the monopoly of land and the consequent helplessness and poverty of the labourer. This is, the constant expectation of a further rise in land value, due to its steady increase with increase of population and advance of industrial development. This expectation leads to speculation in land; and it has all the effect of a combination among landowners to keep up the price. The result is, that land is constantly held for an advance in price, based, not upon present value, but upon the added value that will come with the further growth of population. Hence it happens that--"Labour cannot reap the benefits which advancing civilisation brings, because they are intercepted. Land being necessary to labour, and being reduced to private ownership, every increase in the productive power of labour but increases rent--the price that labour must pay for the opportunity to realise its powers; and thus all the advantages gained by the march of progress go to the owners of land, and wages do not increase. Wages cannot increase, for the greater the earnings of labour the greater the price that labour must pay out of its earnings for the opportunity to make any earnings at all. . . . Begotten of the continuous advance of rent, arises a speculative tendency which discounts the effect of further improvements by a still further advance in rent, to drive wages down to the slave point--the point at which the labourer can just live."

It is not necessary here to go further in this very imperfect exposition of Mr. George's views. It will be seen that they afford a most remarkable theoretical confirmation of the conclusions here reached by an examination of the actual condition of the people under different kinds of land-tenure; and if, as I maintain, these conclusions have now been demonstrated by induction from facts, that demonstration acquires the force of absolute proof when exactly the same conclusion is reached by a totally distinct line of deductive reasoning founded on the admitted principles of political economy and the general facts of social and industrial development. I will now only add the striking passage with which Mr. George concludes that part of his work which specially discusses "The Persistence of Poverty amid Advancing Wealth":--"The ownership of land is the great fundamental fact which ultimately determines the social, the political, and consequently the intellectual and moral condition of a people. And it must be so; for land is the habitation of man, the storehouse upon which he must draw for all he needs; the material to which his labour must be applied for the supply of all his desires; for even the products of the sea cannot be taken, the light of the sun enjoyed, or any of the forces of nature utilised without the use of land or its products. On the land we are born, from it we live, to it we return again--children of the soil as truly as is the blade of grass or the flower of the field. Take away from man all that belongs to land, and he is but a disembodied spirit. Material progress cannot rid us of our dependence upon land; it can but add to the power of producing wealth from land; and hence, when land is monopolised, it might go on to infinity without increasing wages or improving the condition of those who have but their labour. It can but add to the value of land and the power which its possession gives. Everywhere, in all times, among all peoples, the possession of land is the base of aristocracy, the source of power. As said the Brahmins ages ago:--*To whomsoever the soil at any time belongs, to him belong the fruits of it. White parasols and elephants mad with pride are the flowers of a grant of land.*"

We have now to consider the important question, how our present system can be best exchanged for a better one; and also, how we can secure all the benefits which occupying ownership confers, how we can extend those benefits to the largest number and over the widest area, and how most effectually prevent the economical and moral evils of landlordism from again asserting themselves.

# CHAPTER VIII.

## NATIONALISATION OF THE LAND AFFORDS THE ONLY MODE OF EFFECTING A COMPLETE SOLUTION OF THE LAND QUESTION.

SUMMARY OF THE PRECEDING CHAPTERS--THE CONTRAST OF OUR WEALTH AND OUR POVERTY AMAZES ALL FOREIGNERS--OUR POVERTY AND PAUPERISM PERSISTS, NOTWITHSTANDING THE MOST FAVOURABLE CONDITIONS--THE IRISH LANDLORDS FOLLOW THE TEACHINGS OF POLITICAL ECONOMY--EFFECTS OF LANDLORDISM IN THE HIGHLANDS AND LOWLANDS OF SCOTLAND--THE DESPOTIC POWERS OF ENGLISH LANDLORDS--THE COMPLETE AND OVERWHELMING MASS OF EVIDENCE IN FAVOUR OF OCCUPYING OWNERSHIP--THE REMEDIES PROPOSED--FREE TRADE IN LAND SHOWN TO BE COMPARATIVELY USELESS--MR. KAY'S ARGUMENTS IN FAVOUR OF

FREE TRADE IN LAND--SMALL LANDED ESTATES ARE CONSTANTLY ABSORBED BY GREAT ONES--FREE TRADE IN LAND WOULD NOT HELP EITHER THE TENANT OR THE LABOURER--NATIONALISATION OF THE LAND THE ONLY EFFECTIVE REMEDY--OCCUPANCY AND VIRTUAL OWNERSHIP MUST GO TOGETHER--TO SECURE THIS THE STATE MUST BE THE REAL OWNER OR GROUND-LANDLORD--THE STATE MUST BECOME OWNER OF THE LAND APART FROM THE IMPROVEMENTS UPON IT--MODE OF DETERMINING THE VALUE OF THE QUIT-RENT AND OF THE TENANT-RIGHT--HOW EXISTING LANDOWNERS MAY BE COMPENSATED--ALLEGED UNFAIRNESS OF COMPENSATION BY MEANS OF TERMINABLE ANNUITIES--HOW TENANTS MAY BECOME OCCUPYING OWNERS--SUB-LETTING MUST BE ABSOLUTELY PROHIBITED--EVILS OF SUB-LETTING IN TOWNS--MORTGAGING SHOULD BE STRICTLY LIMITED--WHETHER ANY LIMITS SHOULD BE PLACED TO THE QUANTITY OF LAND PERSONALLY OCCUPIED--SUPPOSED OBJECTIONS TO LAND NATIONALISATION--MR. FOWLER'S OBJECTIONS--MR. ARTHUR ARNOLD'S OBJECTIONS--MR. G. SHAW LEFEVRE'S OBJECTIONS--THE HON. G. C. BRODRICK'S

OBJECTIONS--MR. J. BOYD KINNEAR'S OBJECTIONS--HOW NATIONALISATION WILL AFFECT TOWNS--FREE SELECTION OF RESIDENTIAL PLOTS BY LABOURERS AND OTHERS--OBJECTIONS TO THE RIGHT OF FREE-SELECTION--WHY FREE-SELECTION SHOULD BE RESTRICTED TO ONCE IN A MAN'S LIFE--FREE SELECTION WOULD CHECK THE GROWTH OF TOWNS AND ADD TO THE BEAUTY AND ENJOYABILITY OF RURAL DISTRICTS--HOW COMMONS MAY BE PRESERVED AND UTILISED--HOW MINERALS SHOULD BE WORKED UNDER STATE OWNERSHIP--PROGRESSIVE REDUCTION OF TAXATION; ABOLITION OF CUSTOMS AND EXCISE--SUMMARY OF THE ADVANTAGES OF NATIONALISATION--SUMMARY OF THE EVIL RESULTS OF LANDLORDISM--CONCLUSION.

In the preceding chapters we have laid before the reader a body of facts sufficient to form a sound basis for a solution of the Land Problem. They comprise the more essential portions of most of the chief works which have been written on the subject, and it is, perhaps, because these statements and facts in their whole extent, have never before been systematically collected and compared, that the remedies proposed have hitherto been so inadequate, and the arguments by which these remedies have been supported so illogical. Before proceeding to discuss these proposals, or to explain what appears to the present writer the only adequate remedy, it will be as well briefly to summarise the facts and conclusions already established.

*Summary of the Preceding Chapters.*--In the first chapter we have called special attention to the astounding facts of the vast riches and the degrading poverty of our country, which, in their terrible combination and contrast, are unparalleled in the civilised world. Many writers have commented on this fact incidentally, but none (except the American author whose work we have sketched in the preceding chapter) have made it the foundation and key-note of a discussion, or have endeavoured to trace out its causes and its possible cure. To show that I have not overstated the facts of the case, I will here quote the words of the late Mr. Joseph Kay, Q.C., who says:--"The French, the Dutch, the Germans, and the Swiss look with wonder at the enormous fortunes and at the enormous mass of pauperism which accumulate in England side by side. They have little of either extreme." And again:--"The objects which strike foreigners with the greatest astonishment, on visiting our country, and of which they see nothing at all similar in their own countries, are:--(1) The enormous wealth of the highest classes of English society. (2) The intense and continued labour and toil of the middle and lowest classes. And (3) the frightful amount of absolute pauperism among the lowest classes." And as to the condition of the agricultural labourers of England, Professor Fawcett (in his "Political Economy") states, that there are "few classes of workmen who, in many respects, are so thoroughly wretched as the English agricultural labourers. They are so miserably poor that, if they were converted into slaves to-morrow, it would be for the interest of their owners to feed them far better than they are fed at the present time;" while in his "Essays" he says, speaking on the authority of a Parliamentary Report, that the men, women, and children who compose the agricultural gangs which cultivate a wide tract of highly-farmed land "are living in such a condition that some of the worst horrors of slavery seem to be in existence among us in the nineteenth century."

Now this state of things not only co-exists with an unexampled accumulation of wealth, but with a whole series of favourable conditions which few other countries have enjoyed. We had the start of all Europe in the development of the railway system; we had endless stores of coal and iron, which all the world required and bought of us; for a long time we supplied half the population of the globe with cotton and iron goods; we have a greater colonial system than any other country, and a freer outlet for our people and our trade to lands where our own language is spoken; our home-trade is little burdened by fiscal trammels, while we enjoy free imports from all the world; and our capital, London, is, and long has been, the financial and commercial centre of the globe. Surely the amazing anomaly of the degrading poverty of our labourers co-existing with such favourable conditions deserves, not a mere passing notice, but a serious and continued study. It has, however, unhappily, become so familiar to us that most people pass it by as an insoluble problem, and content themselves with suggesting certain possible ameliorations or palliations. In my first chapter I have gone a little further than this, and have endeavoured to define, with some precision, the cause of this frightful anomaly--a cause which the series of facts stated in the subsequent chapters forced me to adopt as the only adequate one, and which I have thus early enunciated as a postulate to be either affirmed or negatived by the evidence adduced subsequently. It is a cause which appears to me to afford the only clue to a general solution of the problem of how to secure the social well-being of the great mass of the community, and it leads irresistibly to the conclusion that the most vital of all the questions of modern civilisation is the proper utilisation of the land.

In the second chapter I have briefly sketched the rise and development of the semi-feudal system of land-tenure now existing in this country, showing that neither its origin nor its history gives it any claim to our respect, or renders it at all likely to be suitable to the wants of a free and civilised people.

In the third chapter I give some account of the effects of

modern landlordism in Ireland. The law has hitherto given to the landlord complete power over the land he holds, to deal with it as he pleases. Millions of people who possess no land nor any other property are absolutely dependent, not for happiness only, but for the power to live, on having a portion of this land to cultivate. Under these circumstances the landlord is master of the situation. He can demand what he pleases for his land; he can let it on what terms he pleases; and he can subject his tenants to any rules or regulations he or his agents think proper. The people *must* have land or starve; so they offer any rent, agree to any terms, and are consequently always the virtual, if not the actual, slaves of the landlord. Hence the perennial misery and crime of Ireland. Hence famines, and evictions, and the shooting of landlords or agents. Some people blame the landlords; but why? The law tells them that their land is their *property*. Political economy tells them to sell it, or the use of it, in the dearest market; that supply and demand regulate the price of all commodities; and that it is best for all that it should be so regulated. They simply act on these principles, which have been drilled into them as the highest teaching of political science; yet the result is a nation in the most hopeless misery to be found anywhere in the civilised world. The only logical conclusion from these facts is, that the law which makes land private property is wrong; and this being so, we can understand why it is that the very same principles of free contract, buying cheap and selling dear, supply and demand as the regulator of price--principles which work *good* for mankind in every other case, work *evil* here. That this *is* the proper conclusion is clearly demonstrated by the necessity for exceptional legislation for the land of Ireland, whereby the greatest modern statesmen and legislators go back to the exploded nostrums of the middle ages, and attempt to regulate the price of this commodity. If land is and should be private property, why determine its fair price or fair rent by Act of Parliament any more than the price of bread or of cloth? The fact that the only way found by Parliament to save a nation from chronic insurrection and a people from chronic misery and starvation *is* thus to interfere in the case of land, proves of itself that land should *not* be private property, but should be held by the State for the free use and general benefit of the community. The question of *how* the land became the property of its present owners is not important. There is, perhaps, hardly an acre of land in Europe but has been at one time or other forcibly taken from some previous holder, and it is not found that the possession of land (as property--not for personal occupation) leads to less evil results when it has been simply purchased or inherited from a purchaser, than when it has been obtained by forcible means in modern or ancient times. It is the act of ownership of land as a property, producing an income by its rents, that leads to all the trouble, not the mode in which the land was acquired by the present or preceding owners. The only logical people are those who, like Lord Sherbrooke and Professor Bonamy Price, maintain that land, being property, should be dealt with like all other property, by free contract between man and man, and that therefore all interference between a landlord and his tenants is contrary to the first principles of political economy--or those who, like Herbert Spencer, Professor F. W. Newman, and others, maintain that the land of a country ought not to be private property at all; and the fact that the unchecked operation of supply and demand, with free contract between purchaser and seller, does produce, in the case of land, endless evils, proves conclusively that the latter position is the true one.

The fourth chapter treats of the effects of landlordism in Scotland, and exhibits a series of facts which, though arising under a totally different set of conditions from those which have prevailed in Ireland, have produced equally lamentable results; and these still further enforce the same doctrine, that land cannot safely be allowed to become private property, to be bought, and sold, and accumulated, and dealt with like other property. Some account is here given of the "clearances" which have been going on in the Highlands for nearly a century, and which are still in operation. The motive for these clearances is usually to obtain a larger or securer rental for the land, either as sheep-farms or as deer-forests; and for this purpose tens of thousands of British subjects have been driven from their homes--often to swell the mass of indigence and crime in the great cities, while the country is being denuded of a hardy, industrious, moral, and intelligent population, to which our army has been indebted for men and officers who, in India and elsewhere, have done the noblest deeds, and added to the nation's roll of fame. Such clearances are a deep injury to the State, and a positive crime against humanity, of the same nature (though less in degree) as despotism or slavery. Yet they are legal; and no power exists which can prevent them, so long as the land--without which no man can live--is allowed to be monopolised by the rich. When the attention of the Home Secretary was called, by Dr. Macdonald, to the recent Leckmeln evictions in Ross-shire, he replied that he could not interfere, because the proprietor had only exercised the *summum jus* of property. That answer is a condemnation of private property in land, because it shows that the greatest of all the evils which arise from it--the power of one man to banish another from his home--cannot be cured so long as it exists.

In the latter part of the same chapter attention is called to the fact that, in the Lowlands of Scotland, where the agriculture is admitted to be the best in the Kingdom, and where there is no lack of capital expended on the land, the condition of the labourer is often as bad as in the worst cultivated parts of England, while his higher wages are wholly due to the competition of the manufacturers for labour. This is a complete disproof of the allegations of those who maintain that, were land freed from entail and settlements and could pass into the hands of men of capital, all the evils of the landlord system would disappear. The fact, however, is, that where the amount of capital expended is greatest, there the evils, as regards the labourer, are at least as great as elsewhere.

The fifth chapter deals with English Landlordism, and it is shown that here, too, the evil results are numerous and wide-spread. The land is badly cultivated; the country is denuded of population while the towns are overcrowded; many of the greatest necessaries of life (which are also its greatest luxuries), such as milk, butter, eggs, poultry, fruit, and vegetables, are all made scarce, dear, and bad by the denial of land to labourers and the middle classes; and these products have to be imported from almost every country in Europe, and even from America, when they could all be abundantly produced at home, and we could have them at our very doors better in quality and far cheaper than now. This is a positive injury to every one--an injury in no way compensated by Free Trade allowing these things to be imported in a more or less stale and deteriorated condition duty free, since the hundreds of millions we pay for them annually to foreigners might be earned by our own rural labourers, keeping them from drink and pauperism, and us from the burthen of supporting paupers.

In England, too, evictions occur as elsewhere, and no man who does not cultivate his own land can feel secure. He may be banished from his home at his landlord's pleasure; and instances are given showing that men *are* thus banished on account of their politics, their religion, their independence, or their love of sport. Every man not a landowner is, in fact, a serf. His lord may be a benevolent despot and he may not feel the chain, but it exists nevertheless; and he cannot be really free when, for no crime or fault whatever, he may be compelled against his will to suffer the punishment of having, at any period of his life, to break up his home and seek a new one. Attention is also called to the enormous and wide-spread evils of over-crowded and ill-built dwellings, with insufficient space of ground for health and recreation, which directly arise from land being a monopoly in private hands. This again is an evil which does not affect a class only, but the entire community, and it is an evil which cannot be got rid of so long as land remains private property, but which may be made to disappear the moment a wise system of nationalisation is effected.

The sixth chapter deals with the question of Occupying Ownership as opposed to Landlordism. A summary is given of the evidence as to the condition of the landholders and labourers in various countries, and it is shown, by an overwhelming mass of evidence, that just in proportion as the cultivator of land has a permanent interest in it is he well-off, happy, and contented. Climate, soil, latitude, government, race, may all differ, but the general law remains true, that the ownership of land by the very persons who cultivate it is beneficial to themselves and to the whole community; that the cultivation of land which belongs to another, and in the improvement of which the cultivator has not a large or an exclusive interest, is injurious to the cultivator and to the whole community. This law is absolute, and has no exceptions. It is not a question of large or small farms; it is a question solely of ownership or tenancy of land. It applies equally to the agricultural labourer with his acre of garden as to the yeoman farming 500 acres of his own land. We English maintain Free Trade, though all the world be against us, because the immutable laws of labour, production, and self-interest prove that the free exchange of the products of labour is for the mutual benefit of all. But in the case of the land, the benefits of occupying ownership are far greater; for they are social and moral as well as material. Free Trade has not diminished drunkenness, Free Trade has not diminished pauperism, Free Trade has not given our labourers decent houses or raised them out of that state of misery which is a disgrace to our civilisation. But occupying ownership *does* do all this wherever it prevails. Just in proportion as it is wide-spread and untrammelled, so do pauperism, drunkenness, and crime disappear, and give place to plenty, peace, and content. If, then, we uphold Free Trade because it is theoretically right and true, and because it makes our riches increase and multiply, ought we not to adopt with equal eagerness that principle of occupying ownership of the soil which is recognised by all enquirers as producing such universally beneficial results, results which are clearly traceable to no less universal and indubitable facts of our mental and moral nature. In the whole field of political and social science there is no induction so complete and so universal as that which connects landlordism and tenancy with a pauperised and degraded population, occupying ownership with a thriving and contented one.

In the seventh chapter I have given a brief sketch of that part of Mr. George's work on "Progress and Poverty" which shows, by a totally distinct line of argument and proof, that private property in land is the direct cause of low wages and pauperism, thus confirming and enforcing the results we have arrived at in the preceding chapter. Having thus set forth a large body of facts, and having found that they point invariably to one conclusion, a conclusion arrived at independently by a writer who has investigated the question from another standpoint, let us proceed to examine the remedies proposed by those earnest and philanthropic writers to whom we are indebted for most of the facts we have made use of, and who all admit the failure of our present land-system and the serious nature of the evils which co-exist with it.

*Free Trade in Land Shown to be Comparatively Useless.*--The great school of English land-reformers, among whom we have the distinguished names of Mr. Bright, Professor Fawcett, Mr. Arthur Arnold, Mr. Thornton, Mr. J. Boyd Kinnear, the Hon. George Brodrick, and the late Mr. Joseph Kay, while fully admitting most of the facts here adduced, and often dwelling upon them at greater length and more forcibly than I have been able to do, all agree in advocating the same universal panacea--the abolition or radical modification of the laws which restrict the transmission and possession of land by means of settlements and entails, so as to bring about a state of things which may be briefly summarised by the term "Free Trade in Land." They all show, with great force and irresistible logic, the evils incident to the system of limited ownership, produced alike by settlements and entails, and by the costly and difficult transfer of land which these necessitate. They urge that the one thing needful is that every acre of land in the country should be in the possession of some one owner, with absolute power to sell or transfer it in any way he pleases to some other absolute owner. They maintain that by this means land would get into the hands of those who have capital to expend on its improvement, and whose interest it would be so to improve it. They maintain, in fact, that what is wanted is not to abolish landlordism, but to arrange matters so that the landlord shall have still greater power than he has now to deal with the land as he pleases. Some of them maintain that this would favour the creation of a class of yeomen or peasant proprietors, by throwing much more land into the market and rendering its sale in small lots inexpensive as well as profitable; while others dwell chiefly on the fact that more capital will thus be diverted to the land. Not one of them seems to recognise anything evil in landlordism itself; not one of them appears to perceive the bearing of the whole mass of the evidence in every civilised country in the world--evidence which proclaims in the most unmistakable manner that the fruits of landlordism are always evil, those of occupying ownership always good.

How is it, it may be asked, that among so many great men who have paid special attention to this subject none have seen, or if they have seen have declared, the inherent evils of landlordism? One such man, and a greater than any of those whose names I have quoted--John Stuart Mill--did see it, and stated his opinion with sufficient plainness; but he did *not* see any practical and just mode of abolishing landlordism, and therefore contented himself with claiming for the State "the unearned increment of the soil." Other land-reformers are most likely deterred by the vast difficulties in the way of such reform; and, though satisfied that landlordism does always produce evil results, do not see any possibility of changing so ancient and so powerful an institution. Before proceeding to show that the problem of radical land reform is not nearly so difficult as has been supposed, when once the source of the evil is detected and it is determined not merely to palliate but to abolish it, it will be well to point out the total insufficiency of the free-trade-in-land panacea to remedy the great and crying evils of landlordism; and, in doing so, we shall refer chiefly to the most authoritative work on the question--Mr. Kay's "Free Trade in Land."

*Mr. Kay's Arguments in Support of Free Trade in Land.*--Mr. Kay's book is throughout an elaborate argument, founded on a copious and most valuable collection of facts; but rarely do we find an argument set forth with such evident care, and yet so entirely illogical and unsound. It is essentially as follows:--Over a large portion of Europe we find peasants cultivating lands of which they are the owners, and they are invariably well-off and contented. In our own country we have mostly large estates cultivated by tenant farmers, and here the labourers are pauperised and discontented. Wherever the former condition prevails *there* is also a free trade in land. With us, and in some other countries where the people are equally wretched, entails and settlements and costly conveyancing prevail; *therefore*"free trade in land" causes the difference; give us "free trade in land" and our country will soon resemble Switzerland or Sweden or Prussia. This is positively the whole argument, and so blindly is it applied that the most vital differences between other countries and our own are slurred over or totally ignored. Thus, he speaks of the misery of the peasants of France before the Revolution, of the abolition of feudal customs and laws, of the peasants having "become the owners of the farms on which they used to labour," and asserts that "the system of peasant proprietorship is literally a system of free trade in land;" but he quite ignores the fact that even before the Revolution there were more than a million of peasant proprietors in France, and that afterwards the enormous Church property and many confiscated estates were sold at low prices to the peasants, who then had no competitors in the market, thus adding, according to Arthur Young, 1,220,000 more to the already large body of French peasant-proprietors. In speaking of Prussia, he refers to the alteration of the "Land Laws" as the one essential thing which has produced the existing peasant-proprietors, ignoring again the fact that there were already in existence an enormous body of peasants cultivating land held under various feudal tenures, often very oppressive, but still, to a great extent, permanent; and that the reforms enabled the peasants to become freeholders on easy terms. And here, too, large ecclesiastical and Crown estates were also sold to the peasants. In England, on the other hand, that beneficial feature of feudalism--the permanent connection of the peasant with the land he cultivates, has been long totally destroyed; the Church lands were all given to feudal lords or court favourites three centuries ago, and have gone to swell great estates, instead of remaining, as in most European countries, to be divided among the people; while the number of wealthy persons seeking to purchase land for speculation or for power is so great, that it is the wildest delusion to suppose that the agricultural labourers of England (rarely able to escape the workhouse in old age) will ever secure an acre of it.

*Small Landed Estates are Constantly Absorbed by Great Ones.*--Mr. Kay himself adduces abundant evidence to this effect. He shows that "the great estates, vast as they already are, are continually devouring the few remaining small agricultural properties," and that "the class of peasant-proprietors formerly to be found in the rural districts is tending to disappear." Mr. Shaw Lefevre, his relative and disciple, further states that--"In some counties, all the land which comes into the market is bought up by the trustees of wills directing the accumulation of land; while in most parts of the country, if a small freehold of a few acres comes into the market, it is almost certain to be bought up by an adjoining owner, either for the purpose of rounding off a corner of his estate, or for extending political influence, or still more often by the advice of the family solicitor, who is always in favour of increasing the family estates." Professor Fawcett also writes strongly on this "greed for land." He says:--"Two or three large proprietors continue increasing their estates until they come at length to think that the whole locality ought to be apportioned among them. If the symmetry of their estates should happen to be disturbed by anyone possessing a few acres of land, he is considered an intruder, and his little freehold is an eye-sore to the great proprietors. A common affects them much in the same way; and in order to achieve the grand object of being able to say that no one else in the neighbourhood possesses a single rood of land, they appeal to Parliament to aid them in destroying these commons over which the public exercise some proprietary rights. A Parliament so largely composed of those who are great landowners, or who wish to become great landowners, respond to such an appeal with cordial sympathy." ("Pauperism," )[1]

*Free Trade in Land would not Help either the Tenant or the Labourer.*--Now, with all these influences at work, and taking note of the enormous fortunes annually made by contractors, merchants, or speculators, as well as those brought home by successful colonists, all seeking investment in land or some form of landed property, what reason is there to suppose that the great bulk of the estates that come into the market will not bc at once absorbed by the various investors of this type, and by speculative builders or by building companies, where the land is suitable for creating a residential district? No facts have been adduced to show that the demand for land by the wealthy will cease or at all diminish, except the totally inapposite fact that much land sold by the Encumbered

Estates Court in Ireland was purchased by the occupying tenants, largely helped by their relations in America. The condition of Ireland, however, neither was nor is at all comparable with that of England. The absentee landlords of Ireland are not generally eager to increase their estates, and there is no constant influx of newly-created wealth ever on the look-out for land, as there is in England and Scotland. It is, therefore, as certain as any anticipated result can be, that "free trade in land" would in no appreciable degree add to the number of yeomen or of peasant-proprietors, or do anything to check their complete extinction. What it would do would be to transfer many estates to the hands of men of capital, and to consign some beautiful demesnes to the speculative builder. But this would in no way benefit either the labourer or the tenant-farmer, or the public at large. We have seen that on some of the best-farmed land in the country the condition of the labourers is a disgrace and a degradation; while alike in Ireland, in the Highlands, and in every part of Europe, it is the new purchasers of land, whether in large or small estates, who are the hardest landlords, who seek to obtain the greatest possible return for their outlay, who buy cheap and sell dear, as they are taught to do by the best-known maxims of political economy--maxims which, when applied to the products of human labour, are beneficial to all parties alike, but which, when applied to the land (which is limited in quantity, which no man can make, and which is as necessary to human existence as the air we breathe), carry with them the inevitable curse of pauperism to the labourer, and the innumerable evils of a half-cultivated and poverty-stricken country to the whole community. For, why do we import eggs to the amount of two and a half millions sterling annually from France, poultry from France and Italy, butter, or some bad imitations of it, to the amount of more than ten millions sterling from various parts of the Continent, rabbits from Belgium, fruits and vegetables from France, Jersey, and America, while milk, which cannot be imported, is constantly adulterated, is only to be had even in the country at an exorbitant price, and often only as a favour? This all happens because our labourers of every kind are landless, and for no other reason whatever. Every English child who cannot get abundance of pure milk, every one who suffers from the want of cheap, fresh, and abundant fruit, vegetables, eggs, butter, and poultry, has the right to protest against this system. The wealthy landowners know nothing of these evils, for they grow all these products themselves; but thirty million people cannot for ever live as if in a desert, or in a state of siege, in order that one million or less may be territorial lords and possess undue political and social power.[2]

*Nationalisation of the Land the only Effective Remedy.*--Having now shown that the panacea of the "free trade in land" school would not sensibly diminish the various evils of landlordism which have been pointed out in the preceding chapters, but that it would, on the contrary, very probably intensify some of them, it remains to be shown that a remedy *can* be found for the terrible disease under which the social organism in our country is labouring, that this remedy may be applied without injury to anyone, and that its results will be in the highest degree beneficial to every class of the community.

Let us first state what are the necessary requirements of a complete solution of the land problem as enunciated in these pages:--

(1) In the first place, it is clear that landlordism must be replaced by occupying ownership. No less radical reform will get rid of the widespread evils of our present system.

(2) Arrangements must be made by which the tenure of the holder of land must be secure and permanent, and nothing must be permitted to interfere with his free use of the land, or his certainty of reaping all the fruits of any labour or outlay he may bestow upon it.

(3) Arrangements must be made by which every British subject may secure a portion of land for personal occupation at its fair agricultural value.

(4) All suitable tracts of unenclosed and waste lands must (under certain limitations) be open to cultivation by occupying owners.

(5) The freest sale and transfer of every holder's interest

in his land must be secured.

(6) In order that these conditions be rendered permanent, sub-letting must be absolutely prohibited, and mortgages strictly limited.

*Occupancy and Virtual Ownership must go together.*--The first of these propositions hardly needs further elucidation or discussion. The whole bearing of the facts adduced in this volume is to show that landlordism *per se* is necessarily evil, while the occupation of land by its real or virtual owners is good just in proportion as the owner is in a position to receive the whole benefit, present and future, of his outlay on the land.

*To Secure this, the State must be the Real Owner or Ground-Landlord.*--It is, however, equally clear that the nature of ownership of land must*not* be the same as that of other property, as, if so, occupying ownership (which alone is beneficial) would not be universally secured. A person must own land only so long as he occupies it personally; that is, he must be a perpetual *holder* of the land, not its absolute *owner*; and this implies some superior of whom he holds it. We thus come back to that feudal principle (which in theory still exists) that every one must *hold* his land from the State, subject to whatever *general* laws and regulations are made for all land so held. The State must in no way deal with individual landowners, except through the medium of special Courts which will have to apply the laws in individual cases. Thus no State *management* will be required, with its inevitable evils of patronage, waste, and favouritism.

It is also essential that the State should be the actual owner of the land, in order that it may be untrammelled in making from time to time such general rules and regulations for its tenure as may be found needful for the public good. If absolute ownership--or what is now termed a freehold--be continued, every such absolute owner becomes an obstacle to needful reform, and the *right* to purchase land (under limitations to be hereafter mentioned) which every Englishman ought to possess would seem a harsh interference with the rights of property. The State alone, as universal landowner, will be able to provide means by which every man, from the labourer upwards, may procure suitable land for his personal occupation; and, unless this is done, fully half the benefits of a good land-system will be lost.

*The State must become Owner of the Land apart from the Improvements added to it.*--It being thus determined that the State must be the only landowner, but that the tenants of the State must be permanent, must be subject to no restrictions or interference in dealing with the land, and must be able to sell or transfer it with a minimum of trouble and expense, we proceed to show how this may be done in the simplest and most beneficial way, and so as to interfere as little as possible with the rights and interests of existing landowners. All previous writers on the possibility of nationalising the land have overlooked a very obvious fact, which is really the key to a practical solution of the problem. This fact is, that all enclosed or cultivated land has its value made up of two distinct portions, easily separable and affording a basis for an important division of ownership. These portions are--firstly, the inherent value, and, secondly, the improvements or additions added to the inherent value by the labour or outlay of the owners or occupiers. The important difference of these two portions of value is, that the one can be maintained, increased, or destroyed by the energy or the neglect of the holder of the land; the other--the inherent value--cannot (except in rare cases) be so destroyed or even deteriorated; for it depends on such natural conditions as geological formation, natural drainage, climate, aspect, surface, and subsoil--or on such general facts and conditions as density of population, vicinity of towns, ports, railroads, or public highways, none of which were created or are capable of being much altered by the individual action of the landholder. This portion of the value of the land, therefore, may conveniently become the property of the State, which may be remunerated for its use by payment of a perpetual *quit-rent*. The other portion, which is that created by the exertions of the landholder or his predecessors--consisting of buildings, fences, drains, gates, private roads, plantations, &c., &c.--should always be the property of the tenant and holder of the land, and it may conveniently be termed the *tenant-right*, because its possession will constitute him a *tenant* of the State, and because it is that portion of the value of landed property which must always belong to the *tenant*, while the land or soil itself remains in the possession of the supreme lord of the soil, the State. The term is familiar from its use in Ireland, as applied to that portion of the value of land which the *tenant* has created by his labour, and which, by custom, he has the *right* to sell or transfer.

As the possibility of practically determining the comparative value of these two elements in landed property has been doubted by some critics--among others, by Professor F. W. Newman, who is favourable to my scheme if it can be worked--it will be well here to say a few words on this supposed difficulty.

*Mode of Determining the Value of the Quit-Rent and the Tenant-Right.*--During the interval between the passing of the Act providing for Nationalisation and the date of its coming into operation--perhaps five, or even ten years--a complete valuation of the landed property of the whole kingdom will have to be made. This valuation must be of the *annual* or *rental value* of the land, and it must be of each field, enclosure, or other separable plot of land, however small--not on estates or holdings. This estimate of the annual value of each plot of land as it stands must then be divided into two parts, the one the value of the landlord's own portion--the future *tenant-right*; the other the inherent value, including that given to it by the community as well as by the cultivation of preceding generations of tenants. The separation of these two values would be by no means a difficult task, as a few considerations will show. By the general custom of the locality it would be found what had usually been done by the landlord, what by the tenant. In most parts of England it would be the *presumption* that the buildings and gates had been provided by the landlord, and this presumption would be acted on by the valuers in the absence of evidence to the contrary. As to fences, the presumption would probably be the other way. Very old enclosures have almost certainly been made by successive occupiers, and where any considerable amount of new fencing had been done by the landlord within living memory, or even beyond it, personal or documentary evidence of the fact would be forthcoming. The expenditure, or rather the work done, by the landlord or his predecessors could thus be ascertained with considerable accuracy, and would form the basis for the valuation.

There are two extreme cases in which the separation of the two values would be easy--the one in which buildings are the main feature of the plot, the other in which nothing has been done to the land but mere enclosure and cultivation. In the former we have the case of house-rent and ground-rent, which any valuer could determine, especially as certain general principles would be laid down for his guidance--as, for instance, that the area of ground occupied by a farm-house, garden, farm-yard or buildings should be estimated at the average agricultural value of the whole farm; while the buildings would be estimated at a fair interest on their approximate cost, less depreciation and repairs, if they were convenient and well suited to their purpose. If, on the other hand, they were badly arranged, badly built, or inconvenient, then a further deduction would have to be made to arrive at their *value*, which is often very different from the *cost* of a thing. In the other extreme are old enclosures which have never been drained, and which, presumably, have had nothing whatever done to them by the landlord or his predecessors, except perhaps supplying gates; and here the *tenant-right* would be a minimum--sometimes perhaps only a few shillings--while the fair rental value of the land, less this amount, would be the quit-rent. In this valuation the State would receive the benefit of the increased value given to the land by the continued cultivation of successive generations of tenants, as well as that due to the increase of population and civilisation in the community; and in every case the sum of these two values--the *tenant-right* and the *quit-rent*--would make up the fair rental value of the farm. The annual value of the tenant-right, capitalised on a scale determined by the durability of these landlord's improvements, would be the sum to be paid him by the tenant who wished to hold the land under the State.

We have thus shown how the two values which make up all landed property may be separated with comparative ease and certainty, and with quite sufficient accuracy. While writing these pages the thing is being done in Ireland by the various Land Courts, so that impracticability can no longer be urged against it. It is, as we have shown, the very foundation of a practicable scheme of land-nationalisation, and even were it more difficult than it is, it would be worth any amount of time and trouble to do it.

There remains only now to consider how existing landlords may be compensated with the least permanent injury to the community for the quit-rents which will henceforth be payable to the State.

*How Existing Landowners may be Compensated.*--In order that the State may become possessed of this portion of the value of all landed property in the kingdom, it must compensate existing landowners and their expectant heirs. This may be done either by its purchase for a fixed sum, or by securing them the full revenue they have hitherto derived from it. For many reasons this last is by far the best way. It would involve no great financial operation, no elaborate determination of absolute value, in which the seller would almost certainly obtain more than his due, to the detriment of the public; while it would at the same time serve to mark a great principle, that the soil itself is, and has always been, the property of the State; and that the State merely resumes its own for the public good, but of course without diminishing the *income* which any living person does or may derive from it.

The period for which such annuities are to last is a matter of detail, but it is clearly better that they should depend upon a certain number of *lives* than be for a fixed term of years, because in the former case the recipient does not suffer the inconvenience and sense of loss caused by the cessation of an important part of his income during his lifetime. That they should not be perpetual is also clear; for that would be to acknowledge a perpetual right of individuals to the land and its produce; it would burthen the land with a permanent tax for the future benefit of persons who would have done nothing whatever to earn or deserve it; and it would help to create and keep in existence a class of pensioned idlers, living upon the labours of others, without the smallest exertion of body or mind on their own part. That there should be some such persons in every highly complex society may in our present state of civilisation be a necessity, but that any great extension of this class is a serious evil is so universally admitted that it would be little less than criminal for any legislature actually to provide for their perpetual existence, a constant burthen on the community, a hindrance to true social advancement. This perpetuation of a large body of persons living on the labours of others is one of the necessary evil results of landlordism. It has been hitherto palliated by the supposed duties which they exercise in the "management" of their estates, and their supposed beneficial influence over the districts in which they reside; but the former have been shown to be injurious, and the latter illusory. Their continued existence for a time, as pensioners on the land, can only be defended on the ground that the property of living individuals should be strictly respected by the State as well as by their fellow citizens. Their accustomed enjoyments and reasonable expectations must not be interfered with. But no such rule applies to the unborn. They have neither expectations nor proprietary rights, and they may be justly disregarded when their supposed rights are opposed to the general well-being of the community.

In accordance with these considerations, the principle that seems most consonant with justice is, to continue the annuity successively to any heir or heirs of the landowner who may be living at the passing of the Act, or who may be born at any time before the decease of the said owner. This would ensure to the owner himself and to all persons in whom he could possibly have any personal interest the same net income from the land which they enjoyed before the passing of the Act. It would take away from them only the right of sale, but as this is the very thing which the majority of English landowners themselves take away from their heirs, and the power to do which they account one of their greatest privileges, they can hardly object to the same thing being done by the State for a great public purpose. It must also be remembered that the annuitants will enjoy the State's guarantee of the income, and so be saved from the fluctuations of annual produce to which landed property is now pre-eminently liable; and, further, that that portion of the value of the land which has been created by themselves or their predecessors--the tenant-right--will still be their own absolutely, either to retain themselves, or to sell to the highest bidder, the power of letting only being taken away as manifestly inconsistent with the public welfare.

*Alleged Unfairness of Compensation by Means of Terminable Annuities.*--The objection to this mode of dealing with landowners most frequently put forward is, to suppose two men with, say, £10,000 each, one of whom invests his money in Consols, the other in land. The former, it is said, derives a perpetual income from his property; the latter intends to do the same, but you change it into a terminable annuity and so rob him. The answer to this is, that the "perpetual income" is purely imaginary. No man can enjoy an income longer than for his life, with the power of leaving it to his next heir. Here his actual enjoyment of it ceases absolutely, and all this enjoyment he retains under the new system. His heir may spend, or give away, or lose the £10,000 in Consols, and his wish or expectation that the money will be increased and go to enrich unborn generations of his family is not a thing to be valued or compensated.[3] It is true that the *selling value* of the land, on the probability of the Act passing, or when it has passed, may be diminished; but, whenever such a diminution of value takes place in any other kind of property from a similar cause, confiscation is not admitted and compensation is not allowed. Many manufacturers have been ruined and many workmen reduced to beggary by the direct action of the State in removing protective duties, on the faith of which they had invested their capital or their manual skill, and in no case have they been compensated for the loss, compensation being refused on the ground that the measure was for the benefit of the whole community, and that they participate in that benefit. In such cases both property and income were often destroyed at one blow, while here the income remains untouched, and even acquires increased stability; and the general welfare will assuredly be advanced to a greater extent by occupying ownership of the land than it has been by the extension of Free Trade to articles of luxury, such as silk and jewellery. The general well-being is, of course, the sole justification for any such interference with any form of property, or with the established condition of society. It has been shown by an overwhelming mass of evidence that the great change here proposed is essential to the welfare of the whole community; and it is certain that no great reform was ever effected with so little interference with the property or the means of enjoyment of individuals as will be necessary here.

It may, however, be doubted whether even the *selling value* of land would be at all diminished by the proposed legislation, and for the following reasons. Till quite recently there has always been much competition for farms, and there is always a great demand for small plots of land at anything like an agricultural value. But when this proposed Act has passed, everyone wishing to purchase land will have to purchase the *tenant-right* only, paying the annual *quit-rent*, as above defined, to the State. This will render the purchase of land very easy, and will certainly bring in more purchasers. The demand for land, either as residential estates, or in small lots for farms or gardens, will probably exceed the supply; and thus the price will rise, perhaps, sufficiently to cover the margin between the value of an annuity for, say three lives, and that of one nominally in perpetuity; and, if it does so, then the landlord will suffer no loss whatever.[4]

*How Tenants may become Occupying Owners.*--Having thus shown how the owner would be compensated for the land itself, we proceed to show how the *tenant-right* would be dealt with, and what would be the position of the purchasers of *tenant-right.*

The land having been acquired by the State, every existing tenant, at the date the Act came into operation, would be entitled to continue in the occupation of his house, his farm, or his land of any description, as a holder under the State, on payment of the fixed *quit-rent*; but to constitute him such a State tenant, he must first purchase or otherwise acquire the *tenant-right*. He will be enabled to do this, either by purchasing it from the landlord under a private arrangement, or, if an agreement as to its value cannot be arrived at, then the official valuer or a "land court," similar to those which administer the Irish Land Bill, may be called in to determine the fair value. As soon as this is paid by the tenant, he becomes the absolute owner of the *tenant-right*, and as such the holder of the land under the State in perpetuity, so long as the quit-rent is paid. The *tenant-right*, which thus carries with it the right to the land (subject to the quit-rent), will be as freely saleable as any other property; it will be capable of being sub-divided, and sold, or bequeathed in portions, and thus the holder of land will, for all beneficial uses, be as much the real owner as if it were a freehold.

As Nationalisation is proposed in order (among other things) to prevent any one being ejected from his house or farm against his will, and as some tenants would not be able to provide the sum necessary to *purchase* the tenant-right, provision must be made (either by authorised Loan Societies or by municipal authorities) for the advance of the sum required, to be repaid by a terminable rental extending over periods of, say, from 14 to 40 years.

*Subletting must be Absolutely Prohibited.*--Such a holder under the State would be absolutely free to use his land as he pleased, just as much as a freeholder is now, because he would be the owner of everything but the land itself, and if he chose to deteriorate his property, that would injure no one but himself. As a rule, he would immensely improve it, because it would be his own. There must, however, be one restriction on his use of the land, which is, that he must not*sublet* it. This is absolutely essential to secure the full benefits of Nationalisation, because, once admit subletting, and landlordism would again rise under another name, and the subtenants would be subject to all the injurious influences and conditions the abolition of which is the very *raison d'être* of the reform. The State, as owner of the land, *can* prohibit subletting, and the importance of doing so is admitted by all who have studied the subject. It is well known that in Ireland the middlemen were often the hardest landlords, while none rack-rent their tenants more than those who have purchased land for the purpose of deriving an income from it. Even where peasant proprietorship largely prevails, its benefits are often neutralised by the more successful owners purchasing farms to let to tenants, and it is the universal testimony that evil results ensue. Mr. Thornton states that:-- "Peasants who let their land to be cultivated by others are, of all landlords, the most griping. Anything but satisfactory is the condition of the actually cultivating class, wherever, on the one hand, landed property is minutely subdivided, and, on the other hand, is not occupied by its owners. Such is the case throughout Flanders generally, and quite saddening are some of the details given by M. de Laveleye with respect to Flemish tenant-farmers." It is, therefore, quite clear that subletting must be prevented and personal occupation be insisted on, and this is a sufficient answer to those who advocate assisting tenants to purchase the *freehold* of their farms, instead of being holders under the State. For wherever, in thickly populated countries, there are small freeholders, they are dying out, owing to the demand for land as an investment. This has been the case, not in England only, but, as we have shown, in many parts of Europe and in America; and it is probable that any such system of purchase would, as the Edinburgh Reviewer already quoted maintains, have to be all done over again after a few generations, while in the meantime it would hardly touch the more important evils which have been shown to be inherent in landlordism.[5]

*Evils of Subletting in Towns.*--Still greater evils arise from subletting in the vicinity of towns, a good illustration of which is furnished by the following statement of the *Daily News* special commissioner as to the present condition of the town of Killarney. He says:--"The great estates of the Lord Chamberlain have curiously enough been equally damaged by the care and carelessness of his ancestors. His great-grandfather was disgusted at the condition of the town of Killarney, and offered any tenant who would build a decent house with a slate roof a perpetual lease of the land it stood upon and the adjoining garden for the nominal rent of four shillings and fourpence per annum, without other important conditions. The result has been that Killarney can boast of as filthy lanes as any in London or Liverpool. The ordinary process, the same as that which formed the hideous slums between Drury-lane and Great Wild-street, now happily demolished, has gone on in Killarney. Tenants under no restrictions gradually converted their gardens into lanes of hovels, and made money thereby, and the result is a concentration in Killarney of filth which would be better distributed on the side of a mountain, and which is under the nose of a landlord who is powerless to apply a remedy."

*Mortgaging should be Strictly Limited.*--Next in importance to the evil of subletting is that of heavy mortgages on the land of the cultivator. Many writers point out this evil, but none suggest any remedy. In Ireland the "Gombeen" men, or usurers, were the curse of the country, while in parts of Austria the small landowners are so deeply indebted to their mortgage creditors that a party has been formed who advocate the annulment of all mortgages on small estates. The State being owner of the land, and the *tenant-right* being its security for the quit-rent, it may properly regulate the proportionate amount to which mortgages may be permitted on landed property, and may only allow them on condition that they are to be extinguished by annual repayments within a definite period, and it might also very properly refuse to allow the same landowner to mortgage his land more than once, on the ground that he who cannot farm except under a perpetual mortgage should either reduce the amount of his land or give way to those who have sufficient capital.

*Whether any Limits should be Placed to the Quantity of Land Personally Occupied.*--Before leaving this part of our subject there is one question that must be clearly answered. What limit, if any, should be placed on the quantity of land one person might hold under the State? The Land and Labour League have proposed "that the lands of the country be divided into cultivable quantities, according to quality, of from two to twenty-five acres," and they further wish all parks and similar large areas of land held for pleasure to be cut up into farms for cultivation. Mr. Fowler, in the "Cobden Club Essays," seems to think that some such scheme of division is an essential part of all systems of nationalisation, and he thus argues against it:--"But forced sub-division is as objectionable as forced accumulation. The one and the other alike interfere with the natural distribution of the land among the people, and ought, therefore, to be alike opposed by those who advocate the principles of Richard Cobden. We have no right to decide that a holding of one size as such is better in itself than another. It is our place to leave people to find out for themselves what suits them best, provided always that we leave them really free."

All this is perfectly true, and it is, therefore, proposed to place no restriction whatever on the quantity of land one man may hold for personal occupation. Some men might wish to farm a thousand acres or more, while others would prefer only ten or twenty. And as for parks, woods, and pleasure grounds, there is not the slightest reason, at present, for interfering with these. When the land is really free to all to be held and cultivated without restriction, there will be ample scope for increased production without interfering with these charming oases of sylvan scenery in the midst of often unpicturesque cultivated fields. But it may be said:--"Would you allow a duke or a millionaire to continue to hold ten or a dozen parks and houses in as many counties, as some of them do now?" Even here I see no need for restrictive legislation so long as the duke retained them for his personal occupation. But, as he could not sublet them, and as the estates attached to each of them would be no longer his, what possible reason could he have for retaining them? Now, they are each the centre and visible indication of an *estate*, and it is a point of honour and dignity to retain them. When the estate was gone there would be no reason whatever for keeping the demesne and house, except in those cases where it was a favourite dwelling. I very much doubt whether, under the conditions here proposed, any proprietor in the kingdom would care about keeping up more than two country houses, and there is certainly no possible reason why he should not do this if he pleases.

It is a strange thing, however, that such men as Mr. Fowler

do not see that under mere free trade in land there could be no such freedom of cultivation as he strongly urges us to allow. The whole mass of evidence adduced in this volume shows a constantly increasing monopoly of land by the rich as the wealth of the country has increased, accompanied by a constantly increasing limitation of freedom in the occupation and enjoyment of land. It is useless "leaving people to *find out* what *suits* them best," when land monopoly absolutely prevents them from *obtaining* what suits them best.

*Supposed Objections to Land Nationalisation.*--Before proceeding to show how the labourers and the public in general are to be directly benefited, it may be well to reply to a few of the chief objections which have been made to all previous schemes for nationalising the land, and to show that none of them are in any degree applicable to that here advocated. We will begin with Mr. Fowler, who, in the work already quoted, refers to schemes of this kind as being usually vague, adding:--"But the general thought of the proposers is clear enough, viz., that the management of land can safely be entrusted to a department of State, and that thus the interests of the people, as such, in the land can be extended, with the best results to the nation." He then goes on to argue that the State could not "manage" land advantageously, any more than Corporations, which notoriously manage it very badly. "We know," he says, "what can be done by private ownership where the law leaves it unfettered, but the experience we have of State management is not encouraging. . . . In State management there is the minimum of private interest with the danger of a maximum of jobbery."

All this is perfectly true if the State were to acquire the *whole* of a landed estate (including the tenant-right), and were to let it out and manage it as an existing landlord does; but it is totally untrue as regards the present scheme, in which no "management" whatever is required or is possible, any more than the State "manages" house property because it collects a land-tax from each householder.

Again, Mr. Arthur Arnold, in his "Free Trade in Land," says:--"The main object for which private property in land is sanctioned by the State, with the concurrence of all rational people, is the belief that such ownership is most successful in promoting production. Production is at present very much neglected, but that is because private ownership is baulked by settlement, and by the "ungodly jumble" of our legal processes. Production would undoubtedly be much greater if private property in land were more firmly and fully established. I cannot think it possible that a Government could promote production with anything like the power which may be obtained from private ownership."

Here again we have the idea of "management," in "Government promoting production." But on our system Government would do nothing but leave production absolutely free under a system of universal "occupying ownership," which has been clearly demonstrated to be the form of ownership which most stimulates "production." Mr. G. Shaw Lefevre, M.P., although an advanced land-reformer, and fully aware of the advantages of any form of occupying ownership, is yet staggered by the practical difficulties in the way of its realisation. At a meeting of the Statistical Society in November, 1880, he said, after referring to the differences between Ireland and England:--"In this country, where the farms were larger, it would require a very large amount to be advanced by the State to enable a tenant to become the owner of his holding, and, apart from all other considerations, he believed the financial difficulties would be insurmountable. But he hoped that with greater freedom in the sale and transfer of land, there would be many instances in England in which ownership would be annexed to the cultivation of land, and the more this condition of things spread, the greater would be the inducements to good agriculture."

By the scheme here developed, however, no advance whatever need be made by the State, while ownership annexed to the cultivation of the land, which Mr. Shaw Lefevre declares to be so beneficial, would become universal.

The Hon. George C. Brodrick, in his excellent work on "English Land and English Landlords," remarks:--"No doubt, it is a perfectly intelligible proposition that all the land in the Kingdom ought to be 'nationalised' and placed under public management, because individual owners cannot be trusted with full dominion over that part of the earth's surface by which and upon which all the natives of England must live, unless they choose to emigrate. It is evident that, apart from all other objections, this doctrine is the very negation of the belief in peasant-proprietorship and 'the magic of property,' being, in fact, an essentially urban sentiment, and inevitably destructive to all independence of rural life. Nor can it be said that our experience of corporate administration, in the case of lands held by collegiate, ecclesiastical, and municipal bodies, as well as by trustees of charities, is such as to recommend the substitution of public for private ownership on a much grander scale." Here we have exactly the same idea of the necessity for "management" by the State as land-owner, and a complete misconception of the real nature of "nationalisation" as here developed.

Even Mr. J. Boyd Kinnear, who, in his valuable work, "Principles of Property in Land," has written so strongly on the evils of landlordism and the benefits of occupying ownership, sees the same supposed difficulties in nationalisation. He asks:--"But how is the State to perform the functions of landlord?" and he proceeds to show, at great length and with irresistible logic, the evils of any interference of the State in the cultivation or use of land. But this is all quite beside the question if the State owns the *land* only, not the improvements on the land, or "tenant-right." The late John Stuart Mill also was only withheld from proposing nationalisation of the land by the same difficulty. In his opening address to the Land Tenure Reform Association he said, speaking of nationalisation:--"I do not know that it may not be reserved for us in the future; but at present I decidedly do not think it expedient. I have so poor an opinion of State management, or municipal management either, that I am afraid many years would elapse before the revenue realised for the State would be sufficient to pay the indemnity which would be justly claimed by the dispossessed proprietors."

This is really the sole objection of the slightest importance that has been urged by most writers of eminence who have made a special study of the subject, and I have sought in vain for any more serious one. It follows that no valid objection has been yet urged which applies to the system of nationalisation here proposed.

*How Nationalisation will Affect Towns.*--However disastrous landlordism has been in the agricultural districts, its evils have been still more severely felt in towns and cities. Here the landlord has been complete master of the situation, and has been able to make his own terms, which the people have been bound to accept. These terms have amounted to the systematic confiscation of the property of others by the custom of building-leases and renewals; and, together with the temptation of large profits to be made by speculation in building sites, have led to cheap and bad building, and frightful overcrowding of the poorer classes in courts, alleys, and cellars. These unsanitary conditions necessarily produce persistent disease as well as many social evils, while they greatly intensify if they do not originate most of the severe epidemics which still periodically attack us. These evils continue in full force to this very day, and under the present system of land-monopoly are quite incurable. As an example of confiscation--strictly legal, but none the less real--I give the following letter, which appeared in the *Echo* of October last year:--

"TO THE EDITOR OF THE ECHO.

"SIR,--Through the medium of your valuable columns allow me space to explain my grievance. Two years ago I purchased a house on the Portman Estate (eighteen years' lease) at £10 10s. per annum. I spent more than £300 to put it into tenantable repair, thinking that I should get a renewal at a fair ground-rent. I applied, and the agent came to inspect the premises, and a few days after sent me the terms as follows:--Lease for 34 years--ground-rent to be £80 instead of £10; fine £1,000 renewal, to be paid from the day of application, or 5 per cent. interest on the £1,000 from that date, which would be principal and interest for eight years, £1,400; improvements to be done as stated in agreement, amounting to about £500, before a new lease is granted; all Viscount Portman's solicitor's fees to be paid by me. For the simple drawing of this agreement I paid £15. The last year of the 34 years' lease the house to be re-decorated throughout; the property to be insured by me in the Portman Fire Office. Upon remonstrating at the exorbitant terms, I received a letter from the agent that I could accept them or not, but in the event of my not accepting I should not have any further opportunity of applying.

"Now, Sir, what right can the landlord have to take away my house? He has never spent 1d. towards its improvement. Of course the ground has increased in value, but that is through the tradespeople, and not through the landlord. The ground-rent is increased eight times; then what right has the landlord to demand £1,400 for a house that I bought, and what right has he to dictate improvements that I have to pay for, so that after the expiration of a few years he may get larger premises, and another larger premium, without him spending a fraction, not even to pay the solicitor for getting the money? It seems incredible that people endure such extortion without seeking redress. I trust that others who are suffering the same wrong will come forward, so that effective action may be taken to alter the law, which beggars tradespeople to enrich the aristocracy.

"Baker Street, Oct. 26. "ENGLISHWOMAN."

This is a typical case--though probably an extreme one--and it well shows how helpless the public are, and how, under the threat of eviction, they can be robbed by the form of free contract and under the protection of the law. We next give one example, equally typical but far more common, of the *kind* of dwelling landlordism provides for the poor.

It is from a coroner's inquest on the body of a child which was killed simply by the foul air of the dwelling, as reported in the *Daily News*, of November 16th, 1881:-- "Last evening Mr. Samuel F. Langham, deputy coroner for Westminster, held an inquest at St. Martin's Vestry Hall, Strand, touching the death of William Howard, aged 11 months, lately living with his parents at No. 6, Hanover-court, Long-acre, who died on Friday, it was alleged from the unhealthy and unsanitary condition of the house.--Mrs. Emily Howard, wife of a labourer, and mother of the deceased, said that her child had been sickly from its birth. At about seven o'clock last Friday deceased was taken with a fit, and it rallied until ten o'clock, when it had another, and died in half an hour. She believed her child had died from the stench that came from the watercloset and yard, which were abominably unhealthy. She had occupied the first floor back for 18 months. She had not made any complaint to the landlord until after the death of the deceased. The cistern was right underneath the window and over the dusthole.--William Howard, the father, said that his window was just over the watercloset, and the stench was sometimes suffocating. *He did not give notice because it was difficult to get another cheap place to live in.*--Mr. Robert William Dunn, surgeon, 13, Surrey-street, Strand, deposed to having attended at the house and finding the child dead. Several people in the house complained of the unhealthy state of the place, one man saying he had never been well since he had lived in the house. The place smelt of sewage. It made him sick when he entered. The deceased died from convulsions.--The Foreman of the jury: I myself am suffering from bad drainage in this neighbourhood, and several people in my house are suffering from the same cause, and the chances are that someone will become seriously ill.--The Doctor: I should not be surprised if typhoid fever were to break out in the house, especially seeing the position of the cistern and the watercloset."

In another inquest reported in the same day's paper in another part of London, the Divisional Surgeon of Police said--"that the parents and two children slept in one bed; that the room was very unhealthy and quite unfit for human habitation." The coroner "had no doubt that, if the wretched, poverty-stricken people could go to clean and decent houses for a little money, such scandals as the Marylebone fever dens would cease to exist. The poor were compelled to herd and crowd and shift for themselves as best they could, and the fever and disease and death went on year by year, notwithstanding the march of science and medical sanitation."

Now, these are the direct results of private property in land under the conditions which prevail in this country. The consolidation of farms, and the destruction of cottages, so much favoured by great landlords and their agents, have driven the labourers from the country into the towns; and land-monopoly in its necessary action brings about the condition of their dwellings above indicated. That the labourers are thus forced to the towns has been shown in my earlier chapters. The fact is clearly proved by the returns of the last census, and public writers have been deploring it, without, apparently, seeing its cause and its only cure; and if further evidence is wanted of the serious character of this movement and its danger to the country, it is to be found in Mr. John Bright's speech at Rochdale, on his 70th birthday. He says:--"There is another question which workmen everywhere should learn and bear in mind--that the labour in the agricultural districts was becoming more and more costly, whilst it was worse in quality, because the younger people, finding that they had no tie to the soil, *that they can never become anything but labourers at very low wages*, are leaving the rural parishes in which they have been born. They are emigrating *to the great towns in the neighbourhood*, and not a few of them are emigrating to the countries across the ocean. The result is that our landed system, with its great estates and farms, *cuts off the labourer almost entirely from the possibility of becoming either a tenant or an owner of the land*,

and as he has no object in remaining there, he goes away. The Education Act now being put in force throughout the rural districts will add greatly to this effect. I had a letter not long ago from a clergyman who had lived many years in the south, and he told me he had noticed the result continually, and he thought it was one which must be seen much more in the future than in the past, because as all young people got some sort of education in the school, although not a thorough education, they were so far educated that they could read the newspaper and see what was being done in other parts of the country and in other countries; and they, looking *with a hopeless feeling at their position*, emigrate therefore to the large towns, in the hope of bettering their condition, or they emigrate to foreign countries, and the result is that only the poorest labour is left behind, whilst it also becomes *costlier* and becomes more and more an increasing burden upon the farmer."

I have called attention, by italics, to a few passages in this weighty paragraph, because they show that up to this very day there is no tendency whatever to better the condition of the rural labourers; while they fully support my contention that the overcrowding of towns, with its inevitable accompaniments of misery, vice, and disease, is the direct product of "our landed system."

The cure of the evils of building-lease confiscation and some of those of overcrowding will probably be effected earlier than complete nationalisation; for already there is a movement on foot for obtaining "tenant-right" for London, and, certainly, the case is exactly analogous to that of the Irish tenant-farmer who has made all the improvements on the land. If justice requires that he should be protected from having his property confiscated, the same rule applies still more strongly in cases where the property on the land bears so large a proportion to the value of the land as it does in the case of the leasehold houses of London and other great cities. The true and only effectual cure for all these iniquities and horrors is, however, to draw back the population from the towns to the country by the natural and healthy process of offering that greatest of all attractions--a free choice to every one of cheap land; and how this is to be done will be shown immediately. Till that takes place some arrangement will have to be made by which the occupiers of town houses may become their owners. With the better class of houses this will follow exactly the same lines as the transfer of the land. The owner of the freehold or of the improved ground-rent will be compensated by a State annuity, while the house itself will be purchased by the tenant at a fair valuation, and, if desired, by means of a terminable rental. As regards the poorer class of houses and those large buildings let out as offices or in flats, either the municipality or some other authorised associations might purchase them, and let them out to such tenants as do not require entire houses or permanent dwellings.

We now pass on to the mode by which labourers and the public might acquire land.

*Free-selection of Residential Plots by Labourers and others.*--The large mass of evidence collected in this volume conclusively shows that innumerable evils arise owing to the impossibility, under the present system, of acquiring land in small plots at agricultural prices. Such an unnatural state of things has been brought about by land monopoly, and so complete is the divorce of the great body of Englishmen from any right of ownership in their native soil, that, when nationalisation permits it, special arrangements must be made to allow of a speedy return to a more healthy condition.

There is no one privilege so beneficial to the members of a community as to have an ample space of land on which to live. Surround the poorest cottage with a spacious vegetable garden, with fruit and shade trees, with room for keeping pigs and poultry, and for storing the house-refuse and manure at some distance from the dwelling, and give the occupier a permanent tenure at a low quit-rent, and the result is absolutely invariable. Such conditions, or anything approaching to them, always produce untiring industry and thrift, always remove the occupiers above poverty and pauperism, always produce health and contentment, always diminish, if they do not abolish, drunkenness and crime.

Under such conditions the poorest cot would soon be improved and made into a comfortable dwelling; the surplus fruit, vegetables, eggs, bacon, and other produce would benefit all the dwellers in the neighbouring towns, while the increased well-being of the rural population would react on all other occupations and revivify our home trade.

Equally important is it to every tradesman to be able to have a country house (if he can afford one) in which to bring up a healthy family, and this blessing a free choice of land at its fair agricultural value would give to thousands to whom it is now an unattainable dream. When the land has been acquired by the nation, every Englishman may claim an equal right to possess a portion of it for personal occupation at its fair value, subject only to the equal rights of others, and to some amount of restriction as to quantity and situation in order not to interfere unnecessarily with agriculture or to inconvenience those already in possession.

The mode in which this great boon may be obtained is simple. Every Englishman should be allowed, *once in his life*, to select a plot of land for his personal occupation. His right of choice will, of course, be limited to agricultural or waste land; it will also be limited to land bordered by public roads affording access to it; it will further be limited to a quantity of not less than one acre or more than five acres, and will cease on any estate from which a fixed proportion, say ten per cent. has been taken during the life of the holder, while it should not apply to very small holdings; and finally, it will be limited by proximity to the dwelling of the occupier of the land, so as to subject him to no unnecessary annoyance. These limitations would be determined in each case by a local Court of the same character as the Sub-Commissions under the Irish Land Act, who would visit the ground, hear the statements of both parties, and finally mark out the lot granted. The Court would also determine the proportion of the quit-rent to be taken over by the new occupier, and the amount to be paid the farmer for his tenant-right of the plot in question.

The limit of quantity has been fixed by the consideration that it is not for the public benefit that a house shall occupy less than one acre of land. Any labourer may easily cultivate this quantity in his spare hours with the assistance of his family, or he may stock it with fruit trees and devote it to poultry runs; while it would afford sufficient space for keeping all disagreeable smells some distance from the house or road, thus avoiding any unhealthiness or public nuisance. The higher limit of five acres is intended for those who want land enough to keep a horse or cow, which thousands would do could they have land with their house at a moderate price; and it need hardly be said how much this would add to the health and enjoyment of a country life. Many have recognised the advantages of such a right of purchase of land, but under no system but Nationalisation is it possible to realise it. Dr. Macdonald in a letter to the *Echo* newspaper well says:--

"There must be freedom of land and its equitable distribution. It is simply scandalous that a poor man cannot get an acre of land for his cottage and garden, while the rich have tens of thousands of acres for parks and sporting grounds. Every person has a natural right to a permanent home in his native land, and how can we expect patriotism if this cannot be obtained? Moreover, the acquisition of a bit of land is the only thing that will raise a man from serfdom to comparative independence. . . . A man with an acre of land of his own is virtually independent, as he has always something to fall back upon when work fails, and it encourages in him a spirit of enterprise and thrift which may enable him to acquire five acres or more in time. He could build himself a comfortable cottage, instead of living in the wretched hovels we see in most of our villages. For an industrious man to grow food for himself and his family on his own land is the straight road to prosperity and happiness; and there is no occupation so healthful and natural, and none so calculated to bring out the best qualities of man's nature as husbandry. Moreover, the prosperity of agriculture very greatly depends on the cultivator having a permanent holding on the land he cultivates. Excessive rents and evictions insure a ruined people and a ruined soil." But he suggests no method of bringing this about except by the purchase of land from existing landowners, and selling it again to labourers--of course, at present monopoly and speculative prices.[6]

*Objections to the Right of Free-selection.*--The only objection that has been made, or that perhaps can be made, to the exercise of this right of selection and purchase of a plot of land, is, that it will injuriously cut up farms and interfere with farming, and that the farmers will violently oppose it. But with the careful restrictions and limitations above indicated, it is absurd to place the small injury or inconvenience it might be to a few farmers against the vast benefit to the acquirers of the land and to the whole community. Do farmers now refuse to take farms when the landlord reserves the right of taking portions to let for building? Are they seriously injured when a railroad or other public work takes some of their land? Yet in both these cases the injury is far greater than would ever be the case under free-selection. For there is in the former cases no limitation to quantity, shape, or position. A man's fields may be cut across diagonally by a railroad, or his best piece of pasture may be taken away to build on, and the farmers have never cried out against this cutting up of their lands, probably because they know it would be useless. It is almost certain that the quantity of land taken for occupation would in most districts be not very large, and might not in many years equal the quantity taken for railroads and the waste-heaps of mines and factories. In this case, too, the farmers would directly benefit by the operation. It would secure them a body of thrifty and industrious labourers, attached to the soil, and therefore always at hand to labour when wanted; while, having resources of their own, they would never require to be set to unprofitable work merely to keep them on, nor would they swell the poor rates by being periodically in the receipt of parish relief. It would also secure a comparatively wealthy rural population, which would aid in keeping the labourers employed at odd jobs when farming work was slack, and would furnish a market for some of the farmers' produce or stock. It must also be remembered that for all land taken from his farm for this purpose the farmer would be fairly and fully compensated, while his objections and wishes would be so far respected as to keep away all intrusion which could be any real injury or annoyance to him. He would, therefore, have no solid grounds for objection to a measure calculated to produce such widely beneficial results, and would probably have the good sense to see that personal predilections must, in this case, as in every other, give way to the public benefit.[7]

*Why Free-selection should be restricted to Once in a Man's Life.*--It may, perhaps, be said, if this free-selection is so beneficial to the community, why restrict it to *once* in a man's life? When he wants to settle in another part of the country why should he not select again? The reason of this restriction is, however, obvious. It is granted once, because, in many districts, all the land being already occupied, the landless Englishman has no means of acquiring land to live upon in the quantities and situations most advantageous to him. He would have to bribe the actual holders with a high price, and even then would often be refused. It is to give him the opportunity of living where he pleases, when he is in a position to require a permanent *home*, but it is not intended to afford the means of speculation, or of making a profit by selecting choice spots, building houses on them, and then selling them. This restriction to one choice will make men very careful not to choose too early, and thus not to throw away their privilege; while, as there will always be a certain number of persons in every part of the country who are obliged by circumstances to sell their lots, these, in addition to the houses always in the market, will enable those who require temporary houses as well as those who have been obliged to part with their selected lots, to find houses more or less suitable to them with greater ease than at present. These considerations show that there will be no great rush for lots, as some critics of the scheme have hastily imagined, but that, except near towns, farmers would be comparatively little troubled by the free-selectors. It must also be remembered that it is often the most worthless parts of an estate that are most desired for residential purposes--bits of healthy upland, or woody spots with a fine view, while the rich, open arable fields, the low meadows, or the open pastures would be comparatively neglected.

*Free-selection would Check the Growth of Towns, and Add to the Beauty and Enjoyability of Rural Districts.*--There can be no doubt whatever that the power of obtaining land where and when required would lead to a steady flow of population from the towns to the country. Villages in all the more picturesque parts of the country which, at the will of great landowners, have remained for generations stationary, would steadily increase in population; but, as building speculation would be almost impossible, they would grow in the most picturesque manner by the addition here and there of single houses, of every size and cost, but never crowded together, so that the rural beauty of the district would not be marred. We should never see then (as we may often see now) noble old trees ruthlessly cut down, because they interfere with building on the narrow strips into which the land-speculator cuts up his lots, while no further additions would be made to those unsightly rows of hideous cottages which the farmer, the manufacturer, or the local speculative builder now provides for the labouring population.

The quantity of land, even in the smallest lots, would enable the occupier to dispose of all the house sewage, in the only natural and economical manner, by applying it to the fertilisation of his own ground; and this application should even be made compulsory, so that no further pollution of streams and no more gigantic drainage works would be necessary. It may, perhaps, be said that the owner of an acre lot would cut it up into three or four smaller lots to dispose of at a profit; but it may safely be predicted that this would not be done. The working man is too anxious to obtain land, and is too keenly alive to the inestimable benefits it confers upon him, to take a smaller quantity than his acre when the amount to be paid for that acre would be merely its agricultural value. No compulsory enactment against the subdivision of lots would be needed, because their subdivision would rarely or never be profitable (*see Appendix*).

*How Commons may be Preserved and Utilised.*--Some reference has been made in the fifth chapter to the way in which so many of our commons have been enclosed, for the sole aggrandisement of landlords and to the injury of all other residents and of the whole community. In some parts of the country, however, extensive commons still remain unenclosed, but usually where there is a very scanty rural population to benefit by them. Such is the case on the borders of Surrey, Sussex, and Hampshire, and there are enormous tracts in Wales, Ireland, and Scotland which, though claimed as private property, have never been enclosed, but remain in an absolute state of nature. On all such lands there can be no claim for *tenant-right*, and they would therefore become the property of the State on payment of annuities, in the one case to the Lords of the Manor, in the other to the present owners, of an amount equal to the average annual proceeds.

When these commons are not very extensive they would, of course, be preserved as common pasture land for the surrounding occupiers and cottagers, who might also have the customary rights of cutting fern or gorse, digging sand, gravel, or peat, under proper supervision of some local authority. All the more extensive of these wastes, however, would afford the opportunity for cultivation by labourers or small farmers, who might have choice of sites, on areas marked out as open to selection, on payment of a low quit-rent, which might be higher than the value of the land as unenclosed pasture, but much lower than that of the surrounding enclosed fields. A limit should be placed to the quantity allowed to be taken by one person, and this need not be high, because the holder would have extensive rights of pasturage over the whole common in addition. Ten acres might be a proper *first* limit, but when this quantity was brought into good cultivation and a house built, another ten acres might be granted on the same terms. In this way the more fertile and sheltered portions of all the great commons, heaths, and mountain wastes of the country might be gradually covered with small farms and cheerful homesteads, while still retaining extensive tracts of unenclosed land as common pasture, and as recreation ground and health-resorts for our ever-growing population. The numerous cases of the reclamation of the worst mountain land in Ireland by tenants with only a temporary occupancy afford us some idea of the beneficial results to our pauperised and landless population of the right to improve and cultivate waste land for their own exclusive benefit, with no fear of the interference of lords of the land or of the manor.

*How Minerals should be Worked under State Ownership.*--In the fifth chapter I have briefly alluded to the evil consequences to the public at large of allowing our mineral wealth to be appropriated by individuals, and our country permanently deteriorated and impoverished for their benefit. I have not, however, yet referred to the unfair manner in which landlords often absorb *all* the profits of mines, leaving nothing whatever to those who have supplied the large capital required to work them. Minerals are usually worked by companies, on short leases, and the landowner is compensated by payment of a royalty on all the produce, not by a share of the profits. This was reasonable in the early days of mining, when no expensive machinery was required, and small parties of working miners, or "adventurers," often with little or no capital, extracted rich ores from near the surface. Then the produce was nearly all profit, and a royalty of one-tenth to one-twelfth of the actual value of the ore extracted was not found to be oppressive. Now the case is very different. Mineral lodes are worked at an enormous depth, and poor ores, neglected by the old miners, are extracted, and the metal obtained from them by complex and expensive operations. Enormous pumping and lifting engines are required, tramroads have to be made, workshops to be built, and coal brought up to the mines at heavy cost. It is not uncommon for the mere working expenses of a mine to be a thousand or fifteen hundred pounds a month, and it is only after ore enough has been extracted to pay this amount that any profits are obtained to pay interest on the capital expended. It thus often happens that for years a mining company never obtains sufficient to pay a single penny of dividend, notwithstanding all possible skill and economy in working the mine. The shareholders lose their whole capital; but not only does the landlord lose nothing, but he receives a large income the whole time from this mine which is really proved to be worthless. The chances of *great* profits in mining cause numbers of such mines to be opened and worked every year, and from all these the landlord alone gets a profit, while everyone else loses. It is a partnership in which one partner supplies a *chance* of something valuable, the other partner a large capital to be spent in proving whether that something valuable exists or not. Yet the partner who gives only the *chance*, and does not risk a penny, secures a *certain* gain, even when his *chance* is proved to be valueless, while the other partners, who advance all the money, risk losing it all, or, if they succeed, share all the gain with the partner who risks nothing.

Under the present system of mining the only equitable

mode of arranging the partnership between owner of the soil and those who find the capital to work a mine would be, that the former should receive a share of the *profits*--not of the *produce*; that is, that the land to be explored should be estimated at a certain portion of the total capital, and the landowner should receive his dividends on that nominal capital *pro rata* with the other shareholders. The present system is simple confiscation, analogous to that of leasehold houses, but even more cruel, since, in many cases, the profit realised would give a fair interest on the capital expended were it not all absorbed in the prior claim of the landlord's "royalty."

When the State owns the land, the more equitable system, of a small fixed quit-rent for the land occupied and a fixed proportion of the profits realised, would be adopted; and it would greatly benefit the mineral industry of the country by rendering the working of many poor ores profitable. In the case of coal and iron, so essential to the well-being of a nation, and, owing to their bulk and weight, most disadvantageous to import from other countries, the State might properly place a heavy duty on their export, which would have the effect of limiting the trade in them to those countries in which they do not exist, while it would stimulate the development of the mineral resources of countries which do possess them but have hitherto depended upon getting them from us at very cheap rates.

As it would be almost impossible to estimate the average value of the produce of minerals in any plot of land, some other mode would have to be adopted in compensating landlords for the minerals they have so unfortunately been allowed to claim possession of. The fair way would probably be for Government to fix the percentage of the whole *profits* which should in future be paid for each class of mines by the workers of mineral property, and to allow each landowner to receive this percentage from the companies or private persons who work the mines during his own life only. Afterwards the same percentage would be paid to the State, which would, however, repay half the amount to the next heir for his life. All new mines opened after the Act came into operation would, of course, wholly belong to the State. Considering the very exceptional character of the mineral wealth of a country, and the enormous fortunes landowners have derived from it without spending or risking a penny, this proposal is, perhaps, hardly fair to the public, and, when land nationalisation is effected, may require to be somewhat modified.

*Application of the Same General Principle to All Other Charges on the Land.*--The principle here developed, by which the land itself becomes the property of the State on payment to the actual owners of an annuity for themselves and their living heirs, is applicable to all kinds of landed property and to all charges whatever upon the land. Tithes, for example, would in this way be extinguished so far as they belong to lay impropriators, and the payments by the future tenants would form part of the State quit-rent. Tithes payable to the clergy would be dealt with in the same way, but the annuities for which they were commuted would, of course, be continued so long as the endowment of the Church continues, and whenever that ceases the revenues would merge into those of the State. In like manner every kind of ground-rent, whether original or improved, whether for terms of years or in reversion, would each be valued on actuarial principles, and commuted into annuities of the same nature and the same duration as those paid to owners of the fee-simple of land. The quit-rent payable by the holder of the land in question would be divided among the several holders of distinct interests in the land in proportions determined by official actuaries, and each would receive the corresponding annuity.

*Progressive Reduction of Taxation; Abolition of Customs and Excise.*--Among the advantages resulting from this scheme of land nationalisation, not the least important would be, the great alleviation of public burdens and reduction of public expenditure. In a very few years after it came into operation some properties would fall to the State, owing to the successive deaths of the two or three generations of heirs. This might happen in some few instances within a year or two, and a regular stream of such cases would certainly begin in ten or twenty years, and would thenceforth increase, till in about a century the whole of the *quit-rents* would be payable to the State. This would enable the Government to take off one by one all the more oppressive taxes, and to gradually abolish altogether the Customs and Excise duties. The effect of this would be to release from unproductive labour the whole body of officials in these departments, whose salaries and office expenses amounted in 1880 to £2,784,316; and if we add to this a proportion of the cost of public buildings, we shall have a saving of £3,000,000 annually, besides a large capital sum derived from the sale of all the offices and warehouses connected with these departments and an income from the quit-rents of the land they occupied. As the net receipts from these two sources of revenues are about £45,000,000, while the quit-rents derived from the whole land of the country will certainly be more than £100,000,000, the same generation which sees nationalisation established will derive the benefit of much of the reduction, while many persons now living may see these injurious taxes wholly abolished. Thereafter there will be a possibility of rapidly extinguishing our huge national debt, which, though capitalists and speculators may find it a convenience, is at once a clog upon industry and a danger to the State.

The benefit to the trade and commerce of the country produced by the abolition of all customs and excise duties cannot be overrated. Mr. Bright has long advocated a "free breakfast table" as the extreme reform in this direction he can even hope for; but nationalisation would afford us the power to obtain absolute freedom in our whole internal trade; and the more important part of this is, perhaps, not the release from money payments, but the freedom from all those vexatious interferences and restrictions which are the greatest clog on the wheels of industry.

These advantages are so enormous, so totally beyond what any other reform can give or promise, that even if they stood alone they would afford a justification for Land Nationalisation. Yet they are really mere incidental effects of the scheme, which rests its claim to support, primarily, on the improvement it would effect in the condition of labourers and producers of all kinds, an improvement which would be social and moral as well as merely physical, and would raise the status and add to the well-being of the whole community.

*Summary of the Advantages of Nationalisation.*--Having now completed our necessarily imperfect survey of this great question, let us endeavour to summarise, in the form of a series of brief propositions, the conclusions we have arrived at, and which, it is maintained, have been demonstrated by an overwhelming body of evidence.

It has been shown that *unrestricted private property in land is inherently wrong, and leads to serious and widespread evils*--for the following reasons:--

BECAUSE--It gives to the class of landowners despotic power over the freedom, the property, the happiness, and even over the lives of their fellow citizens who are not landowners. The wholesale evictions in the Highlands of Scotland and in Ireland, where houses and whole villages have been destroyed and the human inhabitants have been replaced by cattle or deer, often for no crime or fault of theirs, but simply to carry into effect the will of the landlord, are the most glaring examples of the truth of this proposition. Even in England similar cases occur, though less frequently; but the tenant is often coerced in his political rights, is interfered with in the free exercise of his religion, and is generally subject to the will of his landlord in many other ways. In all these cases the State is avowedly powerless to protect the tenants, who are nevertheless told that they are free citizens of a free country, that the Englishman's house is his castle, and that there is no wrong without a legal remedy.

BECAUSE--by possession of the land, which is absolutely essential to all productive labour, and even to life itself, it enables the landowners to absorb all the surplus profits of both labour and capital, keeping down the wages of unskilled labour (which regulates that of labour generally) to the lowest point at which life can be supported, the result being, that large masses of the working people are condemned to exist under unnatural and degrading conditions of poverty, and that pauperism is made chronic among us notwithstanding our ever-increasing wealth. For the same reason it keeps down the rate of interest, enabling large capitalists alone to thrive, while small capitalists can hardly live. In all civilised countries, and at various periods of history, the same phenomena have been observed--where land is cheap, wages and interest are comparatively high; where land is dear, both are comparatively low.

BECAUSE--the divided and often conflicting interests it creates in the soil check permanent improvement, limit the variety of crops and of agricultural industry, and seriously diminish production. This evil is admitted to be great even where leases are granted, but is at its maximum under the system of yearly tenancies which are now the rule in this country.

BECAUSE--it has to a large extent caused and now perpetuates pauperism, by depriving the labourer of any rights in the soil of his native land, and destroying to a large extent his home feelings and interests. This has been aggravated by the enclosure of so many of the commons, which were the labourers' heritage from the past, by the clearing estates of cottages to avoid the burthen of poor-rates or to make "show villages," and by leaving the poor to the mercy of speculators for their dwellings, usually of the most wretched character, without land or gardens, and often far removed from the scene of their daily labours.

BECAUSE--it interferes with the freedom which every citizen of a free country should have of obtaining a healthy dwelling (in proportion to his means) in any part of the country he may prefer, and with a sufficiency of land around it for health, recreation, and garden cultivation, at approximately the same cost of agricultural land. He is now forced to live only where landowners will allow him, in houses erected by speculative builders for show rather than for health, comfort, and permanence, on land costing from ten to a hundred times its agricultural value, or leased out for a term of years in order finally to be confiscated by the landlord for the aggrandisement of his successor.

BECAUSE--it has led and still leads to the enclosure or appropriation of all unenclosed lands for the exclusive benefit of landowners, thus depriving the entire population of the country of rights they have enjoyed from time immemorial; to the stopping of footpaths, the destruction of roadside greens, and the exclusion of the people from much of the wild and beautiful scenery of their native land.

BECAUSE--it gives to a limited class the power of permanently impoverishing the country for their private benefit by the excessive export of minerals, which, being limited in quantity and not producible by man, should be jealously guarded for the use of the nation, with due regard to the needs of our successors.

BECAUSE--it gives to individuals a large proportion of

the wealth created by the community at large. All land has doubled in value--much of it has increased a hundred-fold or even a thousand-fold in value during the present century; and this increased value, due to the growth, industry, and enterprise of the people at large, has become the property of a body of men who, for the most part, have had the very smallest share in creating it.

BECAUSE--it involves the continued existence of a large body of citizens living in idleness on revenues derived from the labour and skill of the working classes, and who constitute therefore, a permanent and injurious burden on the industry of the people.

For these reasons it is essential to the well-being of the community that unrestricted private property in land be abolished.

And further:--

BECAUSE--in every one of these cases in which the present system of Landlordism produces evil results, and carries with it the curse of pauperism and crime, a well-guarded system of Occupying Ownership under the State is calculated to produce beneficial results--to diminish pauperism and crime, and to add to the general well-being of the whole community--it therefore becomes necessary that some such system of Land Nationalisation as that here sketched out be speedily established.

I conclude with a quotation from Mr. J. Boyd Kinnear's

important and instructive volume:--

"Who does not see how much happier England will be when, instead of one great mansion surrounded by miles beyond miles of one huge property, farmed by the tenants-at-will of one landlord, tilled by the mere labourers, whose youth and manhood know no relaxation from rough mechanical toil, whose old age sees no home but the chance of charity or the certainty of the workhouse, there shall be a thousand estates of varying size, where each owner shall work for himself and his children, where the sense of independence shall lighten the burdens of daily toil, where education shall give resources, and the labour of youth shall suffice for the support of age."

Working men of England! I have here shown you how this improved social condition may be brought about. It is for you to make your voices heard and insist that it be made the question of the day by your chosen representatives in the Legislature.

*Notes, Chapter Eight*

1. In an article on the Land Question in the *Edinburgh Review* of October, 1871, the same view is forcibly upheld. It is shown by the testimony of M. de Laveleye that even in Belgium peasant properties are diminishing, on account of facilities of sale and the general desire for land by capitalists. In the Eastern States of America also small farms are being

bought up for investments or for residential purposes, and the writer continues:--"If you could divide England into lots; if you could restore the imaginary times of village communities and joint ownership of the soil; still, if, at the same time, you left the disposal of land free, the same result would recur. Landlordism would revive and grow again. After a period of transition capital would very certainly re-assume its ordinary predominance, and the land would be engrossed once more. Nothing could prevent this, except the enactment and enforcement of agrarian laws. This, and no other, is the price which we must pay for reducing our landed property to the condition of comparative level for which Mr. Mill wishes, and of absolute level which alone will content his more advanced disciples. Does it not stand to reason that if the sale and purchase of land were perfectly easy and free, those persons would buy most land and give the best price for it who had most money to buy it with?"

2. As an authoritative exposition of the "free trade in land" arguments and views, we may refer to Mr. William Fowler, M.P., who, in the "Cobden Club Essays" (Vol. II, ), argues justly against the scheme of the late J. S. Mill that it would render the charges against land uncertain and fluctuating, and would thereby diminish its value as a secure investment. He maintains throughout his essay that the great thing, and the only needful thing, is to cause capital to be expended on the land, and for this purpose he advocates the

removal of all restrictions on its ownership and its transfer. This, he believes, will do all that is necessary for the labourer, by rendering it the interest of the landlord to house and feed him well, just as the farmer houses and feeds his horses well. But this very same argument was used in the case of slavery. It was said that slaves *could not* be seriously ill-treated, or maimed, or murdered, because it was against the *interest* of their owners to deteriorate their own property. Yet no fact is more certain than that they were so ill-treated, or that in many cases they were systematically worked out, it being found cheaper to exhaust them and buy others than to keep them in old age. So, the fact is certain (and has been proved in the preceding chapters) that, however much capital is expended on the land, the labourer does *not* benefit. On the highly cultivated farms of the lowlands of Scotland, the cottages and bothies in which the hinds are lodged are often bad and insufficient, as bad at least as in the worst cultivated parts of England. It does not do, therefore, to look at this question solely from a landlord-and-tenant point of view, and treating the labourer solely as a part of the necessary "stock" of the farm. Yet this is what Mr. Fowler and the free-trade-in-land men do. We find it stated that, "a good cottage can only be considered self-supporting in the same sense that good stables and good cattle-sheds are self-supporting, and *the only hope that the labourer can have of being properly housed is, that the landowners should accept the position that good cottages conveniently placed pay, in the same sense that good farm offices so placed pay.*" And it is assumed that the only reason why landlords do not act on this principle is, that they have only life-interests in the land. To support this view it should have been shown that *wherever* an estate is not encumbered by entails, the cottages are ample and convenient, but no attempt whatever has been made to do this, while the universality of bad, dear, and inconvenient cottages over the *whole* country, and the absence of all adequate provision of garden ground attached to them, is a strong proof that this is *not* the only or the chief cause of the deficiency. On the other hand, it is a fact established by overwhelming evidence, that wherever the labourer possesses land from which he cannot be ejected at the will of his landlord or his employer, he invariably secures for himself decent house-accomodation, while he has also that feeling of independence and security which is the foundation of every social and political virtue. The labourer, therefore, has a right to refuse to be treated as a mere portion of the farming stock, to be housed well or ill as the landlord chooses; and the placing him in this position is the condemnation of "free trade in land," as the panacea for all the evils connected with the land-system, put forward by the Cobden Club School of Reformers.

3. Not only is the supposed "perpetual income" derived from Consols or any other form of investment non-existent

as regards any living owner, but it may be shown to be altogether unjust in principle and impossible in fact. Let us see what the contrary assumption--that interest on capital paid in perpetuity is altogether right and expedient--leads us to. The surplus capital of each generation will be invested to produce a "perpetual income" for all succeeding generations. But as each generation creates more surplus capital, its amount, and that of the "perpetual income" derived from it, will go on increasing; and without approaching perpetuity we should very soon arrive at a state of things in which this interest would be of so vast an amount that the workers--the producers of all wealth--could not possibly pay it. This period would arrive sooner because, with the increase of the "perpetual incomes," those supported in idleness on these incomes would also increase continually; and we come, at last, to the *reductio ad absurdum*, that the "income" would be so great that it would support everybody if there was only anybody else to pay it! It is evident that before long the result must be, either a revolution, in which all such incomes would be swallowed up, or a progressive decrease in the purchasing power of money, which, if the "income" were really perpetual, would inevitably end in its becoming worthless. As a matter of fact we see this tendency already in action, in the constantly increasing cost of living with the constantly decreasing rate of secure interest. The conception of "perpetual income" is therefore a fallacy from two distinct points of view. on

4. In order to render any diminution even of the selling value of the land less probable, the annuity might be extended to three generations certain, in the direct line, that is, to the actual owner, his sons, and grandsons, as well as to any collateral or other heirs living at the time the Act came into operation. As it is practically certain that the power of entail, and, perhaps, that of transmitting any property to unborn heirs, will be abolished long before Nationalisation is effected, and as land could then be used only for personal occupation, the value of such an annuity would be very great to those who wished to secure a competency to their family during the two generations after them, because they could do this in no other way so easily and so securely. There will, therefore, in all probability, be a great demand for these annuities by trustees and others.

5. This would not prevent temporary subletting by permission of the Courts, to keep house or land for minors, and in other analogous cases.

6. The permanent possession of a plot of land would have the effect of securing the labourer of all kinds from that absolute dependence on the capitalist which, as pointed out in my first chapter, is one great cause of poverty and pauperism. It would be the first and greatest step in bringing about the state of things which Professor Cairnes recognised as that which alone would elevate the labourer. He says:-

-"It appears to me that the condition of any substantial improvement of a permanent kind in the labourer's lot is, that the separation of the industrial classes into labourers and capitalists which now prevails shall *not* be maintained; that the labourer shall cease to be a mere labourer" (, Cairnes, "Some Leading Principles," &c.). Now the possessor of land would be a capitalist as well as a labourer. He would be in a position to bargain on equal terms with his employer. He would be, what he is not now, a free man.

7. In the *Contemporary Review* of March 1882, the Rev. W. L. Blackley, (author of the admirable scheme of National Insurance now exciting so much attention) endeavours to demonstrate the absurdity of this proposal "by a very simple process of arithmetic." He shows clearly that if every man and woman over 20 years of age should claim his or her five acres, the whole agricultural land of the country would not suffice to supply them. It is surprising that a writer so acute and logical as Mr. Blackley usually is did not see the futility of such an objection. Its whole force depends on the supposition that such classes of people as domestic servants, City clerks, small tradesmen, and shopkeepers, and the whole body of unmarried men and women, should have the desire and the means of suddenly quitting their present mode of life and *purchasing* or *renting* five acres of land each for *personal occupation*! As well might a person reading for the first time of the 100 acre lots offered in Canada and Australia, almost

for nothing, and knowing the high wages of mechanics and domestic servants in those countries, jump to the conclusion that these same classes will at once emigrate *en masse*, and thus leave England entirely destitute of workers. Let us, however, see what are the actual probabilities of the case.

The total number of families in Great Britain is about six millions, and it is with families we have to deal, since single men and women do not, as a rule, occupy separate houses, much less land. Of these about a million will be comprised in the categories of landowners, farmers, merchants, and the official and professional classes, whose wants as regards land for personal occupation are already, for the most part, supplied. Of the remainder, about three millions are town dwellers, and probably only a small percentage of these would be in a position to utilise land in the country. Perha per cent. would be a sufficient estimate, but to give ample margin we will take 16 per cent., or about half a million in all, and most of these would not care to have more than an acre or two. There remains the poorer country dwelling families, mostly labourers, mechanics, and village tradesmen, and of these a larger proportion--perhaps half the whole number--might take advantage of the right of pre-emption within the first ten years. This would make, together, one and a half million families; and if we put the average amount of land taken by each at two acres, we arrive at a total of three millions of acres thus occupied, or rather less than 10 per cent. of the whole agricultural land of the country. Probably, however, a portion of this amount would be taken from the commons and waste lands, which could be had at a cheaper rate. The quantity thus taken would no doubt go on slowly increasing, and possibly, in the course of centuries, the bulk of the whole land of our country might come to be occupied in small farms or residential plots, the produce of which would, in most cases, be supplementary to the gains of some industrial occupation. But so far from there being anything to dread in this, if the illustrative facts adduced in this volume teach us one thing more clearly than another, it is that such a consummation would be an unmixed blessing--that it would give us a healthy, happy, and contented population, in which want and pauperism would be unknown, while our land would be covered with a succession of gardens and of cottage farms as in the Channel Islands, producing far more both of human food and human happiness than it could produce in any other way.

---

# APPENDIX I.

## ON THE NATIONALISATION OF HOUSE PROPERTY.

It has been already intimated (see ) that house property may be advantageously dealt with on the same general principles as the agricultural land of the kingdom, but details were avoided, because it was felt that this part of the scheme was beset with exceptional difficulties and was open to many objections. A fuller consideration of this subject, after reading the criticisms to which my proposals have given rise, and after discussion with friends who consider the crucial test of the practicability of land-nationalisation to be its applicability to towns, enables me now to treat it more fully; and I therefore propose to indicate a method by which it may be effected. I wish however clearly to state that the proposals which follow are put forth as suggestions--not as the only method by which the problem may be solved. They will, at all events, serve to show how nationalisation *can* be applied in towns, and will thus afford an answer to the cry of "impracticable" which is always raised if no workable plan is sketched out.

*The State should resume possession of Agricultural Land first--of land occupied by house property, &c., at a later period.*--Much consideration of the effects likely to follow nationalisation have convinced me of the importance of this proposition. When all the agricultural and waste lands of the kingdom are resumed by the State and rendered available for personal occupation in the manner indicated in the latter part of Chap. viii. (p-224), there will inevitably result an outflow of the congested population of the large towns into the country. All villages and small towns which have long remained in an almost stationary condition, owing to the impossibility of obtaining land from the great landlords, will at once start into healthy life and growth. Numbers of persons who have been hitherto unable to obtain a country residence with a few acres of land in the district of their choice, except perhaps at an exorbitant price, will, so soon as land is obtainable everywhere, build houses for themselves, and thus there will arise a large demand for labour and a considerable extension of trade all over the country. Many labourers, mechanics, and small tradesmen, who have left their native town or village and are struggling vainly to earn a living in some great town, will then be able to return to their former homes, attracted both by the fresh demand for labour and by the enormous boon of being able to obtain plots of land at low rents and on a permanent tenure. The effect of this outflow of population will undoubtedly be, that rents and house property generally must fall in value considerably below the monopoly prices they have hitherto commanded. On the worse class of houses the fall will be considerable, on the better class probably little if any. Numbers of houses will become temporarily vacant, while the worst of all will have to be destroyed as uninhabitable.

Some of the evils of land-monopoly in towns will thus be removed merely by the free access which nationalisation will afford to rural land; but other evils will remain, and in order to remove these it will be necessary for the State or the Municipality to become the sole ground-landlord, while every householder should be able, if he desires it, to obtain possession of his house or premises on the easiest terms. The most convenient arrangements, and those best adapted to secure the full benefits of nationalisation to the entire community will probably be somewhat as follows:--

*How House-property may be dealt with.*--When the free-selection of rural land for dwellings, the opening up to cultivation of the more extensive wastes, and the subdivision of large farms, have brought down ground-rents in towns to their true value (which may perhaps be effected in about ten years after the complete nationalisation of agricultural land), the entire house-property of the country will be in a condition to be advantageously dealt with on the principles already laid down in this volume.

Application being made by any person desirous of purchasing his house and premises, the local Land Court (established to carry out nationalisation) will cause a valuation to be made of the property, separating the value of the ground-rent from that of the buildings or other improvements on the land, and the occupier will then be entitled to purchase the latter, either by payment of the amount of the valuation or by means of a terminable rental extending over a period not exceeding, say, fifty-five years; and on paying this amount or this rental, as well as the annual ground-rent, he would become the virtual owner of the dwelling-house or premises. Persons who do not wish to purchase their houses might remain as tenants, but in this case the Municipality or the local Land Court would become the landlord, receiving the rents from the tenant and applying them to the payment of the terminable annuity awarded to the former landlord in lieu of ground-rent and also in liquidation of the amount at which the buildings, &c. upon the land have been valued. The terminable rental by which this last is to be paid would be always so adjusted to the valuation as to secure the public from loss. In this way the Municipalities or other local authorities would gradually become possessors of large quantities of house-property which they would be always ready to sell at very low prices to any occupier desirous of purchasing them.

*Additional powers of Municipalities.*--In order to provide

for the wants of an increasing population, every municipality should have power to take any land required for the use of its inhabitants, either for health and recreation, for the sites of public buildings, or for the erection of dwelling-houses, paying only the official valuation price. Thus the needs of every locality would be provided for without trouble, delay, or unnecessary expense.

*Replies to some objections.*--Some of my critics have objected that the complete stoppage of speculative building would be highly injurious to the community and ruinous to many builders. I reply to this, that people would still build houses, and that, owing to the land on which they must be built being so much cheaper, larger and better houses would be built than now, so that the building trade would not suffer, except in so far as it had already built beyond the needs, or in a style unsuited to the wants of the community. It will hardly be urged that people should continue to live in bad or unsuitable houses in order that builders may thrive.

Fear has also been expressed that many who require houses, but who have neither the means nor the inclination to build them, would suffer. But such a fear is quite groundless, for Society will, as it always does, adapt itself to new conditions; while failing other means of supply the local authorities will always be able to meet a public want. It must be remembered, too, that the large number of houses which, under the present system are always "to let," will have to be absorbed before there is really a pressing want of new houses. When most people own the houses they live in, and it becomes the general custom for houses to be built only when people require them, instead of by speculators on the chance of finding tenants (who often leave some other house vacant), unoccupied houses will be comparatively unknown. It will then be perceived that the many thousands of houses now always standing empty represent a vast loss of capital entirely due to the system of speculative building arising out of landlordism.

*Concluding remarks.*--Without going into further details it has, I think, been now made clear that the principles of Land Nationalisation as developed in this work, can be applied to house-property as well as to agricultural land; and that by so applying them the ever-increasing value of ground-rents in populous centres which now go to enrich individuals and give them injurious power over their fellow-men, will, as the annuities to landlords expire, form an ever-increasing fund for the expenses of government, and will ultimately render other taxes as well as local rates, altogether unnecessary.

# APPENDIX II.

## STATE-TENANTS *VERSUS* FREEHOLDERS.[1]

When Nationalisation of the land is advocated, a great many people reply: "I don't see the good of Nationalisation; I prefer Freeholders to State-tenants". Let us therefore see what are the comparative advantages of the two modes of tenure.

In order that the greatest number of people may become freeholders, many Liberals advocate the abolition of all restrictions on the sale and transfer of land. They say, make every man who owns land an absolute owner, with power to sell, or divide, or bequeath as he pleases, and plenty of land will come into the market. Then, every one who wants land can buy it, if able to do so; and if the mode of transfer is also made simple and cheap, everything will have been done that needs be done. We shall then have free trade in land; there will be no limited or encumbered estates, and capital will flow to land and develop its resources.

But people who talk thus forget that we have already

had two great experiments of this nature, both supported by these very arguments, and that both have utterly failed. Thirty years ago the dreadful condition of the Irish peasantry was imputed to the prevalence of entailed and encumbered estates, the owners of which had no money to spend on improvements, and a most radical measure was passed, by which all these estates were brought into the market and sold to the highest bidder. But the result was not as expected. Capital flowed into the country, but with no benefit to any one but the capitalist. English manufacturers and speculators became owners of Irish land, and sometimes laid out money on it; but they were harder landlords than those whom they replaced; they looked upon the land they had bought merely as a means of making money, and utterly ignored the equitable or customary rights of the unhappy tenants. Irish distress was not in the least degree ameliorated by this drastic measure from which so much was expected; and it is now rarely spoken of, while legislation on totally different lines has been found necessary.

The second example of the utter uselessness of pouring capital into a country so long as the people are denied any *right* to the use of land is afforded by Scotland. In the early part of this century, the great demand for wool made sheep-farming profitable, and many of the Highland landlords were persuaded that they could double their incomes by establishing great sheep farms on their vast estates. They did so. Many thousands of valuable sheep were introduced; much money was spent in fencing and in building new farm houses for the Lowland farmers, while the rights of the hereditary dwellers on the soil were utterly ignored, and, by a series of barbarous evictions, these poor people were banished to the sea shore, or forced to emigrate. The result was, for a time, beneficial to the landlords, who proclaimed the scheme a great success; but it was most disastrous to the people, who, ever since, have been kept in a state of perpetual serfdom and pauperism. The present condition of the Highlands is a direct consequence of the application of capital to the land by landlords while the rights of the people were ignored; and the result of these two great experiments in Ireland and Scotland should teach us that any similar experiment in England cannot possibly lead to good results. It is true the conditions of society in England are different. There are here more capitalists, ever competing for the possession of land; but "free-trade" would simply enable those capitalists who desire land to obtain it more easily. What chance would the poor man have against such competitors? With population, wealth and manufactures ever increasing, as they are in England, the poor man will have less and less chance of getting land, so long as it is to be obtained solely by purchase and there is neither compulsion to sell, nor right to buy at equitable prices.

As land is ever getting scarcer in proportion to population, and in private hands must necessarily be a monopoly, it offers the greatest temptation to speculators, who, even now, frequently buy up estates offered for sale and resell them in small plots at competition prices which no poor man can afford to give; and this will continue to be the case so long as land is treated as a commodity to be bought and sold for profit. We maintain that this is a monstrous wrong and should never be permitted. Land is the first necessary of life, the source of food and of all kinds of wealth, and a sufficiency of health and enjoyment is absolutely needed by every one. It is a political crime to permit land to be monopolised by a few, to allow the wealthy to enjoy it for mere sport or aggrandisement while thousands live in misery and have to suffer disease and want because they are denied the right to live and labour upon it.

In order that all may have equal rights to use and enjoy the land of their birth, it must become, not theoretically only but actually, the property of the State in trust for all; and for all to derive equal advantages from it, those who occupy it must pay a rental to the State for its use. This is the only way to equalise the advantages derived by the several occupiers of land of different qualities and in different situations,--the only way to enable the whole community to benefit by the increased value which the community itself gives to land.

The use of land is two-fold. Its chief and primary use is to supply to every household in the kingdom, the conditions for healthy existence, and whenever possible, some portion at least of their daily food. When all are thus supplied with the land necessary for a healthy home, the remainder should be devoted to cultivation in such a way as to produce the maximum of food, and at the same time to support and bring up the maximum number of healthy and happy food producers. All experience shows that these two things go together, and that in any country the maximum of food is produced when the greatest possible population lives upon and by the land. At one extreme we have the great farms of S. Australia, and California, cultivated with the minimum of human labour and producing a net return of about ten bushels of wheat per acre, and at the other extreme, the allotments of our farm labourers, producing food to the value of £40 per acre.

But in order that our labourers and mechanics may each be enabled to have, say, an acre of land to live on, and an acre or two more to cultivate, if they require it, with the power of getting a small farm of, from 10 to 40 acres, whenever they have obtained money enough to stock it, the land must be *let*, not *sold* to them. For at first a man wants all his little capital to enable him to cultivate even the smallest plot of land, and if he has to buy it, even by the easiest instalments, he is to that extent crippled. Moreover it is a bad thing for him to *own* the land absolutely, because he is then open to the temptations of the money-lender.

Instead of economising and pinching in bad seasons, he borrows money and mortgages his land, and thus falls under a tyranny as bad as that of the hardest landlord. In every part of the world the small freeholder falls a victim to the money-lender.

As a State-tenant the occupier would have all the essential rights and advantages of a freeholder. His tenure would be practically perpetual. He would have the right to sell or bequeath his holding, or any part of it, just as freely. His rent would never be raised on account of any improvements made by himself, but only on account of increased value of ground-rent, due to the growth of population or other general causes, which would affect all the ground around as well as his. He would therefore enjoy all the rights, all the privileges, and all the security which a freeholder enjoys. But he would have this great advantage over the freeholder, that he need not sink one penny of his capital in the purchase of the soil; and thus, for one man who could save money enough to acquire a farm or a homestead by purchase, two or three would be able to become State-tenants, with money in their pockets to stock their land or build their house, and to live upon till their first crops were gathered. Those who maintain the superiority of freeholds, therefore, speak without knowledge; the superiority is all the other way.

There is one more point to be considered, which is of great importance, that under a general system of small freeholders, one half of these would very soon be ruined by the other half--would be obliged to sell their farms to money-lenders or lawyers, and thus great estates would again monopolise the land. The way this would necessarily come about (as it always has come about) is as follows. Suppose there are a body of peasant proprietors all over the country. Their land necessarily varies in quality and position, and, therefore, in value from fifteen or twenty shillings an acre up to two, three, or four pounds an acre; and all being freeholders, none of them pay rent. But the owner of the better land can afford to sell his produce of all kinds at a lower rate than the owner of the inferior land, because prices which will enable the former to live and save money, will be starvation to the latter. Hence an unequal competition will arise between the two classes, in which the one must necessarily starve out the other. The payment of rent in proportion to the *inherent value of the land* equalises the position of all. The occupier of poor land at a low rent can fairly compete with the occupier of rich land at a high rent; and thus while a system of *small proprietors* is sure to fail, a system of *small occupiers*, under the State, combines all the essential elements of stability.[2]

Thus far we have considered the question solely from the economical and practical point of view, but the great superiority of State-tenants over freeholders is equally apparent when we treat it as a question of justice. Land necessarily increases in value as population and civilisation increase, and that increase being the creation of the community at large, is justly the property of the community. By a system of State-tenants we shall obtain this increase for the benefit of all, by means of a periodical reassessment of the ground rents payable to the State; but if we create a body of small freeholders we shall perpetuate injustice and inequality. A. and B. may acquire two farms at the same cost, and may bestow the same labour and skill in the cultivation of them. But in 30 or 40 years the value of the two may be very different. Minerals may be discovered or some new industry may spring up, causing the farm of A. to become the site of a populous town, while that of B. remains in a secluded agricultural district; so that, while the children of the one are earning their living by honest labour, the children of the other may be all living in idleness by means of wealth which they have not created and to which they have no equitable claim, and to the same extent the community at large is robbed of its due. If, on the other hand, we establish a system of State-tenancy over the whole country, the natural increase of land-value by social development will produce an ever-increasing revenue even if existing landlords continue to be paid the incomes they now receive from land, so that in addition to all the other advantages of the system, we shall acquire means of bringing about a steady diminution of taxation by which all alike will benefit.

Briefly, to sum up the argument: SMALL FREEHOLDERS ARE BAD because:--

1.--Money must be sunk in the *purchase* which can be better invested in the *cultivation* of the soil.

2.--The number of men who can advantageously acquire small farms is therefore greatly reduced.

3.--The unearned increment of the land is taken from the community, who create it, and is given to individuals.

4.--The inheritors of these small farms of different qualities of land will compete unequally with each other, and those holding the poorer land must sooner or later sell their farms, or fall into the hands of the money-lender. The system, therefore, contains within itself the elements of decay and failure.

IN ALL THESE RESPECTS STATE-TENANCY IS GREATLY TO BE PREFERRED TO SMALL FREEHOLDINGS, AND A GENERAL SYSTEM OF STATE-TENANCY CAN ONLY BE SECURED BY A COMPLETE NATIONALISATION OF THE LAND.

*Notes, Appendix II*

1. Originally written for the Land Nationalisation Society, and published by them as a tract (No. 15).

2. This danger has been attempted to be obviated on the continent by the farms consisting of scores of hundreds of scattered patches of land of different qualities. But this

system renders economical cultivation impossible, and the remedy is worse than the disease.

---

THE END.